THE
CLASSIC *f*M
HALL OF FAME

THE
CLASSIC *f*M
HALL OF FAME

DARREN HENLEY
SAM JACKSON
TIM LIHOREAU

Illustrated by Lynn Hatzius

E&T

Published in 2011 by Elliott & Thompson Ltd
27 John Street, London WC1N 2BX
www.eandtbooks.com

ISBN: 978-1-90764-217-3

Text © Darren Henley, Sam Jackson and Tim Lihoreau
Design © Elliott & Thompson, Illustration © Lynn Hatzius
The authors have asserted their moral rights.

9 8 7 6 5 4 3

A CIP catalogue record for this book is available from the British Library
Printed in Italy by Printer Trento

The publisher would like to thank the following record labels for CD artwork included in this book:

BIS: Edvard Grieg/ *Holberg Suite* Classic FM: Samuel Barber / *Violin Concerto*; Philip Glass / Violin Concerto No. 1; Modest Mussorgsky / *Pictures at an Exhibition* Deutsche Grammophon: Johannes Brahms / *Violin Concerto in D*; George Handel / *Sarabande*; Giuseppe Verdi / *La traviata* EMI: Johann Sebastian Bach / *Cantata No. 147*; Hector Berlioz / *Symphonie fantastique* (from Title: *Berlioz: Symphonie fantastique/La Mort de Cleopatre* Artist: Sir Simon Rattle Release: *Symphonie fantastique* op. 14 Date: 1 Sep 2008 Copyright: P 2008 The copyright in this sound recording is owned by EMI Records Ltd.); Johannes Brahms / *A German Requiem* (from Title: Brahms: *Ein deutsches Requiem (A German Requiem) Op. 45* Artist: King's College Choir, Cambridge Release: Brahms: *Ein deutsches Requiem (A German Requiem) Op. 45* Date: 2 Oct 2006 Copyright: P 2006 The copyright in this sound recording is owned by EMI Records Ltd.); Léo Delibes / *Lakmé* (from Title: *Lakmé* Artist: Natalie Dessay Release: *Lakmé* Dessay Plasson Date: 15 Sep 1998 Copyright: P 1998 EMI Music France); Antonín Dvořák / *Rusalka*; Antonín Dvořák / *Symphony No. 9 in E minor*; Edward Elgar / *Cello Concerto in E minor*; Edvard Grieg / *Piano Concerto in A minor* (from Title: *The Ultimate Grieg Album* Artist: Leif Ove Andsnes Release: *Ballad for Edvard Grieg* Date: 13 Aug 2007 Copyright: This compilation P 2007 by EMI Records Ltd.); Joseph Haydn / *The Creation*; Gustav Holst / *The Planets*; Karl Jenkins / *The Armed Man* ((from Title: *The Armed Man (A Mass For Peace)* Artist: Karl Jenkins Release: *The Armed Man (A Mass For Peace)* Date: 10 Sep 2001 Copyright: P 2001 The copyright in this sound recording is owned by Karl Jenkins Music Ltd under exclusive licence to Virgin Records Ltd); Wolfgang Amadeus Mozart / *Clarinet Concerto in A*; Jean Sibelius / *Symphony No. 5 in E flat* (from Title: *Rattle: Sibelius Complete Symphonies* Artist: Sir Simon Rattle Release: *Rattle: Sibelius Complete Symphonies* Date: 3 Sep 2007 Copyright: This compilation P 2007 by EMI Records Ltd.); Pyotr Ilyich Tchaikovsky / *Nutcracker* (from Title: *Tchaikovsky: The Nutcracker Standard Version* Artist: Sir Simon Rattle Release: *Tchaikovsky: The Nutcracker Standard Version* Date: 6 Sep 2010 Copyright: P 2010 The copyright in this sound recording is owned by EMI Records Ltd.); Hallé: Edward Elgar / *The Dream of Gerontius* Hyperion: Johann Sebastian Bach / *Goldberg Variations*; Ludwig van Beethoven / *Symphony No. 7 in A*; Sergei Rachmaninov / *Piano Concerto No. 2 in C minor*; Maurice Ravel / *Pavane pour une infante défunte* London Philharmonic Orchestra: Pyotr Ilyich Tchaikovsky / *Symphony No. 6 in B minor* Naxos: Marie Joseph Canteloube de Malaret / *Songs of the Auvergne*; Ralph Vaughan Williams / *Five Variants of Dives and Lazarus* Nonesuch: Henryk Górecki / *Symphony No. 3* Onyx: Claude Debussy /*Suite bergamasque*; Felix Mendelssohn / *Violin Concerto in E minor* RCA: Aaron Copland / *Rodeo*; Gustav Mahler / *Symphony No. 1 in D* SDG: Johann Sebastian Bach / *The Brandenburg Concertos* Sony Leonard Bernstein / *Candide*; Ludwig van Beethoven / *Symphony No. 5 in C minor*; Aaron Copland / *Appalachian Spring*; Nigel Hess / *Ladies in Lavender* Supraphon: Bedřich Smetana / *Má Vlast* Virgin: Franz Schubert / *Piano Quintet in A* Virgin Veritas: Johann Sebastian Bach / *Mass in B minor*

All pictures are subject to copyright and may not be photocopied, scanned or reused without the owner's prior consent. Artwork is credited to the source supplied and does not necessarily represent the image copyright holder. The publisher is happy to give specific credit to copyright holders in any future edition on request.

Contents

Introduction

We first launched the Classic FM Hall of Fame in 1996. We had no idea back then that we were giving birth to a phenomenon. It has become so much more than just an annual chart – spawning a daily radio programme and a whole series of bestselling CDs.

Since we started our quest to identify the United Kingdom's favourite pieces of classical music, we have produced fifteen annual charts. Each one offers a snapshot of our listeners' favourites at a given point in time. We are often asked how we go about compiling the chart. What happens is that at the beginning of each year, we ask our listeners to send us their top three all-time classical favourites. Every single one of those votes is registered on a computer, which creates a running tally of the relative positions of each of the pieces. The final chart is produced just before Easter. Classic FM's team of music producers then sets about the unenviable task of fitting all 300 works into one 48-hour countdown, which is broadcast from dawn to dusk on Good Friday, Easter Saturday, Easter Sunday and Easter Monday.

The chart on which we have based this book is a distillation of all of those fifteen years of charts, which we broadcast in full at the beginning of 2011. How did we arrive at this 'ultimate' Classic FM Hall of Fame? Well, we took the annual Top 300 from 1996 to 2010 and created a new Top 300 based on each work's relative position in the annual countdowns. That means that all the works that have seen their popularity ebb and flow over the decade and a half since the Classic FM Hall of Fame began receive a chart position based on an aggregation of their achievements over the full period. New works entering the chart in more recent years (in many cases because they hadn't actually been composed as far back as 1996) are more likely to appear further down our chart because they don't benefit from listeners' votes in the early years of the countdown.

During the first five years of the chart, one composer reigned supreme: Max Bruch. In 1996, he surprised all of us by beating the likes of Mozart and Beethoven to take the No. 1 spot with his *Violin Concerto No. 1*. At No. 300 the same year was another work by Bruch, *Kol Nidrei*. So a lesser-known composer, born in Cologne in 1838, not only topped but tailed our debut chart. That Bruch found himself at the top of the chart was all the more remarkable when you consider that, by the time he died in 1920, his music had drifted out of fashion to such an extent that his reputation had dwindled to almost nothing. It also proves that looks count for very little with Classic FM listeners – a German contemporary of Bruch once said of him, 'In personal appearance, he is by no means as majestic as one would suppose from his works.'

Bruch maintained his place in pole position a further four times, confounding the pundits who claimed that his early success was merely a fluke. But, in 2001, Classic FM's listeners voted Rachmaninov's *Piano Concerto No. 2* into the top spot. Forever linked to that classic romantic movie moment on a railway platform in the film *Brief Encounter*, the work also enjoyed five years at the peak of the chart through until 2005. Prior to the work's spell at the top, Rachmaninov was a constant bridesmaid to Bruch's bride, taking the No. 2 position each year.

Then in the year that we all celebrated his 250th birthday, Wolfgang Amadeus Mozart knocked Rachmaninov from his perch with his *Clarinet Concerto*. But his stay at No. 1 was short-lived, with our first English work topping the poll in 2007, when Vaughan Williams climbed to the top spot with his beautifully wistful *The Lark Ascending*. At the time of writing, this work continues to fly high, having been ahead of the rest each year until 2010. It marks an enormous success for a piece of music that made its chart debut at No. 18 in 1996 – hence its relatively low position in the 'chart of charts', which follows over the next few pages.

In the aggregated chart, which we have used as the basis for this book, the four works that have held the No. 1 position in our fifteen annual charts take the top four positions in our 'ultimate' countdown. With Vaughan Williams's *The Lark Ascending* in fourth place, Bruch's *Violin Concerto No. 2* comes in third, having seen its support wane since the early days of the Hall of Fame. Mozart might have taken the crown only once in our annual charts with his *Clarinet Concerto*, but the work is rewarded for its consistently high ranking by coming in at No. 2. That means that the overall winner in our search for the UK's favourite classical work over the past fifteen years is Rachmaninov's *Piano Concerto No. 2*.

Cinema successes and failures always have a part to play in our annual charts, and in 1998 there was one movie that hit the headlines more than any other. There are very few superlatives that haven't already been used to describe the film *Titanic*. Among the eleven Oscars it won was that for Best Dramatic Score. Classic FM listeners gave this award their seal of approval by voting James Horner's majestic score into the No. 75 slot, the second highest new entry to the chart that year. No round-up of movie soundtracks that feature in our Top 300 would be complete without mention of John Williams, whose four entries in our aggregated chart, including *Schindler's List* and *Star Wars*, put him well ahead of any other film composer. Another of Williams's soundtrack successes, *Harry Potter*, together with Howard Shore's music from *The Lord of the Rings* are relative newcomers to the Hall of Fame, both having been released since we began our series of charts fifteen years ago. The two films have since given birth to major franchises of their own.

In 1997, the highest new entry in the chart was *Adiemus*, which shot in at No. 134. The haunting voice of Miriam Stockley performing Karl Jenkins's breakthrough work was one of the biggest-selling records of the 1990s. Jenkins has become the most popular living composer, with *Adiemus* eventually being eclipsed by his even more wildly successful *The Armed Man: A Mass for Peace*. Living composers continue to be well represented in the chart, with the likes of Patrick Hawes, Nigel Hess, Paul McCartney and Jon Lord all earning their places in the pages of this book.

Operatic works have performed strongly every year and Bizet's *The Pearl Fishers* has consistently been the highest-placed representative of the genre. In terms of choral music, that hardy perennial of choirs across the land, Handel's *Messiah* has regularly appeared ahead of the rest of a chasing pack, which includes masterful works from nearly all the other big-hitting composers.

Some pieces become popular with Classic FM listeners because of particular pro-grammes on the station. Among these are the music of the eighteenth-century Italian Jesuit priest, Domenico Zipoli, and in particular his beautiful *Elevazione*; Arvo Pärt's deeply minimalist music, such as *Spiegel im Spiegel*, has grown in popularity since the countdown first aired, while the Italian composer Ludovico Einaudi (*Le Onde*) and American Jay Ungar (*The Ashokan Farewell*) have enjoyed great success based on the airplay that they have received on Classic FM.

It's always surprising how many 'one-hit wonders' appear in the chart each year – pieces from composers with one magnum opus that puts all their other work in the shade. It seems ironic that among them are some of the greatest pieces of classical music ever written: Pachelbel's *Canon in D*, Mascagni's *Cavalleria rusticana*, Holst's *The Planets* and Allegri's *Miserere*. At the other end of the scale comes Mozart, who has had more entries in the chart each year than any other composer, beating Beethoven into second place every time. Edward Elgar has been a consistent performer, flying the flag as our most prolific home-grown composer in terms of number of entries in the chart.

This book contains details of all 300 entries in our aggregated Hall of Fame, along with biographical information about the main composers whose music features in the chart. You will find a list of the complete Top 300 works in our all-time Classic FM Hall of Fame at the front of the book. This is followed by detailed entries for each of the works that feature in the chart arranged alphabetically by the composer's surname. For composers who have more than one entry, these are ranked according to each piece of music's relative position in the Top 300, with the most popular work coming first.

We've also made a recommendation for a recording of each of the works, which we believe shows off the music at its best. Of course, in many cases there are hundreds, if not thousands, of different recordings of each work from which we have had to choose. There will always be a good deal of subjectivity involved in narrowing our choice down to a single CD or download. In making our selection, we have relied on the database of thousands of recordings that we keep at Classic FM, so you will find that our choices tend to reflect what you hear on the radio.

The Classic FM Hall of Fame is very much a living, breathing entity, reflecting fashions and events in the world around us. For this reason there can never be a single definitive chart − only a series of snapshots of tastes at any given moment in time. Each year the chart changes, so who knows which composers will come to the fore, which film scores and operas will capture our collective imagination, or which long-forgotten pieces will be revitalised by a new recording. Whatever they may be, you can rest assured that we will be here at Classic FM to share your delight in discovering them.

Darren Henley
Sam Jackson
Tim Lihoreau

Classic FM, March 2011

A WORD ABOUT
CLASSIC *f*M

Classic FM is the UK's only 100 per cent classical music radio station. Since we began broadcasting in September 1992, the station has brought classical music to millions of people across the UK. If you've yet to discover for yourself the delights of being able to listen to classical music twenty-four hours a day, you can find Classic FM on 100–102 FM, on Digital Radio, online at www.classicfm.com, on Sky channel 0106, on Virgin Media channel 922 and on FreeSat channel 722.

Classic FM Magazine is published monthly, containing full details of the station's programming, as well as the latest news and interviews from the world of classical music. A free CD accompanies each month's magazine, which is available from most newsagents.

Among Classic FM's many CD releases is a range exclusively available from HMV. The Classic FM Full Works series provides top-quality recordings of many of the most popular classical works, played in full by world-famous musicians. Priced at just £5.99, these CDs are perfect for both the dedicated collector and for those who are just discovering classical music. You can find out more at www.classicfm. com/fullworks.

Classic FM works particularly closely with six orchestras around the UK, with the aim of encouraging new listeners to enjoy the power and passion of hearing a live orchestra playing in the concert hall. Check the station's website to find out if the Royal Scottish National Orchestra, Northern Sinfonia, the Orchestra of Opera North, the Royal Liverpool Philharmonic Orchestra, the Philharmonia Orchestra or the London Symphony Orchestra are performing near you.

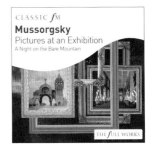

The Classic FM Full Works series

Classic FM has a long history of working to develop the next generation of classical music lovers, supporting organisations such as Music for Youth, which runs the annual Schools Proms at the Royal Albert Hall in London, and The Prince's Foundation for Children & the Arts, which has worked with the Philharmonia Orchestra to deliver an annual orchestral music education project to thousands of children across the UK, thanks to funding from the radio station's charity appeal. Currently, the Classic FM Foundation is raising money to enable the Nordoff Robbins music therapy charity to deliver thousands of extra therapy sessions to disabled and disadvantaged children and young people around the country.

For more information about any part of Classic FM, log on to our website at www.classicfm.com

The Top 300 Chart

1	Sergei Rachmaninov	*Piano Concerto No. 2 in C minor*
2	Wolfgang Amadeus Mozart	*Clarinet Concerto in A*
3	Max Bruch	*Violin Concerto No. 1 in G minor*
4	Ralph Vaughan Williams	*The Lark Ascending*
5	Edward Elgar	*Cello Concerto in E minor*
6	Ludwig van Beethoven	*Piano Concerto No. 5 in E flat (Emperor)*
7	Ludwig van Beethoven	*Symphony No. 6 in F (Pastoral)*
8	Edward Elgar	*Enigma Variations*
9	Ludwig van Beethoven	*Symphony No. 9 in D minor (Choral)*
10	Johann Pachelbel	*Canon in D*
11	Samuel Barber	*Adagio for Strings*
12	Edvard Grieg	*Piano Concerto in A minor*
13	Camille Saint-Saëns	*Symphony No. 3 (Organ Symphony)*
14	Ralph Vaughan Williams	*Fantasia on a Theme by Thomas Tallis*

15	Georges Bizet	*The Pearl Fishers*
16	Gustav Holst	*The Planets*
17	Antonín Dvořák	*Symphony No. 9 in E minor (From the New World)*
18	George Frideric Handel	*Messiah*
19	Wolfgang Amadeus Mozart	*Requiem*
20	Sergei Rachmaninov	*Symphony No. 2 in E minor*
21	Antonio Vivaldi	*The Four Seasons*
22	Pietro Mascagni	*Cavalleria rusticana*
23	Gregorio Allegri	*Miserere*
24	Joaquín Rodrigo	*Concierto de Aranjuez*
25	Gabriel Fauré	*Requiem*
26	Jean Sibelius	*Finlandia*
27	Felix Mendelssohn	*Violin Concerto in E minor*
28	Wolfgang Amadeus Mozart	*Piano Concerto No. 21 in C*
29	Gustav Mahler	*Symphony No. 5 in C sharp minor*
30	Ludwig van Beethoven	*Symphony No. 7 in A*
31	Sergei Rachmaninov	*Rhapsody on a Theme of Paganini*
32	Johann Sebastian Bach	*Concerto in D minor for Two Violins*
33	Ludwig van Beethoven	*Symphony No. 5 in C minor*
34	Pyotr Ilyich Tchaikovsky	*1812 Overture*
35	Nikolai Rimsky-Korsakov	*Scheherazade*
36	Sergei Rachmaninov	*Piano Concerto No. 3 in D minor*

37	Ludwig van Beethoven	*Piano Sonata No. 14 in C sharp minor (Moonlight)*
38	Pyotr Ilyich Tchaikovsky	*Piano Concerto No. 1 in B flat minor*
39	Ludwig van Beethoven	*Violin Concerto in D*
40	Dmitri Shostakovich	*Piano Concerto No. 2 in F*
41	Tomaso Albinoni	*Adagio in G minor*
42	Gabriel Fauré	*Cantique de Jean Racine*
43	Pyotr Ilyich Tchaikovsky	*Symphony No. 6 in B minor (Pathétique)*
44	Bedřich Smetana	*Má Vlast*
45	Dmitri Shostakovich	*The Gadfly*
46	George Gershwin	*Rhapsody in Blue*
47	Sergei Prokofiev	*Romeo and Juliet*
48	Giuseppe Verdi	*Nabucco*
49	Frédéric Chopin	*Piano Concerto No. 1 in E minor*
50	Johann Sebastian Bach	*Toccata and Fugue in D minor*
51	Wolfgang Amadeus Mozart	*The Marriage of Figaro*
52	Carl Orff	*Carmina Burana*
53	George Frideric Handel	*Solomon*
54	Edvard Grieg	*Peer Gynt Suite No. 1*
55	Giuseppe Verdi	*Requiem*
56	Johann Sebastian Bach	*Brandenburg Concertos*
57	Charles-Marie Widor	*Organ Symphony No. 5 in F minor*
58	Pyotr Ilyich Tchaikovsky	*Swan Lake*

59	George Frideric Handel	*Zadok the Priest*
60	Richard Strauss	*Four Last Songs*
61	Giacomo Puccini	*Madama Butterfly*
62	Felix Mendelssohn	*Hebrides Overture (Fingal's Cave)*
63	Wolfgang Amadeus Mozart	*The Magic Flute (Die Zauberflöte)*
64	Frédéric Chopin	*Piano Concerto No. 2 in F minor*
65	Franz Schubert	*Piano Quintet in A (Trout)*
66	Claude Debussy	*Suite bergamasque*
67	Wolfgang Amadeus Mozart	*Concerto in C for Flute and Harp*
68	Giacomo Puccini	*La bohème*
69	Jean Sibelius	*Symphony No. 5 in E flat*
70	Jules Massenet	*Thaïs*
71	Wolfgang Amadeus Mozart	*Ave verum corpus*
72	Wolfgang Amadeus Mozart	*Solemn Vespers*
73	Ludwig van Beethoven	*Symphony No. 3 in E flat (Eroica)*
74	Wolfgang Amadeus Mozart	*Eine kleine Nachtmusik*
75	Pyotr Ilyich Tchaikovsky	*Symphony No. 5 in E minor*
76	Gustav Mahler	*Symphony No. 2 in C minor (Resurrection)*
77	Jean Sibelius	*Karelia Suite*
78	Johann Sebastian Bach	*St Matthew Passion*
79	Aram Khachaturian	*Spartacus*
80	Maurice Ravel	*Boléro*

81	Jean Sibelius	*Symphony No. 2 in D*
82	Johannes Brahms	*Violin Concerto in D*
83	Jean Sibelius	*Violin Concerto in D minor*
84	Pyotr Ilyich Tchaikovsky	*Violin Concerto in D*
85	Johann Strauss II	*By the Beautiful Blue Danube*
86	Giuseppe Verdi	*La traviata*
87	Jay Ungar	*The Ashokan Farewell*
88	Johann Sebastian Bach	*Mass in B minor*
89	Pyotr Ilyich Tchaikovsky	*Nutcracker*
90	Modest Mussorgsky	*Pictures at an Exhibition*
91	Edward Elgar	*The Dream of Gerontius*
92	Richard Wagner	*Tristan and Isolde*
93	Franz Schubert	*String Quintet in C*
94	Richard Wagner	*Tannhäuser*
95	Giuseppe Verdi	*Aida*
96	Léo Delibes	*Lakmé*
97	Richard Wagner	*Die Walküre*
98	Antonín Dvořák	*Cello Concerto in B minor*
99	Georges Bizet	*Carmen*
100	George Frideric Handel	*Water Music: Suites*
101	Henryk Górecki	*Symphony No. 3 (Symphony of Sorrowful Songs)*
102	Thomas Tallis	*Spem in Alium*

103	Gabriel Fauré	*Pavane*
104	Edward Elgar	*Pomp and Circumstance Marches*
105	Pyotr Ilyich Tchaikovsky	*Romeo and Juliet*
106	George Butterworth	*The Banks of Green Willow*
107	Ludwig van Beethoven	*Romance No. 2 in F*
108	Wolfgang Amadeus Mozart	*Così fan tutte*
109	Camille Saint-Saëns	*Carnival of the Animals*
110	Johann Sebastian Bach	*Cantata No. 147*
111	Hector Berlioz	*Symphonie fantastique*
112	Johannes Brahms	*A German Requiem*
113	Camille Saint-Saëns	*Danse macabre*
114	Max Bruch	*Scottish Fantasy*
115	Aaron Copland	*Appalachian Spring*
116	Wolfgang Amadeus Mozart	*Clarinet Quintet in A*
117	Antonio Vivaldi	*Gloria in D (RV 589)*
118	Ludwig van Beethoven	*Piano Concerto No. 4 in G*
119	Karl Jenkins	*The Armed Man (Mass for Peace)*
120	John Williams	*Schindler's List*
121	Antonín Dvořák	*Rusalka*
122	Erik Satie	*Gymnopédies*
123	Ludwig van Beethoven	*Piano Sonata No. 8 in C minor (Pathétique)*
124	Howard Shore	*Lord of the Rings*

125	Pyotr Ilyich Tchaikovsky	*The Sleeping Beauty*
126	Edvard Grieg	*Holberg Suite*
127	Johannes Brahms	*Piano Concerto No. 2 in B flat*
128	Ludovico Einaudi	*Le Onde*
129	Wolfgang Amadeus Mozart	*Symphony No. 40 in G minor*
130	Ralph Vaughan Williams	*Fantasia on Greensleeves*
131	Alexander Borodin	*In the Steppes of Central Asia*
132	Franz Schubert	*Symphony No. 9 in C (Great)*
133	Charles Gounod	*Mors et Vita*
134	Johann Sebastian Bach	*Cello Suites*
135	Arvo Pärt	*Spiegel im Spiegel*
136	Felix Mendelssohn	*Symphony No. 4 in A (Italian)*
137	Ralph Vaughan Williams	*Five Variants of Dives and Lazarus*
138	Giacomo Puccini	*Tosca*
139	Aaron Copland	*Fanfare for the Common Man*
140	Samuel Barber	*Violin Concerto*
141	Johann Sebastian Bach	*Orchestral Suite No. 3 in D*
142	Pyotr Ilyich Tchaikovsky	*Symphony No. 4 in F minor*
143	Karl Jenkins	*Adiemus – Songs of Sanctuary*
144	Alexander Borodin	*Prince Igor*
145	Antonio Vivaldi	*Mandolin concerto in C (RV 425)*
146	Wolfgang Amadeus Mozart	*Piano Concerto No. 23 in A*

169	Antonio Vivaldi	*Motet in E*
170	Ennio Morricone	*The Mission*
171	Domenico Zipoli	*Elevazione*
172	Wolfgang Amadeus Mozart	*Symphony No. 41 in C (Jupiter)*
173	Vincenzo Bellini	*Norma*
174	Joseph Haydn	*Trumpet Concerto in E flat*
175	M. J. Canteloube de Malaret	*Songs of the Auvergne*
176	Edward Elgar	*Violin Concerto in B minor*
177	C. Willibald von Gluck	*Orpheus and Eurydice*
178	Gustav Mahler	*Symphony No. 1 in D (Titan)*
179	Robert Schumann	*Piano Concerto in A minor*
180	Pyotr Ilyich Tchaikovsky	*Capriccio Italien*
181	Franz Schubert	*Symphony No. 8 in B minor (Unfinished)*
182	John Rutter	*Requiem*
183	Francisco Tárrega	*Recuerdos de la Alhambra*
184	Ludwig van Beethoven	*Bagatelle No. 25 in A minor (Für Elise)*
185	Giacomo Puccini	*Gianni Schicchi*
186	John Williams	*Harry Potter*
187	Ralph Vaughan Williams	*English Folk Songs Suite*
188	Richard Wagner	*Siegfried*
189	Richard Addinsell	*Warsaw Concerto*
190	Niccolò Paganini	*Violin Concerto No. 1 in D major*

191	Johannes Brahms	*Symphony No. 4 in E minor*
192	Edward Elgar	*Symphony No. 1 in A flat*
193	Johann Strauss I	*Radetzky March*
194	Richard Wagner	*Lohengrin*
195	Sergei Prokofiev	*Symphony No. 1 in D (Classical)*
196	Hans Zimmer	*Gladiator*
197	Alexander Borodin	*String Quartet No. 2 in D*
198	William Walton	*Crown Imperial*
199	Edward Elgar	*Chanson de Matin*
200	Ludwig van Beethoven	*Piano Concerto No. 3 in C minor*
201	George Frideric Handel	*Sarabande*
202	Edward Elgar	*Introduction and Allegro for Strings*
203	Hamish MacCunn	*The Land of the Mountain and the Flood*
204	Antonín Dvořák	*Symphony No. 8 in G*
205	Richard Strauss	*Der Rosenkavalier*
206	Ludwig van Beethoven	*Piano Concerto No. 1 in C*
207	Dmitri Shostakovich	*The Unforgettable Year 1919*
208	Peter Maxwell Davies	*Farewell to Stromness*
209	Maurice Ravel	*Pavane pour une infante défunte*
210	Henry Purcell	*Dido and Aeneas*
211	Frederick Delius	*The Walk to the Paradise Garden*
212	Igor Stravinsky	*The Firebird*

213	John Williams	*Saving Private Ryan*
214	Ludwig van Beethoven	*Triple Concerto in C*
215	Gerald Finzi	*Eclogue*
216	Johannes Brahms	*Symphony No. 1 in C minor*
217	Richard Wagner	*The Mastersingers of Nuremberg*
218	Tomaso Albinoni	*Oboe Concerto in D minor Opus 9 No. 2*
219	Claudio Monteverdi	*Vespers*
220	Patrick Hawes	*Quanta Qualia*
221	Johannes Brahms	*Piano Concerto No. 1 in D minor*
222	Johann Sebastian Bach	*Cantata No. 208*
223	Edward Elgar	*Serenade in E minor for Strings*
224	Ludovico Einaudi	*I Giorni*
225	Sergei Rachmaninov	*Piano Concerto No. 1 in F sharp minor*
226	Jean Sibelius	*The Swan of Tuonela*
227	Johannes Brahms	*Symphony No. 3 in F*
228	Ralph Vaughan Williams	*The Wasps*
229	Gustav Mahler	*Symphony No. 8 in E flat (Symphony of a Thousand)*
230	Richard Wagner	*Götterdämmerung*
231	Ludwig van Beethoven	*Choral Fantasia in C minor*
232	Giuseppe Verdi	*Rigoletto*
233	Charles Gounod	*St Cecilia Mass*
234	Max Bruch	*Kol Nidrei*

235	Antonio Vivaldi	*Concerto in D for lute (RV 93)*
236	Modest Mussorgsky	*A Night on the Bare Mountain*
237	John Tavener	*Song for Athene*
238	Frederick Delius	*La Calinda*
239	Wolfgang Amadeus Mozart	*Sinfonia concertante in E flat for Violin and Viola*
240	Edward Elgar	*Sea Pictures*
241	César Franck	*Panis angelicus*
242	Edward Elgar	*Salut d'Amour*
243	Franz Liszt	*Hungarian Rhapsody No. 2 in C sharp minor*
244	Frédéric Chopin	*Nocturne in E flat major Opus 9 No. 2*
245	Giovanni Battista Pergolesi	*Stabat Mater*
246	Zbigniew Preisner	*Requiem for My Friend*
247	Gustav Mahler	*Symphony No. 4 in G*
248	Benjamin Britten	*Four Sea Interludes (from Peter Grimes)*
249	Hubert Parry	*I Was Glad*
250	Wolfgang Amadeus Mozart	*Exsultate, jubilate*
251	Gioachino Rossini	*The Barber of Seville*
252	Karl Jenkins	*Requiem*
253	George Gershwin	*Piano Concerto in F*
254	Jacques Offenbach	*The Tales of Hoffmann*
255	Giulio Caccini	*Ave Maria*
256	Nigel Hess	*Ladies in Lavender*

257	Johann Sebastian Bach	*Cantata No. 140*
258	Maurice Ravel	*Piano Concerto in G*
259	Aram Khachaturian	*Masquerade Suite*
260	Hector Berlioz	*L'Enfance du Christ*
261	Franz Schubert	*Ave Maria*
262	John Stanley	*Trumpet Voluntary*
263	Sergei Rachmaninov	*Vespers (All-Night Vigil)*
264	Johann Strauss II	*Die Fledermaus*
265	Johannes Brahms	*Symphony No. 2 in D*
266	Max Bruch	*Violin Concerto No. 2 in D minor*
267	John Rutter	*A Gaelic Blessing*
268	Edvard Grieg	*Lyric Pieces*
269	Karl Jenkins	*Palladio*
270	Aaron Copland	*Rodeo*
271	Felix Mendelssohn	*Elijah*
272	John Barry	*Dances with Wolves*
273	Ralph Vaughan Williams	*Symphony No. 5 in D*
274	Hubert Parry	*Jerusalem*
275	Ralph Vaughan Williams	*A Sea Symphony*
276	Frederick Delius	*On Hearing the First Cuckoo in Spring*
277	Antonín Dvořák	*Slavonic Dances*
278	Wolfgang Amadeus Mozart	*Mass in C minor (Great)*

279	Ralph Vaughan Williams	*A London Symphony*
280	James Horner	*Titanic*
281	William Walton	*Spitfire Prelude and Fugue*
282	Paul McCartney	*Standing Stone*
283	Franz Lehár	*The Merry Widow*
284	Jean-Philippe Rameau	*Les Indes galantes*
285	Johann Nepomuk Hummel	*Trumpet Concerto*
286	Franz Schubert	*Impromptu No. 3 in G flat*
287	Léo Delibes	*Coppélia*
288	Gaetano Donizetti	*Lucia di Lammermoor*
289	Antonio Vivaldi	*Concerto in G for Two Mandolins (RV 532)*
290	Pyotr Ilyich Tchaikovsky	*Serenade for Strings*
291	Leonard Bernstein	*Candide*
292	Jon Lord	*Durham Concerto*
293	Sergei Prokofiev	*Lieutenant Kijé*
294	Morten Lauridsen	*O Magnum Mysterium*
295	Giuseppe Verdi	*La forza del destino*
296	Gerald Finzi	*Clarinet Concerto*
297	John Barry	*The Beyondness of Things*
298	Pyotr Ilyich Tchaikovsky	*Piano Concerto No. 2 in G*
299	Joaquín Rodrigo	*Fantasia para un gentilhombre*
300	Joseph Haydn	*Cello Concerto No. 1 in C*

The Classic FM
Hall of Fame

RICHARD ADDINSELL
(1904–1977)

Warsaw Concerto

If you're looking for a piece of music that divides opinion, look no further than this work. Beloved by many for its Rachmaninov-esque melodies and nostalgic sound-world, it's also remembered for its repeated occurrence in Spike Milligan's autobiography as 'the bloody awful *Warsaw Concerto*'. Despite sounding like a full-blooded Romantic piano concerto, the piece was actually composed for the 1941 film *Dangerous Moonlight*, a World War II love story with a sweeping soundtrack to match the romance of the plot. The film's producers apparently had their eyes on Rachmaninov: he, they thought, would be the perfect man to write the score. But if you're Rachmaninov, you can afford to turn down the odd commission here and there – and so, when the first-choice composer said 'thanks but no thanks', the job of penning the music for *Dangerous Moonlight* fell to Addinsell. Despite all that, it's fair to say that even he passed on much of the work, too: it fell to the arranger and orchestrator Roy Douglas to knit together the melodies and turn them into a fully orchestrated, heart-on-your-sleeve concert piece.

The composer's unashamed use of indulgent harmonies and grand Romantic gestures goes a great way towards explaining why the *Warsaw Concerto* remains hugely popular today. And while the music lives on, you would struggle to find a decent crowd of people who can remember the movie.

RECOMMENDED RECORDING

Roderick Elms (piano); Royal Philharmonic Orchestra; José Serebrier (conductor).
Classic FM: CFMCD 46.
CHART POSITION 189

TOMASO ALBINONI
(1671–1751)

Adagio in G minor

Albinoni was a Baroque composer who had a financially rather well-cushioned life, thanks to the shares he inherited in his father's stationery firm, which manufactured playing

3

cards, among other things. In 1945, the Italian academic Remo Giazotto published a book on Albinoni entitled *The Violin Music of the Venetian Dilettante*. Albinoni was just one area of expertise for Giazotto. Others included the composers Vivaldi and Busoni, as well as the music of the Baroque and Classical periods in general in Giazotto's native Genoa.

The academic's expertise on the life and music of the stationer's son led him to complete an Albinoni fragment, which he said he had discovered in the Saxon State Library in Dresden, while he was trying to salvage manuscripts after it was bombed in the Second World War. This produced what is known as the 'Albinoni *Adagio*', but should surely, at the very least, be called the 'Albinoni–Giazotto *Adagio*'. Late on in life, Giazotto changed his story, denying that the piece was based on a fragment of Albinoni's original composition at all. Instead, he wanted the world to know that he, Giazotto, had written the whole thing himself and Albinoni hadn't played any part in it. Nevertheless – and whatever the truth – the name 'Albinoni's *Adagio*' sticks.

RECOMMENDED RECORDING

I Solisti Veneti; Claudio Scimone (conductor). Erato: 2292-45557-2.

CHART POSITION 41

Oboe Concerto in D minor Opus 9 No. 2

Unlike the famous *Adagio*, there is no question mark hanging over the authorship of one of Albinoni's best-known works for oboe. During his lifetime, the self-styled Venetian dilettante became famous across Europe, chiefly for his operas. He was determined not to let the inheritance of his father's paper and stationery company get in the way of composing and he soon divested himself of any day-to-day

operational duties. This left him free to spend much of the 1720s (when he would have been in his fifties) touring the most fashionable international opera houses, overseeing his works. It meant that he found himself in the front line when it came to experiencing the latest advances in the music of the period. He was one of the first in Italy to write for the oboe – an emerging new instrument. This concerto is a near-perfect example of the species.

RECOMMENDED RECORDING

Pierre Pierlot (oboe); I Solisti Veneti; Claudio Scimone (conductor). Erato: ERA 450 992 1302.

CHART POSITION 218

GREGORIO ALLEGRI
(1582–1652)

Miserere

This piece is the stuff of legends. Well, one particular legend, to be precise. Mozart, when he was a teenager, so the story goes, once heard Allegri's *Miserere* being performed in the Sistine Chapel. The precocious young composer apparently scurried home and wrote down the entire work from memory. Wonderful as the story sounds, it's almost certainly apocryphal: it would have been highly likely that Mozart would have come across the *Miserere* before, given its already significant popularity in musical circles.

The work itself is a sublime nine-voice setting of Psalm 51: *Miserere mei, Deus, secundum magnam misercordiuam tuam* ('Have mercy upon me, O God, after Thy great goodness'). As you listen to the heavenly sound of each interweaving voice, it's fascinating to think that Allegri composed the piece for two separate choirs: one of four voices, and the other of five.

Allegri was a devout Catholic, having been trained as a priest, and he worked with the Vatican's Papal Choir right up until his death. Karl Proske, former Canon of Ratisbon Cathedral, described the composer as a man whose music was imbued with his religious faith and personal sense of justice, saying Allegri was 'a model of priestly peace and humility, a father to the poor, the consoler of captives and the forsaken, a self-sacrificing help and rescuer of suffering humanity'.

RECOMMENDED RECORDING
Choir of New College, Oxford;
Edward Higginbottom (conductor).
Erato: 3984 295882.
CHART POSITION 23

B

JOHANN SEBASTIAN BACH
(1685–1750)

Concerto in D minor for Two Violins
Double Concerto

Today, around half a million people live in Leipzig, a city that boasts one of the oldest and most respected orchestras in the world, the Gewandhaus, as well as two opera houses, a couple of music festivals and much more besides. However, when Bach arrived in Leipzig in 1723, he inherited a professional music staff of four town pipers, three violinists and one apprentice. At the age of forty-eight, he had taken what seemed to him to be a backward move in his career, becoming Kantor of St Thomas's. He built up his force of musicians by recruiting from his school and the nearby university. Composed in 1717, the 'Bach Double', as it is often called, came with him from his previous job in Cöthen, but seven years after he had arrived in Leipzig, he made a transcription for two harpsichords. Many of Bach's orchestrations were for purely pragmatic reasons,

so we might presume that none of the three fiddlers were up to playing it in its original form. However, when the Cöthen version of the work was lost, Bach specialists were able to reconstruct it from the harpsichord version. The slow movement is surely one of Bach's most sublime creations.

RECOMMENDED RECORDING
Daniel Hope (violin); Marieke Blankestijn (violin); Chamber Orchestra of Europe. Warner Classics: 2564625452.
CHART POSITION 32

Toccata and Fugue in D minor

This work might as well be called 'The Organ'. For many, the instrument Stravinsky called 'the monster that never breathes' seems to come alive in this piece, which might have been written to make the listener believe that the organ talks, proving Stravinsky wrong. This is perhaps all the more striking when one realises that, since

right Johann Sebastian Bach: Toccata and Fugue in D minor

Johann Sebastian Bach

1685-1750

'Johann Sebastian Bach has done everything completely, he was a man through and through.'

FRANZ SCHUBERT

This German composer was the most famous of a large musical family. Alongside Handel, he was one of the greatest composers of the Baroque period. He was also an organist and director of church music, which is why lots of his works are religious.

Orphaned as a child, he became a chorister when he was fifteen. Four years later, he walked from his home in Arnstadt to Lübeck to hear a performance by his favourite composer, Buxtehude. The teenager then walked all the way back to Arnstadt, a total journey of some 420 miles.

Bach's career began in Weimar as an organist and court musician. Then he took a job in Cöthen, before eventually going to live and work in Leipzig for almost three decades.

He was without doubt a diligent composer, but that very much went with the territory of writing for church choirs. There was an expectation that a steady stream of new choral works would be

DID YOU KNOW?

Alongside composing, Bach also found time to teach music to many of his children. He had twenty in total – so, an entire class of young musicians!

composed for his choirs to perform. Although a hard worker, Bach was not the quiet bookish don that one might imagine. Instead, he often had blazing rows with his

employers and was even locked up for disloyalty on one notable occasion. As well as his choral works, Bach wrote some of the finest examples of secular Baroque keyboard and orchestral music.

It was not until after his death that Bach's true greatness was recognised. Towards the end of his life, rather than his huge output being hailed as that of a master composer, he began to be overshadowed by his sons Carl Philipp Emanuel, Johann Christian, Johann Christoph Friedrich and Wilhelm Friedemann, all of whom were successful composers of the day.

Bach was a fan of two things: coffee and numbers. Lots of his pieces play games with numbers, inaudibly. And he wrote a whole cantata about coffee.

the 1980s at least, there has been a growing body of opinion that the work is not even by J. S. Bach. As with a lot of Bach's music, there is no surviving manuscript by the man himself – something that is not enough in itself to cast a stain on the work's credentials. It is more the complete originality, the one-off nature and the very un-Bach-like characteristics that lead some musicologists to doubt its provenance. If Bach did write it, say the believers, it was probably when he was very young – possibly between the ages of eighteen and twenty-two. The finest performances, such as the one recommended below, prove that, no matter who actually wrote it, it's a masterpiece of epic proportions.

RECOMMENDED RECORDING
Daniel Chorzempa (organ).
Pentatone: PTC5186127.
CHART POSITION 50

The Brandenburg Concertos (BWV 1046-51)

There is no doubt that J. S. Bach did write the *Brandenburg Concertos*. However, he would not have recognised them by that name. When he penned the six concertos, almost certainly during his time at Cöthen (presumably for various members of the Cöthen Court Orchestra) the composer gave them the title 'Concertos for Several Instruments'. It was only his decision to package them up as a present for Christian Ludwig, the Margrave of Brandenburg (a margrave is roughly on a par with a marquis) that gave them their title.

Sadly for Bach, there appears to be no record of him ever having received a reply from the Margrave – and certainly not the one he desired: 'Thank you, Herr Bach, here's a large bundle of money and a job.' Indeed, there is no evidence the Margrave himself even heard them played.

Each of the six concertos appeals most to different listeners, from the galumphing First, the more 'stately-home' styling of the Second, the homely Third, the lofty Fourth and the galloping Fifth right through to the joyous Sixth.

RECOMMENDED RECORDING
English Baroque Soloists; John Eliot Gardiner (conductor). SDG: SDG707.
CHART POSITION 56

St Matthew Passion

Good Friday 1727 in Leipzig was a particularly good Friday. When Bach had first arrived, four years earlier, he had no doubt wowed his employers – not to mention the congregation – with that year's Easter offering, the *St John Passion*. Bach was ushered to Leipzig on the promise of a very large salary indeed, so the splendour of the work was probably timely. Given that he was responsible for providing weekly music at not one, but two, churches, for teaching singing to the schoolchildren, for training the choir, for teaching Latin (although, in the end, he farmed this part out to a deputy), he could surely be forgiven for thinking he was doing enough. Indeed, one of the reasons for Bach's constant use of existing chorale tunes as the basis for his extended cantatas was not just familiarity to his audience, but also sheer necessity. Four years into the job, though, he decided to compose another major choral piece. The *St Matthew Passion* is a monster of a work for two orchestras with extra words by Bach's favourite poet, Picander.

RECOMMENDED RECORDING

Anthony Rolfe Johnson (tenor, Evangelist); Barbara Bonney (soprano); Ann Monoylos (soprano); Anne Sofie von Otter (alto); Michael Chance (alto); Howard Crook (tenor); Olaf Bär (baritone); Cornelius Hauptmann (bass); English Baroque Soloists; Monteverdi Choir; John Eliot Gardiner (conductor). Deutsche Grammophon Archiv: 4297732.

CHART POSITION 78

Mass in B minor

There are several reasons why many Bach-lovers regard the B minor Mass as the pinnacle of his work. Size, for one, singles it out, even when compared to his previous titans, the *St John Passion* and the *St Matthew Passion*. It also contains some of the most engaging passages of music that he ever wrote, such as the opening five-part *Kyrie eleison*. Composed around 1748–49, it came at the end of Bach's life, when he had only one year left to live.

When the work is heard in its entirety, the listener comes away with the impression that this is a piece of music the composer had been building up to writing for the whole of his life. It therefore seems ironic that much of this best-loved work was 'bottom-drawer' music – music that Bach had either put by earlier or recycled. Indeed, he didn't even give the work a name. So this bundled collection of itinerant manuscripts simply bears the names of its

individual sections, save for the *Missa*, which he transplanted wholesale from some fifteen years earlier. Despite being a motley disarray of homeless Mass sections on paper, it sounds completely wonderful.

RECOMMENDED RECORDING

Barbara Schlick (soprano); Catherine Patriasz (soprano); Charles Brett (alto); Howard Crook (tenor); Peter Kooy (bass); Chorus and Orchestra of Collegium Vocale, Ghent; Philippe Herreweghe (conductor). Virgin Veritas: 6931972.

CHART POSITION 88

Cantata No. 147

If we translate the title of the most popular section of Bach's cantata a little more accurately than the now ubiquitous English version we know, it comes out something like 'Jesus remains my joy, my heart's comfort and essence', rather than 'Jesu, joy of man's desiring'. Indeed, the rest of the translation bears precious little relation to the actual German text, written by the lawyer and poet Salomo Franck. Accuracy of words aside, this exquisite movement – choral interludes between that divine, undulating melody – might be best seen as a mere key to unlocking the rest of the cantata, entitled *Herz und Mund und Tat und Leben* (which translates as 'Heart and Mouth and Deed and Life'). Bach, in his quest to supply music for umpteen venues throughout his life, recycled the cantata – adding the now favourite section only the second time around. Originally destined for the last Sunday of Advent, the reworked version became a setting for May's Feast of the Visitation. Thank goodness, in some respects, for the composer's pretty oppressive work schedule. And a great example of recycling making sense.

RECOMMENDED RECORDING

Susan Gritton (soprano); Lisa Milne (soprano); Michael Chance (counter-tenor); Ian Bostridge (tenor); Michael George (bass); Choir of King's College, Cambridge; Academy of Ancient Music; Stephen Cleobury (conductor). EMI Classics: 5569942.

CHART POSITION 110

Cello Suites

Rarely has a composer managed to pare his music down to its absolute essence as Bach did in his *Cello Suites*. Perhaps there are three reasons for this: one, we're dealing with a genius composer; two, their solo nature – forcing Bach to astound his listener with clever and sometimes fiendishly difficult ways of maximising the instrument; and three, the fact that the cello is often considered the nearest instrument to the human voice. It somehow captures the feeling of exposed honesty, of complete naturalness, as the greatest voices do.

There are six suites in all, each with six movements. There are no surviving manuscripts in Bach's own hand, so musicians have relied on a copy written out by his second wife, Anna Magdalena. Her role as a scribe has even led some musical historians to paint her as a sort of Bacon to Bach's Shakespeare, with the suggestion that she actually wrote many of the cello suites herself.

The eminent cellist Pablo Casals kicked off the craze for recording all six in the 1920s – he'd found a second-hand copy of the music in a charity shop when he was just thirteen years old. Today, stunning complete versions abound.

RECOMMENDED RECORDING

Yo-Yo Ma (cello). Sony: SM2K89754.

CHART POSITION 134

Orchestral Suite No. 3 in D

Bach wrote a total of four orchestral suites, although his definition of an orchestra is pretty loose, as the group of musicians performing the work might be as small as a string quartet, a handful of woodwind players, some trumpets and a percussionist. The most popular of the suites is the Third, which was written, along with the others, during the last period of his life in Leipzig. It comes in five movements and, from the outset, it feels like 'civic' music, perhaps reflecting the fact that Bach was a public servant, rather than an aristocrat's in-house musician. In Germany and France, these works tend to be known as *ouvertures*, which is also the designation of the first movement in each case. The *Air* (the second movement) has now been reclaimed in its original form after a period being primarily known as a transcription by August Wilhelmj, which made it a party piece playable on only one string of a violin – hence its nickname *Air on the G string*. For an entire generation, this piece will forever be linked to Hamlet cigars, after being used in a long-running and highly popular television advertising campaign.

RECOMMENDED RECORDING

Scottish Chamber Orchestra. Regis: RRC1160.

CHART POSITION 141

Goldberg Variations

The story behind this work is one of music's best, with a cast of three. First, a count: Count Kaiserling, who suffered from insomnia. Second comes his much put-upon musician, the eponymous Johann Goldberg. Finally, there is Bach. When Kaiserling was up all night, he would make Goldberg play in the adjacent antechamber. Bach's reputation as a fine composer reached the ears of Kaiserling, so Goldberg was sent to him to be well tutored. When Bach heard of the plight of Goldberg's boss, he penned the work. It was a genre of music into which he had never before ventured, thinking variations almost a form of musical 'sheep counting' (in the most respectful sense) and thus perfect for an insomniac. Luckily for Bach, and also for Goldberg, the new composition helped to ensure that Kaiserling was out for the count. For his troubles, Bach was said to have been paid a goblet full of gold louis d'or.

RECOMMENDED RECORDING
Angela Hewitt (piano). Hyperion: CDA30002.
CHART POSITION 155

Cantata No. 208

Not many works in this book are known by three completely different names. Although best known for *'Sheep May Safely Graze'*, this particular work is described as Bach's *Hunting Cantata* – a reference to its secular subject matter. Its beacon aria is the ninth movement, *Schafe können sicher weiden*. To explain that line, sheep may graze safely where there's a good shepherd who stays awake and where there's a good nobleman watching over a blissful nation. Why did Bach set such a line? Well, because he was writing this music for the birthday of Duke Christian in 1713 and he knew which side his bread was buttered. The commission also gives rise to its third name, the *Birthday Cantata*.

RECOMMENDED RECORDING
Concentus Musicus Vienna;
Nikolaus Harnoncourt (conductor).
Warner: 2564 692592.
CHART POSITION 222

Cantata No. 140

The opening words of this cantata, *Wachet auf*, which translates as 'Sleepers Awake', contains a tune written by a Lutheran pastor called Philipp Nicolai. It caught Bach's attention during his golden Leipzig period. It wasn't unusual for Bach to transform original melodies by other chorale and hymn-tune composers into his own works of art. The most famous section of this cantata is Part IV: 'Zion hears the watchmen calling' and it is here that Nicolai's tune features.

The first performance of this most beautiful of wake-up calls was on 25 November 1731, which was the 27th Sunday after Trinity – the specific day for which the work was written to be performed. It is notable that there can be only 27 Sundays after Trinity in years when Easter falls early. As a result, this now famous

---

left Johann Sebastian Bach: Cantata No. 208

cantata was, in fact, rarely heard in the years after it was written.

RECOMMENDED RECORDING
Monteverdi Choir; English Baroque Soloists; John Eliot Gardiner (conductor).
SDG: SDG171.
CHART POSITION 257

SAMUEL BARBER
(1910–1981)

Adagio for Strings

For many, it was its use in the film *Platoon*. For others, it was William Orbit's *Pieces in a Modern Style* project. But very few of us can claim to have first experienced Barber's *Adagio for Strings* in its original form: as part of a string quartet. The American composer wrote his String Quartet Opus 11, in 1936 – and considered himself happy with the result. But he had one of the twentieth-century's greatest conductors to thank for what became a new and far more profitable life for this relatively unknown piece. Arturo Toscanini spotted a hit when he heard its second movement, and urged Barber to arrange it for full string orchestra. The composer wisely took the advice on board – and, in 1938, Toscanini premiered the new work with the NBC Symphony Orchestra. Millions of Americans were listening as it was broadcast on the radio, and *Adagio for Strings* quickly became a huge success.

The solemn, heart-wrenching sadness of the music has lent itself to a range of powerful uses beyond the concert hall. *Adagio for Strings* was played at the funeral of Albert Einstein, can be heard on all sorts of commercials and movie soundtracks, and has become a modern day hit among trance music pioneers, who have taken the hypnotic harmonies composed by Barber and used them to create very different, high octane sounds. The composer also arranged a choral version of the work, the *Agnus Dei*, in 1967.

RECOMMENDED RECORDING
Detroit Symphony Orchestra; Neeme Järvi (conductor). Chandos: CHAN 9169.
CHART POSITION 11

Violin Concerto

Given the great success of the *Adagio for Strings*, Samuel Barber could have been forgiven for resting on his musical laurels in the late 1930s. But the American composer was having none of it: he set about working on his only *Violin Concerto* in 1939, just a year after the *Adagio*'s premiere.

Initially, the composer's reasons for cracking on with a new work were primarily financial: he'd been commissioned to write a violin concerto by one Samuel Fels, father to one of Barber's classmates at the Curtis Institute of Music and a Philadelphia industrialist. Fels was a wealthy man, but a seemingly demanding one, too. Far from letting Barber compose at a distance, Fels, it's said, gave continued feedback on what he did and didn't like. At first, the work was too simplistic. Barber's solution? Add a fiendishly challenging finale. Fels's response? It had become too complex. Back and forth they went, the composer duly making changes against his wishes – presumably because he knew that a worthwhile pay cheque awaited him at the end of his endeavours.

Today, it's the soulful, intense middle movement of the concerto that guarantees its enduring popularity. The violin seems at times to be almost wrestling with the orchestra, before reaching a position of serene contentment – only to find itself wrought in conflict again a few moments later. Stunning stuff.

RECOMMENDED RECORDING
Joshua Bell (violin); Baltimore Symphony Orchestra; David Zinman (conductor). Classic FM: CFM FW 004.

CHART POSITION 140

JOHN BARRY
(1933–2011)

Dances with Wolves

Kevin Costner directed and starred in *Dances with Wolves*, a 1990 Western, which hoovered up seven Oscars, including Best Picture and Best Director. With a running time of nearly three hours (the director's cut comes in just four minutes shy of four hours), it truly was a saga, and one that worked. Made for just $22 million, it eventually took more than $184 million at the box office.

The British film composer John Barry's sweeping string sounds suited the epic nature of the story's Sioux-soaked skylines perfectly. As well as the main *John Dunbar Theme*, the *Love Theme* is eloquent and ever so slightly haunting; while the music used to accompany Two Socks (the 'star' wolf) is

both shifting and beautiful.

The full score rewards extended listening. Don't be put off by titles such as *Two Socks at Play* or *Stands with a Fist Remembers*. These are meat and drink to a film composer whose primary role is to write music that accompanies exactly what is happening on screen at any given moment. Unsurprisingly, the CD remains in demand more than two decades after the movie's premiere.

RECOMMENDED RECORDING
John Barry conducts a Studio Orchestra. Epic Soundtrax: EK 63555.

CHART POSITION 272

The Beyondness of Things

As with so many composers, understanding the key events in the life of John Barry Prendergast (his original name) leads to a deeper understanding of his music. After a youth spent as a projectionist in his father's York cinema, he was bathed from an early age in the rich choral music of the English tradition, going for lessons with Francis Jackson, the Organist at York Minster. But it is probably his later youth – as pop star with the John Barry Seven and musical director for Adam Faith – that informs this album more.

Coming at the end of a life in the cinema, this collection of pieces marries Barry's tried-and-tested cinema style with the earlier 'three-minute-thirty' quick-hit singles. Pieces such as *Nocturnal New York* are like film scores in miniature, sweeping you up in their wake and enveloping you in the classic Barry sound. The title track is the CD's show-stealer, allowing the English Chamber Orchestra's lush string sound to come across at its best. At times, you can almost hear history playing out in front of you: *Kissably Close* doffs the cap, in style only, to the classic score of *Midnight Cowboy*, reminding us of John Barry's genius. Beautiful, lush sounds.

RECOMMENDED RECORDING
English Chamber Orchestra; John Barry (conductor). Polygram: 460009.

CHART POSITION 297

LUDWIG VAN BEETHOVEN
(1770–1827)

Piano Concerto No. 5 in E flat
Emperor

Every portrait of Beethoven seems to drive home the impression that he was a composer whose music was tempestuous, brooding and muscular. And while that was certainly the case, the masterful *Emperor Concerto* is proof of the tenderness and beauty that runs like a thread through this great man's music.

At the time of writing this concerto, Beethoven was very much straddling the divide between the Classical and Romantic periods. The work itself seems to be breaking out of conventional boundaries – almost as if a new kind of music is being born. The sheer length of the opening movement belies convention; the serene second movement flows directly – and unusually – into the finale; and the overt romance of the music looks ahead to a musical period that was at that time still in its infancy.

At its premiere in Vienna in 1812, the soloist was one Carl Czerny – a fine composer in his own right and a man who studied under Beethoven. Apparently, the work's nickname derived not from Beethoven but from a comment made by one of Napoleon's officers, who

was stationed in Vienna at the time. It was 'an emperor of a concerto', the man supposedly exclaimed. Indeed it was. And the name has stuck ever since.

RECOMMENDED RECORDING
Alfred Brendel (piano); Vienna Philharmonic Orchestra; Simon Rattle (conductor). Philips: 4627812.

CHART POSITION 6

Symphony No. 6 in F
Pastoral

As you listen to the sublime opening movement of this bucolic symphony, you can't help but feel Beethoven would sympathise with those of us who have spent many a summer's journey stuck in heavy traffic, yearning to arrive at our rural destination. We hear the buoyant, optimistic, almost skipping melody that begins the symphony, and we're instantly transported to calmer scenes. Beethoven promises an 'awakening of pleasant feelings upon arriving in the country'; if this music had a scent, it would be freshly cut grass and fields of bluebells, or maybe even a whiff of the farmyard.

Originally dubbed 'recollections of life in the country', Beethoven's *Symphony No. 6* is his homage to the great outdoors. The composer was, in many ways, an urban man, known and revered in Vienna, and central to the city's reputation within European culture at the time. And yet, as the five descriptively titled sections of this piece so amply prove, he also had a joyous view of the countryside and all it contains. The work is one of the first real examples of what became known as 'programme music':

---

right Ludwig van Beethoven: Symphony No. 6 in F

Ludwig van Beethoven

1770-1827

'If anyone has conducted a Beethoven performance, and then doesn't have to go to an osteopath, then there's something wrong.'

SIR SIMON RATTLE

Along with Mozart, Beethoven has a strong claim on the title 'the world's greatest classical composer', and he is revered as one of the undisputed kings of classical music. He wrote everything: concertos, an opera, choral works and pieces for solo instruments – you name it – but his speciality was the symphony.

Beethoven led a tough life, often beaten, early on, by his alcoholic father. He gave his first public concert when he was seven years old, becoming a court organist in Bonn when he was still a teenager. Fifteen years younger than Mozart, Beethoven played for the older man in Vienna in the hope that he would give him lessons. Mozart agreed but in the end Beethoven travelled back to Bonn to care for his ailing mother.

Instead, a few years later, Beethoven became a pupil of Joseph Haydn, who was another of the greats of the Classical period. Beethoven made

> ## DID YOU KNOW?
> We have Beethoven's father to thank for encouraging in him a love of music. Beethoven Senior taught his son the piano from the age of four.

rapid progress in Vienna, where he was by then living. Soon he was acknowledged as being the best keyboard player in the city.

From his mid-twenties onwards, he was at his

most productive, with a steady stream of chamber works to his name. His First Symphony was composed before his thirtieth birthday.

In Beethoven's twenties, his doctor told him that he was going deaf and during his thirties he totally lost his hearing. It is remarkable to think that such was Beethoven's talent that he could continue to compose amazing music even though he himself was unable to hear it.

Given the challenges that going deaf must have presented to a composer, particularly at a time when medical science was not particularly advanced, it is not difficult to understand the frustrations that Beethoven must have suffered and he could be an irascible and difficult man.

music that tells a specific story or paints an aural picture of a particular scene. Just one of the many ways in which Beethoven was a groundbreaking composer.

RECOMMENDED RECORDING
Budapest Festival Orchestra; Iván Fischer (conductor). Channel Classics: CCS SA 30710.

CHART POSITION 7

Symphony No. 9 in D minor
Choral

This is arguably the greatest symphony ever composed: the summit of Beethoven's achievements, a masterful musical celebration of the human race and a massive work that makes all who hear it feel better about life. And yet, Beethoven himself never actually heard it. By the time his *Symphony No. 9* was premiered on 7 May 1824, he was profoundly deaf. The man who had done more than anyone before him to change the way we hear music had become one for whom sounds could no longer exist – and the bitter irony of this was not lost on him. Despite his deteriorating hearing, though, Beethoven persevered with writing this mammoth symphony. Encouraged, no doubt, by his status as the composer of the moment, he penned a colossal work. But, when Beethoven conducted its premiere, he was famously unaware of the rapturous response his Ninth Symphony received. It took one of the musicians to alert him to the cheering audience – and that was only at the end of the second movement.

Beethoven's *Symphony No. 9* is famous for its setting of Friedrich Schiller's poem 'Ode to Joy' – a text the composer had been fascinated with for over twenty years: 'Mercy from the final judge! The dead shall live! Brothers, drink and chime in, all sinners shall be forgiven and hell shall be no more!' Triumphant words that perfectly match the power and scale of Beethoven's immortal music.

RECOMMENDED RECORDING
Twyla Robinson (soprano); Karen Cargill (mezzo-soprano); John MacMaster (tenor); Gerald Finley (bass); London Symphony Orchestra and Chorus; Bernard Haitink (conductor). LSO Live: LSO0092.

CHART POSITION 9

Symphony No. 7 in A

It's tempting to feel sorry for Beethoven's *Symphony No. 7*. Hidden away amid the Fifth (the most famous opening four notes in the history of classical music), the Sixth (how could anyone fail to love the 'Pastoral'?) and the mighty colossus that is his Ninth, you feel as if the Seventh is a work that could easily get forgotten. That fate has arguably befallen *Symphony No. 8* – but not *No. 7*. The raw power and drama found in Beethoven's *Symphony No. 9* seem, in many ways, to be receiving their first full outing here. There's a visceral quality to the music – not least in the almost crazed finale when the musicians appear to be playing as if their lives depend on it. In the case of the premiere, those orchestral musicians included fellow composers Meyerbeer, Spohr and Moscheles, with Beethoven himself on the podium.

Described by Wagner, no less, as 'the apotheosis of the dance', this four-movement symphony begins in grave, sombre tones. Not for Beethoven the stirring opening to the Fifth, or the lilting, sunny start to the Sixth; instead, the orchestral colours are dark, creating a sense of foreboding about what's to come. The lightness of touch in later parts of the symphony – particularly the third movement – is therefore surprising, with some parts seeming very consciously to link back to the light-hearted mood of the *Pastoral*. The unbounded finale, meanwhile, was apparently summed up by Tchaikovsky as 'a whole series of images, full of unrestrained joy, full of bliss and pleasure of life'.

RECOMMENDED RECORDING
Scottish Chamber Orchestra; Charles Mackerras (conductor). Hyperion: CDS 44304.
CHART POSITION 30

Symphony No. 5 in C minor

If you had to pick one musical phrase in the whole of classical music known by more people than any other, it would surely be the opening two bars of Beethoven's *Symphony No. 5*. But what does it mean? As with many other classical works, critics have been all too keen to assign to this symphony the character of Fate knocking at the door. But, aside from an assertion to that effect by Beethoven's friend Schiller, there's very little evidence to suggest that it was the composer's intention. Instead, could it simply be the case that Beethoven's musical genius led him to write an outstanding, gripping melody? His creative juices were certainly flowing in the early 1800s: work on the *Symphony No. 5* began shortly after the premiere of his mighty *Eroica* – a symphony similarly imbued with thrilling melodic lines from start to finish.

Vienna must have been an incredibly exciting city to live in at this time. Just imagine

being at the premiere of Beethoven's Fifth in 1808: a concert where the warm-up material was the premiere of the *Pastoral*. By the time Beethoven stepped up to the podium to conduct *Symphony No. 5*, the audience must have wondered how any composer could come up with another tune to match what they had just heard. And yet, as this four-movement symphony amply proves, this composer was only too ready to share more extraordinary music with the world.

RECOMMENDED RECORDING
Basel Chamber Orchestra; Giovanni Antonini (conductor). Sony Classical: 8869 7648162.
CHART POSITION 33

Piano Sonata No. 14 in C sharp minor
Moonlight

Despite its nickname, in Beethoven's mind this was never the *Moonlight Sonata*. Instead, the rather pedestrian title of *Piano Sonata No. 14* was what the composer seemed perfectly content with. But when the German critic Ludwig Rellstab described the sonata's famous opening movement as being akin to moonlight flickering across Lake Lucerne, he created a description that would go on to outlive the composer.

In many ways, Beethoven was a revolutionary. More than any other composer of his day, he was responsible for pushing convention and welcoming in the Romantic era of classical music. This work is a prime example of his refusal to follow the status quo: not for Beethoven the traditional fast–slow–fast pattern of how it was then perceived a sonata should sound. Instead – and astonishingly for the time – he chose to open with a slow, hypnotic set of arpeggios (this is where the notes of a chord are broken up and played one after another, instead of all at the same time). The storm and drama certainly comes, but not until the second movement, a section audiences of the time would have expected to be reflective and calm. Just one of the ways in which Beethoven was prepared to turn the predictable on its head and create whole new forms of music.

Today, the *Moonlight* (or the 'sonata in the style of a fantasia', as Beethoven preferred to subtitle it) stands as the composer's most famous and most loved solo piano piece.

RECOMMENDED RECORDING
Steven Osborne (piano). Hyperion: CDA 67662.
CHART POSITION 37

Violin Concerto in D

Nine symphonies, five piano concertos, thirty-two piano sonatas, stacks of chamber music and plenty more besides. Beethoven's output in nearly every musical genre was prolific – so it's perhaps surprising that he wrote only the single concerto for one of the most popular instruments of his day: the violin.

This work, which is now so firmly accepted as one of the greats of the repertoire, was something of a slow burner. Unlike many other pieces by the great composer, it certainly didn't become an instant hit. The concerto was rattled off by Beethoven in a remarkably short space of time. He took just a few weeks to compose it in the winter of 1806, and it was premiered within days of

its completion on 23 December. This was a fairly rushed affair. The soloist hadn't had time to learn his part, so spent a good deal of the concert sight-reading. It's hard to imagine Beethoven being too pleased with such an approach.

Beethoven's only two other works of note for the violin were his *Romance in G Opus 40*, and *Romance in G Opus 50*, completed a few years before this concerto. Lyrical and spacious in tone, they couldn't be more different from the *Violin Concerto*'s most famous movement: a zesty, spirited finale making dazzling use of the instrument's melodic range.

RECOMMENDED RECORDING
Maxim Vengerov (violin); London Symphony Orchestra; Mstislav Rostropovich (conductor). EMI Classics: 3364032.
CHART POSITION 39

Symphony No. 3 in E flat
Eroica

Of all the works in the history of classical music, this is the one that definitively closed the door on the Classical period and ushered in fully the start of the Romantic era. Composed in 1803, the piece was very much written in the shadow of the two symphonic masters, Mozart and Haydn. Between them, they had defined the symphony for their era. Their music certainly contained passion and emotion, but it was always restrained within set structures. These structures were becoming tired, though, and a new music was ready to burst forth.

Step forward Beethoven, prepared once again to break the rules. Here, for the first time, the composer was determined to take his listeners on a sublime musical journey. The degree to which the *Eroica* was inspired by Napoleon is something that musicologists continue to debate today. But, in essence,

TOP COMPOSERS

1	Wolfgang Amadeus Mozart	*20 entries*
2	Ludwig van Beethoven	*17 entries*
3	Pyotr Ilyich Tchaikovsky	*13 entries*
4=	Johann Sebastian Bach	*11 entries*
4=	Edward Elgar	*11 entries*
6	Ralph Vaughan Williams	*9 entries*
7	Johannes Brahms	*8 entries*
8=	George Frideric Handel	*7 entries*
8=	Franz Schubert	*7 entries*
8=	Antonio Vivaldi	*7 entries*
8=	Richard Wagner	*7 entries*

it's not the real question here. Instead, the question is: can we hear what Beethoven is communicating from deep within his soul? Can we hear the themes of struggle and triumph in this victorious music?

Beethoven's status as the most important composer of his time was pretty much confirmed in an instant with this one mighty work. After hearing it, audiences were gripped. They wanted more. And as they were about to discover, Beethoven was determined to set about giving them just that.

RECOMMENDED RECORDING
Minnesota Orchestra; Osmo Vänskä (conductor). BIS: SACD 1516.

CHART POSITION 73

Romance No. 2 in F

Many of Beethoven's most popular works are epic in scale, programmatic in style and even semi-autobiographical in nature. Here, though, the composer treats us to what can, in comparison with his mighty symphonies and concertos, appear to be something of a musical lollipop.

Beethoven composed his *Romance No. 2* in 1803 and the sweet, innocent melodies belie the altogether more tumultuous events of the composer's personal life at the time. His ability to create astonishing music throughout this period can all too easily lead us to forget the cruel experience of his suffering from gradual deafness. At the same time as writing the *Romance in F*, Beethoven was forced to come to terms with his condition, probably for the first time.

The delicate, youthful phrasing of the violin line suggests a composer finding some brief respite through the escapism of writing music. Indeed, Beethoven seems to have continually found solace in this way throughout the early 1800s, when his awareness of his deteriorating hearing was at its most acute. During this period, the *Moonlight Sonata* and his *Symphony No. 2* were just two of the other works he composed.

Here, all angst is absent from the page. In its place, we find music that suggests that all is well. As Beethoven knew all too clearly, though, this was far from the case.

RECOMMENDED RECORDING

Anne-Sophie Mutter (violin); New York Philharmonic Orchestra; Kurt Masur (conductor). Deutsche Grammophon: 4713492.

CHART POSITION 107

Piano Concerto No. 4 in G

Just imagine that you are the most famous composer in the world. Your public adores you. You've had huge success already with all sorts of works. And now, you've written your fourth piano concerto. Deciding who should play the solo piano part could surely be considered an afterthought. Every pianist in Europe would jump at the chance – wouldn't they?

Apparently not. At least, not in the case of Beethoven's *Piano Concerto No. 4*. After com-

pleting this concerto in 1806, the composer struggled to find anyone to perform it. So the work sat on a shelf, gathering dust, until its public premiere on 22 December 1808. The eventual soloist? One Ludwig van Beethoven. The man clearly had astonishing stamina. In the same concert, he conducted the premiere performances of his *Symphony No. 5* and *No. 6*!

Beethoven has Felix Mendelssohn to thank for the continued popularity of his *Piano Concerto No. 4*. The piece was in danger of being eclipsed by the many other great works being composed by Beethoven at the time – not least, those two symphonies. Some twenty-five years after its composition, though, Mendelssohn championed it in concert halls across Europe, performing it in England in 1847. In many ways, it remains eclipsed today, primarily by the *Emperor Piano Concerto* that was to follow it. But Beethoven has only himself to blame for that.

RECOMMENDED RECORDING

Richard Goode (piano); Budapest Festival Orchestra; Iván Fischer (conductor). Nonesuch: 7559 799283.

CHART POSITION 118

Piano Sonata No. 8 in C minor
Pathétique

The Swiss composer and conductor Edwin Fischer said, 'For Beethoven, the sonata form is not a scheme that can be used in caprice one day and abandoned the next. This form dominates everything he imagines and composes; it is the very mark on his creation and the form of his thought – an inherent form, a natural one.' And of the 32 piano sonatas composed by Beethoven, only the *Moonlight* challenges this one in the popularity stakes.

The *Pathétique* hails from the early part of Beethoven's career: the late 1700s, a time when the traditions of the Classical period were still dominant and Beethoven himself was largely content to compose within these constraints. For the best part of two hundred years, musicians have debated the true reason for its nickname. Some sources suggest Beethoven himself added the subtitle *Pathétique*, while others imply it was the work of his publisher, albeit with the composer's blessing.

The key of C minor – often a perfect vehicle for tragic, deeply emotive music – is Beethoven's key of choice here, leading many to believe it was directly inspired by Mozart's *Piano Sonata No. 14*, composed in the same key less than two decades previously. While there might be links, many of these are arguably tenuous. The music is undeniably Beethoven's, and shows a young composer already thoroughly at ease with the concept of sonata form and clearly able to use it to convey deep meaning.

RECOMMENDED RECORDING
Maurizio Pollini (piano). Deutsche Grammophon: 4748102.
CHART POSITION   123

Egmont Overture

During 1809 and 1810, Beethoven composed both the overture and the incidental music to Goethe's play *Egmont*, depicting the life of the Count of Egmont, a Flemish nobleman who was executed as part of a conspiracy in 1567.

If the *Pathétique Sonata* sits in Beethoven's early period, and the *Choral Symphony* is the musical embodiment of his later years, the *Egmont Overture* finds itself squarely in the middle. In many ways, the work harks backwards and yet it also looks forwards prophetically. The stately, austere orchestral opening, so beloved of Beethoven and clearly

evident in early works such as the *Eroica Symphony*, is absolutely present here. But so is the thrilling, climactic ending, drawing together themes heard throughout the work and weaving them into a powerful finale.

In a letter to Goethe, Beethoven's friend Bettina von Brentano explained the composer's fascination with Egmont, writing that he had told her, 'Goethe's poems exert a great power over me not only by virtue of their content but also their rhythm; I am put in the right mood and stimulated to compose by this language, which builds itself into a higher order as if through spiritual agencies, and bears within itself the secret of harmony.'

RECOMMENDED RECORDING
German Chamber Philharmonic Orchestra; Daniel Harding (conductor). Virgin Classics: 5453642.
CHART POSITION   163

Bagatelle No. 25 in A minor
(Für Elise)

Stick with learning the piano long enough as a child, and it's only a matter of time before your teacher puts this one on your music stand. Beethoven's *Bagatelle No. 25 in A minor* is rarely referred to in such grandiose terms; instead, all who know and love it refer to it simply by its nickname. A nickname that, frankly, should never have existed. Beethoven did indeed include a dedication on the manuscript, but it was 'Für Therese'. Poor Therese must have been slightly miffed when, thanks to a rather slapdash copywriter called Ludwig

right Ludwig van Beethoven: Bagatelle No. 25 in A minor

24

Nohl, the dedication on the published version of the work was to someone quite different.

Nowadays, *Für Elise* is undoubtedly one of Beethoven's most famous works. It seems almost strange then that, at the time it was composed, the piece was relatively incidental. It certainly didn't provoke much of a reaction and apparently Beethoven himself was never fully satisfied with the work, returning to it some years later and trying, unsuccessfully in his eyes, to revise and refine it. Ultimately, 'Für Elise' wasn't even published until 1865, nearly forty years after Beethoven's death.

The enduring popularity of the work now, though, means it even has its own website: www.forelise.com. Beethoven would surely approve, don't you think?

RECOMMENDED RECORDING
Vladimir Ashkenazy (piano).
Classic FM: CFM FW 049.
CHART POSITION 184

Piano Concerto No. 3 in C minor

The most soulful of all Beethoven's music is arguably found in his piano concertos. If you need any proof, listen to the middle movement of either his *Piano Concerto No. 1* or of this, his *Piano Concerto No. 3*. There's a beauty and elegance here that truly confirms Beethoven's status as the one composer who quickened the pace of change in classical music by welcoming in the Romantic era that was to follow.

It's all too easy to attempt to create rather tenuous links between composers when no such links truly exist – but in the case of this piece, Beethoven owes an undoubted debt to Mozart. The great Austrian composer's *Piano Concerto No. 24* directly inspired Beethoven here, from its key signature of C minor through to intricate details of phrasing and orchestral colour within each movement.

As was the custom with most of Beethoven's works for piano, the composer himself performed as soloist on the night of the premiere. His *Piano Concerto No. 3* was premiered alongside the oratorio *Christ on the Mount of Olives* and the *Symphony No. 2* and, never one known for his organisational skills, Beethoven performed most of the concerto from memory – not through choice, but because he'd run out of time to transcribe the piano part!

RECOMMENDED RECORDING
Martha Argerich (piano); Mahler Chamber Orchestra; Claudio Abbado (conductor). Deutsche Grammophon: 4775026.
CHART POSITION 200

Piano Concerto No. 1 in C

Rather confusingly, Beethoven's *Piano Concerto No. 1* is actually the second piano concerto he composed. The first, however, was published after this one, hence the slight numerical anomaly. To place any real emphasis on this fact, though, would be somewhat pedantic. The two concertos were composed in very quick succession, right at the start of the young Beethoven's career and they display very similar approaches in terms of the harmonious relationship between piano and orchestra.

This concerto certainly seems more polite than, say, the Fourth, or the *Emperor*. Beethoven hadn't yet decided to champion the idea of the piano and orchestra performing as one, in interweaving dialogue. Instead, there's a respectful distance between the two; they exist very much as separate voices. That's not to say the work is disappointing – just that it's absolutely a product of its time. Quite simply, for this concerto to make sense, it could have been composed only within Beethoven's early period.

Despite its relative conservatism, his *Piano Concerto No. 1* did provoke quite a response in its day. At its premiere in Prague, the audience reacted favourably but with surprise – proving that, even when he was starting out, Beethoven was already sowing the seeds of musical revolution and challenging pre-conceived ideas as to what any given musical structure should contain.

RECOMMENDED RECORDING
Yevgeny Kissin (piano); London Symphony Orchestra; Colin Davis (conductor).
EMI Classics: 50999 20631123.
CHART POSITION 206

Triple Concerto in C

The very name *Triple Concerto* is slightly misleading here. At first glance, you might expect a three-for-the-price-of-one concerto experience, with the violin, cello and piano all happily co-existing as genuine soloists. But what Beethoven gives us is something slightly different.

In many ways, it's an odd work: there's very little conversation between the instruments and the orchestra, with nearly everything of interest being played by the soloists. Although that's to be expected to some degree, all of Beethoven's other concertos still appear to have orchestral material that, when heard alone, remains pretty compelling. And there's a real risk that in any performance of the piece the intended interplay between the three soloists is diminished by the individual musicians' desire to ensure that they come out on top when an audience asks afterwards, 'Who was the best?'

The finest performances of the *Triple Concerto*

are therefore those where ego is removed, allowing the music to become the sole star. The work has chamber-like qualities; indeed, it's easy to wonder whether an entire orchestral accompaniment was really necessary – but that was Beethoven's call to make, not ours.

Composed in 1803, the *Triple Concerto* remained unperformed for five years, until its outing at a summer music festival in Vienna in 1808.

RECOMMENDED RECORDING
Pierre-Laurent Aimard (piano); Thomas Zehetmair (violin); Clemens Hagen (cello); Chamber Orchestra of Europe; Nikolaus Harnoncourt (conductor).
Warner: 2564 606022.
CHART POSITION 214

Choral Fantasia in C minor

Of everything Beethoven composed, this is one of his most intriguing works. The unusual instrumentation he chose would certainly not have been something to which audiences of the time would have been accustomed. Indeed, you could easily believe the *Choral Fantasia* to be a piano sonata, given the expansive solo passage at the start. On top of that, the structure is a little strange: what exactly led Beethoven to split it into just two movements? The duration is also puzzling. With such a grand title, coupled with the fact that Beethoven was now known for writing large-scale symphonies and concertos, the audience at its premiere must surely have wondered why it was all done and dusted in little over twenty minutes.

When the *Choral Fantasia* was first performed in 1808, Beethoven had a number of things on his mind. After all, this was the very same concert where, among other works, he was introducing two of his best-loved symphonies

(*Nos. 5* and *6*) to the world for the first time. Far from being a slick affair, the *Choral Fantasia*'s birth was a difficult one. The performance was clunky, the sense of ensemble between the musicians poor, and the reception decidedly lukewarm.

RECOMMENDED RECORDING
Hélène Grimaud (piano); Swedish Radio Choir; Swedish Radio Symphony Orchestra; Esa-Pekka Salonen (conductor). Deutsche Grammophon: 4717692.
CHART POSITION 231

VINCENZO BELLINI
(1801–1835)

Norma

In the same year that Darwin set sail in his *Beagle*, Bellini rocked the Milan opera world with not one but two operas. The Sicilian was just thirty years old and at the absolute pinnacle of his musical life, commanding huge fees and producing operas at a rate of knots. *La Sonnambula* had already done very well for him in March 1831, transferring to Paris and London almost as soon as the sets could be painted. Later in the year, far from resting on his laurels, Bellini produced his most enduring hit: a lyric tragedy in two acts centred on a druid called Norma, the daughter of the chief druid, Oreveso.

The brightest shining jewel in its vocal crown is the exquisite *'Casta Diva'* – an aria Bellini rewrote some eight times. It comes from Act I and is Norma's 'song to the moon', as it were. Having cut some mistletoe, she sings to the lunar goddess, praying for peace – as well as hoping for luck when trying to defeat the Romans.

Maria Callas made the song her own for a few generations of opera-lovers, although,

today, it has been reclaimed by singers such as Cecilia Bartoli.

RECOMMENDED RECORDING
Cecilia Bartoli (soprano); Orchestra of the National Academy of Saint Cecilia; Myung-Whun Chung (conductor).
Decca: 4782249.
CHART POSITION 173

HECTOR BERLIOZ
(1803–1869)

Symphonie fantastique

Most portraits of composers tend to paint a similar picture: austere, grumpy and – to put it bluntly – fairly unattractive. They certainly don't tend to scrub up well. And yet, many of the shots of Hector Berlioz tell a different story. He cut a dashing figure, with a mop of wavy hair and a lean build. Berlioz was something of a ladies' man, and his *Symphonie fantastique* was famously inspired by a sexually charged and passionate relationship with the Irish actress Harriet Smithson. Berlioz was obsessed with her – so much so, in fact, that she initially thought him to be insane – but this was lust rather than love. The couple eventually married but were far from blissfully happy. Instead, it transpired that she'd accepted his advances only for financial reasons, and they eventually parted company in 1841.

Symphonie fantastique was premiered in 1830, three years before the couple's tempestuous marriage, during one of Berlioz's periods of intense infatuation with the young Harriet. It's one long, musical expression of his passion for her, from the perspective of a struggling artist who, despite his clear gifts, is mired in depression and seeking solace for the fact that his cries of desire go unanswered.

The subject matter becomes more and more fantastical, going from *Reveries* in the first movement through to the final *Dream of Witches' Sabbath* in the final movement, via the *March to the Scaffold* in the penultimate movement. Listen out for the loud chord at the end, representing the cutting off of the artist's head, and the subsequent falling of said head into the basket below.

RECOMMENDED RECORDING
Berlin Philharmonic Orchestra; Simon Rattle (conductor). EMI Classics: 50999 21622403.
CHART POSITION 111

L'Enfance du Christ

Of all the great composers, Berlioz certainly isn't remembered as a man of faith, despite his strict Catholic upbringing. And yet, three of the composer's most important and substantial works have a religious basis. First came his mighty *Requiem* in 1837; that was followed twelve years later by the *Te Deum*; and then Berlioz produced the oratorio *L'Enfance du Christ*, dating from 1854. It's a huge work, which took four years to compose, and depicts not just the childhood of Christ but also Herod's mass murder of infants in Judea, which led to the fleeing of Mary, Joseph and Jesus.

L'Enfance du Christ is a creation of supreme beauty. The best-known section, *The Shepherds' Farewell*, is a glorious blend of warm woodwind sounds, sublime choral harmonies and sensitive orchestral accompaniment. Berlioz was certainly a passionate composer, with a love of writing very red-blooded, romantic music. He was also clearly capable of creating music with a sense of complete serenity, touching simplicity, and ethereal beauty.

Berlioz whipped up a storm of praise wherever he went, and the premiere performance of *L'Enfance du Christ* was met with euphoric appreciation by the Parisian audience. Subsequent performances across Europe received an equally rapturous response, much to the composer's delight.

RECOMMENDED RECORDING
Yann Beuron (Narrator/Centurion); Karen Cargill (Marie); William Dazeley (Joseph); Matthew Rose (Herod); Peter Rose (Father/Polydorus); Tenebrae Choir; London Symphony Orchestra; Colin Davis (conductor). LSO Live: LSO0606.
CHART POSITION 260

Candide

The journey of *Candide* from 1956 failed comic operetta to perpetual Classic FM Hall of Fame favourite is as intriguing as the hero's journey within the work itself. In the operetta, Candide (sung by a tenor) experiences numerous fabulous disasters and tortuous plot twists. In real life, the operetta itself seems to have had just as many ups and downs.

It received a disappointing premiere in 1956 and had to be fitted with a completely new libretto in 1973, after the original librettist withdrew her permission for her words to be used. After numerous minor makeovers, it was finally set in stone with the composer's 1989 refurbishment, which took the essence of the 1956 and 1973 versions, blending them with parts from 1958 and 1971 settings. If you factor in the revelation that some music

he had written for *Candide* was 'borrowed' by the composer for another of his great works, *West Side Story* – 'One Hand, One Heart' was intended originally for *Candide* – then it makes it all the more surprising that it has endured. Could it be that the *Overture*, which seems to be written in the key of life, is the reason for its success? For an exuberant version, the composer's own with the New York Phil is hard to beat.

RECOMMENDED RECORDING

Overture only: New York Philharmonic Orchestra; Leonard Bernstein (conductor). Sony: SMK63085.

CHART POSITION 291

GEORGES BIZET
(1838–1875)

The Pearl Fishers

You have to wonder how Bizet would feel about our response to *The Pearl Fishers*, were he alive today. This three-act opera lasts around eighty minutes and has an exotic plot, rich orchestral imagery and a number of arias to boot. And yet, it's almost solely remembered today for an extract that many think is a stand-alone piece of music: *The Pearl Fishers' Duet*.

Sung by the characters Zuria and Nadir, caught in a love triangle with the one girl they're both after, the duet has been performed thousands of times in its own right in the concert hall. Jussi Björling and Robert Merrill capture Bizet's music magically in their definitive 1950s recording. Bryn Terfel also joined forces with Andrea Bocelli to perform it at the Classical BRIT Awards in 2003;

there was a warmth and passion in their rendition that the young Bizet would surely have approved of.

Not received well at the time, the full-length opera has never really garnered much critical acclaim. That's understandable, though; Bizet was, after all, only twenty-four when he began composing it, and it was by no means his most mature work. The famous duet alone arguably contains enough musical magic to more than justify the continued popularity of *The Pearl Fishers* – even if 74 minutes of the opera remain largely unknown.

RECOMMENDED RECORDING

(*The Pearl Fishers' Duet* only) Jussi Björling (tenor); Robert Merrill (baritone); RCA Victor Symphony Orchestra; Renato Cellini (conductor). RCA: 4479133.

CHART POSITION 15

Carmen

Bizet's two famous operas couldn't be more different. The first, *The Pearl Fishers*, is cruelly remembered for containing only one hit. *Carmen*, by contrast, is so packed full of memorable melodies that it's guaranteed an almost permanent position as the world's most popular and most frequently performed opera. From the barnstorming orchestral *Prelude* to the macho *Toreador's Song*, via the sexy *Habanera* and sultry *Seguidilla*, this is like a nineteenth-century collection of three-minute pop songs from start to finish.

Carmen is set in Seville and stretches across four acts. Its steamy nature shocked audiences at the time. In fact, Bizet was seen as quite the rebel for having set to music something so apparently salacious. Every man loves Carmen – and they're not afraid to show it. She drives men wild, flirts outrageously, and is an all-round good-time girl. The risqué plot, sexual tension and typically exotic music all

left Georges Bizet: Carmen

fuse together to create a universally appealing opera that absolutely cements Bizet's position within the history of the genre. Here was a composer who wrote mass-market music in the very best sense of that phrase. Today, nearly 150 years on from its premiere performance, it remains hugely popular the world over – and of that Bizet would have been proud.

RECOMMENDED RECORDING
Julia Migenes (soprano); Placido Domingo (tenor); Ruggero Raimondi (bass-baritone); Chorus of Radio France; French National Orchestra; Lorin Maazel (conductor).
Erato: 2292 452072.

CHART POSITION 99

ALEXANDER BORODIN
(1833–1887)

In the Steppes of Central Asia

When Queen Elizabeth II celebrated her Silver Jubilee, Britain celebrated with new coins, commemorative mugs and nostalgic street parties. When Alexander II of Russia held his Silver Jubilee, in 1880, among other things he commissioned Borodin to compose a symphonic poem. It was intended to be the soundtrack to a *tableau vivant* – a slightly curious and now largely forgotten art form in which actors pose, motionless, in a set, often lit to resemble a painting.

Quite how they would have coped standing motionless for the full seven or eight minutes of Borodin's music, we'll never know. The 'production' was called off after an attempted assassination. Rimksy-Korsakov rescued it, though, for the 1880 season with his Russian Opera Orchestra and it has since become a concert favourite. It's not hard to see why. The music, as well as being crammed full of great tunes, is beautifully comprehensible: the listener can easily hear the Russian troops and Central Asians travelling across the steppe. Both have their own melodies, which briefly meet, working perfectly over each other, before the Asian music wafts off into the distance and the Russian theme is left alone.

RECOMMENDED RECORDING
Kirov Orchestra; Valery Gergiev (conductor).
Philips: 4708402.

CHART POSITION 131

Prince Igor

Many musical historians regard *Prince Igor* as Borodin's magnum opus. But, strictly speaking, it should really be considered as his 'magnum opus infectus' – his great unfinished work. Despite spending some eighteen years working on it, by the time Borodin died, aged fifty-four, *Prince Igor* was still incomplete. The main string to Borodin's bow was chemistry: he was a professor at the St Petersburg Academy of Medicine. That meant that the huge four-act epic that started life as *The Lay of the Host of Igor* was always going to have a job competing for his attentions.

So, in 1887, when Borodin died – in full national dress, it should be added (he suffered a heart attack at a ball) – and Rimsky-Korsakov, with Glazunov, began the hugely unenviable task of sifting through his belongings, the score of *Prince Igor* loomed large. As Rimsky-Korsakov later wrote in his memoirs, 'Glazunov ... was to fill in all the gaps in Act

III and write down from memory the *Overture* played so often by the composer, while I was to orchestrate, finish composing, and systematise all the rest that had been left ...' All things considered, they did a wonderful job.

RECOMMENDED RECORDING
Nikolai Putilin, Galina Gorchakova, Evgeny Akimov, Sergey Aleksashkin, Vladimir Vaneev, Olga Borodina. Kirov Opera & Ballet, Valery Gergiev. Philips DVD: 0741739
CHART POSITION 144

String Quartet No. 2 in D

Musically speaking, the time of the *String Quartet No. 2* was the beginning of the end for Borodin. It was written when he was in his late forties and at exactly the period when finding time for music was becoming nigh on impossible. As a successful chemist (in Russia, they refer to one particular reaction – that of silver salts with carboxylic acids and halogens –as the 'Borodin Reaction') he felt compelled to devote more and more of his time to his important scientific work, at the expense of his music.

Nevertheless, when he was forty-eight, and just one year after the composition of *In the Steppes of Central Asia*, he found himself with a free summer to compose. In between visiting the odd festival – and his friend Liszt, to whom he dedicated *In the Steppes of Central Asia* – he composed his *String Quartet No. 2*. As with most things Borodin wrote, it is not short of tunes, something that proved a blessing when the writers of the musical *Kismet* came to use his music. The jaunty second movement provided them with *'Baubles,*

Bangles and Beads', while the third stumped up the show-stopping *'This is My Beloved'*. Unsurprisingly, the Borodin Quartet performs a mean version.

RECOMMENDED RECORDING
Borodin String Quartet. Onyx: ONYX4002.
CHART POSITION 197

JOHANNES BRAHMS
(1833–1897)

Violin Concerto in D

Brahms lived and worked under the shadow of Beethoven throughout his career. Brahms was very conscious of this – indeed, it was one of the main reasons why he took so long to compose a symphony – and in the case of this violin concerto, there is an obvious parallel to be made between the two composers' works. Both wrote only one concerto for this most popular of instruments. Neither had any personal experience of playing the violin and therefore had to rely heavily on others to interpret their music and to guide its progress. And, despite all this, both composed a violin concerto that would end up in every great soloist's repertoire, and in every lover of the instrument's CD collection.

In Brahms's case, the inspiration and guide for the piece was his great friend, the violinist Joseph Joachim. The raw and rugged sound of the outer movements is contrasted with an *Adagio* of exquisite, silky beauty, with an intimacy that very few composers have truly been able to create. Nowadays, it remains as one of only a handful of violin concertos that, along with Beethoven's, simply has to be performed by any world-class violinist.

RECOMMENDED RECORDING
Vadim Repin (violin); Leipzig Gewandhaus
Orchestra; Riccardo Chailly (conductor).
Deutsche Grammophon: 477 7470.
CHART POSITION 82

A German Requiem

What is so 'German' about this requiem, then? Why the additional word in the title? After all, we never refer to Fauré's 'French Requiem' or Mozart's 'Austrian Requiem'. So, what was at the root of Brahms giving his work such a proudly nationalistic name?

For the answer, we need to consider the nature of religious faith in Germany at the time. Here was a country where Luther had come to prominence, and where Catholicism was by no means the sole expression of Christian belief. By choosing Luther as his inspiration, and describing this work overtly as *A German Requiem*, Brahms was expressing what it meant to be German. He was also setting direct biblical passages, rather than choosing as his text the liturgies of a particular church.

Rather like one of the best contemporary requiems, that of Classic FM Composer in Residence Howard Goodall, *A German Requiem* is not primarily a Mass for the Dead. Instead, it is intended as comfort for those who mourn and who feel the pain of the death of others. By the time he began writing the work in 1865, Brahms had just experienced such loss extremely personally: his mother had died that very same year.

RECOMMENDED RECORDING
(piano-duet version) Susan Gritton (soprano);
Hanno Muller-Brachmann (bass-baritone);
Jose Gallardo (piano); Evgenia Rubinova
(piano); Choir of King's College,
Cambridge; Stephen Cleobury (conductor).
EMI Classics: 3669482.
CHART POSITION 112

Piano Concerto No. 2 in B flat

Both of Brahms's piano concertos are gargantuan works. At nearly fifty minutes in duration, this one lasts longer than any other major Romantic piano concerto by quite some stretch. And talking of stretch – any soloist wanting to master the piano passages needs to have very wide hands and extremely nimble fingers. The composer begged to differ, however, wryly commenting to a friend that this was simply a 'tiny, tiny piano concerto'.

Brahms was an absolute master of writing for the piano. He knew the sonorities of the instrument so well. As this expansive, four-movement concerto demonstrates, he was able to blend beauty with fire and tenderness with drama in the most remarkable of ways. From the rich, spacious opening of the first movement, we become immediately aware that Brahms is going to take his time to unveil his musical themes and ideas. The most well-known section – a thrilling, energetic finale – is very much the summit of the piece, the culmination of everything that has come before. To get a real feel for the scale of his *Piano Concerto No. 2*, it is worth giving Brahms fifty minutes of our time. Experience this from start to finish, and be

Johannes Brahms
1833-1897

'It is not hard to compose, but it is wonderfully hard to let the superfluous notes fall under the table.'

JOHANNES BRAHMS

Now known to many as one half of the rhyming slang for 'drunk', in his early career Brahms earned a living playing piano in brothels around his native Hamburg. He continued to tour as a pianist and was regarded as a master of every type of music, except for opera, to which he never turned his hand.

Brahms might have been musical in the daytime, but at night his snoring was a far from sweet sound. One conductor, forced to share a room with him, described how 'the most unearthly noises issued from his nasal and vocal organs'.

Brahms would never have won the award for 'best-turned-out composer'. He seems to have had particular problems in the trouser department. He hated buying new clothes

and often wore baggy trousers that were covered in patches and nearly always too short. Once, his trousers nearly fell down altogether in the middle of a performance. On another

DID YOU KNOW?

Brahms gained admirers for his looks as well as his music. As a teenager, his flowing blond locks, impressive physique and sea-blue eyes made many a girl swoon.

occasion, he took a tie from around his neck and looped it around his waist in place of a belt.

Brahms was friendly with the composer Robert

Schumann and his wife Clara, who was also a composer, but was better known as a virtuoso pianist. Schumann, who was older than Brahms, recognised just how talented the younger man was – both as a piano player and as a composer. When Schumann died, Brahms became quite besotted with Clara, although she never allowed the relationship to progress beyond friendship.

Despite the big differences in the music that they wrote, Brahms was also a firm friend of the Viennese waltz king and bandmaster, Johann Strauss II. When Mrs Strauss once asked Brahms for an autograph, he wrote out a few bars of Strauss's greatest hit, *By the Beautiful Blue Danube*, with the note, 'Sadly, not by Brahms!'

captivated by one of the giants of all Romantic music.

RECOMMENDED RECORDING
Marc-Andre Hamelin (piano); Dallas Symphony Orchestra; Andrew Litton (conductor). Hyperion: CDA 67550.
CHART POSITION 127

Symphony No. 4 in E minor

It might have taken Brahms quite some time to write a symphony but once he had premiered *No. 1* in 1876, there really was no stopping him. By 1884, he was penning this, his final one – and given that it had taken him the best part of fifteen years to complete *Symphony No. 1*, we'd consider that to be pretty good going!

There's an evergreen feeling to this symphony – an almost autumnal sound. Having struggled for so long to find his own authentic voice amid the noise that followed Beethoven's death, Brahms sounds free here; musically liberated. Rich orchestral colours abound, and melody after melody flows right across the orchestra. The triumphant sound of the finale is impossible to avoid, with Brahms using every instrument of the orchestra to drive onwards to the most thunderous and joy-filled conclusion.

Self-doubt, while never overcoming Brahms, was certainly something he struggled with. In the case of his *Symphony No. 4*, he worried for a long time that it wasn't worthy of a full orchestra, and he originally had it performed in a setting for two pianos so he could get some feedback from a few trusted friends. Better that than to premiere it in its complete version, only for ridicule to ensue. Brahms needn't have worried, though; the work was warmly received at its premiere and has remained loved ever since.

RECOMMENDED RECORDING
Berlin Philharmonic Orchestra; Simon Rattle (conductor).
EMI Classics: 50999 26725420.
CHART POSITION 191

Symphony No. 1 in C minor

Beethoven's *Symphony No. 9* was – and still is – an undisputed masterwork. Audiences went wild for it; critics asked whether it could ever be equalled; and frankly, composers such as Brahms wondered whether they might as well pack up and head home. After all, how could anyone follow that?

Brahms's chamber music output was prolific but when it came to composing a symphony, he struggled deeply. It took him nearly fifteen years to compose this, his *Symphony No. 1*, with frequent revisions made to the score over that period. Even at its premiere, he remained sceptical about whether anyone would like it. So many versions had been torn up, edited and begun all over again. With that many changes to the original material, how could Brahms be sure that he had finally come up with something worth sharing?

This great composer had nothing to fear, though. Hans von Bülow (himself a composer, conductor and pianist, just like Brahms) famously described this work as 'Beethoven's Tenth'. No greater compliment could have possibly been paid. At the age of forty-three, Brahms had finally produced a symphony that both he and his public were happy with. Thankfully, they didn't have to wait nearly as long for the arrival of another: he wrote the Second the following year.

RECOMMENDED RECORDING
London Philharmonic Orchestra; Vladimir Jurowski (conductor). LPO: LPO0043.
CHART POSITION 216

Piano Concerto No. 1 in D minor

Although nowadays Brahms is often remembered for his full-blooded, large-scale works, at the time of writing his *Piano Concerto No. 1*, he was a very different composer. Brahms's comfort zone was music for solo piano. Indeed, it was the music that book-ended his life. And this particular work was his very first creation for the instrument on a more epic scale. Never before had Brahms composed something with such depth, orchestration and duration.

It's not surprising, then, that his *Piano Concerto No. 1* was written over a full four-year period. The composer was clearly at pains to ensure its premiere was a success – not least because he was already known as something of a piano expert. Brahms no doubt feared accusations of an inability to transfer his chamber-music success into this altogether grander form.

Sadly for Brahms, his worst fears were realised. The piece was dismissed by those in the know and, in its day, it was never held in such high esteem as other Romantic piano warhorses of the period. Now, however, it's a very different story: this is one of the best-loved and most frequently performed piano concertos in the world.

RECOMMENDED RECORDING
Nicholas Angelich (piano); Frankfurt

Radio Symphony Orchestra; Paavo Järvi (conductor). Virgin Classics: 50999 5189982.
CHART POSITION 221

Symphony No. 3 in F

As you listen to this richly Romantic symphony, you get a real sense that Brahms had very much hit his stride as a composer. It had taken until he was well into his forties before he felt able to write a symphony. Yet, once Brahms started, there was evidently no stopping him. By the time he reached this, his third and penultimate symphony, in 1883, he had clearly found his own voice. Sweeping, lyrical string lines and beautifully autumnal woodwind passages make this a delight from start to finish.

While some other great composers had a reputation for being curmudgeonly, Brahms was of an altogether sunnier disposition. If you're in any doubt, listen for the musical clue that runs through this symphony: the notes F–A flat–F occur repeatedly, and allude to the composer's own saying, 'frei aber froh' – which translates as 'free but happy'.

There's a risk that this symphony could suffer from a sort of musical version of middle-child syndrome. The novelty of the *Symphony No. 1*, coupled with the fire and joy of the *No. 4*, can leave the *No. 3* being almost forgotten. The problem is compounded by the fact that it's the shortest of the four symphonies Brahms composed. It's also the most lyrical and, arguably, the most finely crafted, which goes some way towards explaining its enduring popularity today.

RECOMMENDED RECORDING
WDR Symphony Orchestra; Semyon
Bychkov (conductor). Avie: 2051.
CHART POSITION 227

Symphony No. 2 in D

On 30 November 1877, the great conductor
Hans Richter stood at the podium before the
Vienna Philharmonic Orchestra for the premiere performance of Brahms's *Symphony No.
2*. Brahms's *Symphony No. 1*, in the brooding
key of C minor, had been premiered the year
before and was pretty austere in tone. The
rich, wistful melodies Brahms had become
known for were certainly there, but in rather
sombre form.

It's not surprising, then, that many expected
his second attempt at a symphony to inhabit
a similar sound-world. Brahms himself stoked
such beliefs, writing to his publisher barely a
month before the premiere that the work 'is
so melancholy … you will not be able to bear
it. I have never written anything so sad, and
the score must come out in mourning'.

Brahms was, quite simply, pulling his publisher's leg. He knew all too well that his
Symphony No. 2 was full of warmth, brimming with optimism and overflowing with
lush, joyful melodies. The very fact that he
felt able to joke about the work suggests a
composer who was deeply comfortable in
his own skin and perfectly at ease with the
music he had created. Not for Brahms the
worry of acceptance that cast a shadow over
his *Symphony No. 1*; instead, he was evidently
very satisfied with his creation. As you listen
to the final few bars of the fourth movement,

you sense that Brahms felt victorious. He'd
waited years to compose symphonies – but
the wait was definitely worth it.
RECOMMENDED RECORDING
Philharmonia Orchestra; Christoph von
Dohnányi (conductor). Signum Classics:
SIGCD 132.
CHART POSITION 265

BENJAMIN BRITTEN
(1913–1976)

Four Sea Interludes
from Peter Grimes

Despite reports that Benjamin Britten paced
nervously at the back of the Sadler's Wells
theatre when *Peter Grimes* was first performed,
this work is now regarded by many as the
greatest English opera ever written. It certainly marked a revival of post-war English opera.

The seeds for *Peter Grimes* were sown not
on these shores, but in Los Angeles. Having
left war-struck Britain in 1939, he chanced
on George Crabbe's poem *The Borough* in a
second-hand bookshop in Los Angeles, and
started transforming it into what would become only his second opera, ready for its
premiere in 1945.

Back in the UK, he launched the rebirth
of English opera with the story of the tragic,
lonely fisherman, who was both cantankerous
and misunderstood. By way of contrast from
the often tense vocal machinations, four orchestral interludes pepper the score and, long
before the first night, Britten had decided
that they should stand alone, too. They have
arguably become more popular than the opera

right Benjamin Britten: Four Sea Interludes

Max Bruch
1838–1920

'In personal appearance, Bruch is by no means as majestic as one would suppose from his works.'
ANONYMOUS CONTEMPORARY

Bruch enjoyed a long career as a teacher, conductor and composer. If Brahms lived his life in the shadow of Beethoven, then Bruch had the same relationship with Brahms – always seemingly one step behind a great composer who was both his compatriot and his contemporary.

He was a rather short-tempered man and his tenure as Principal Conductor of the Liverpool Philharmonic Orchestra between 1880 and 1883 was a rather stormy affair. Although his time in Liverpool wasn't entirely happy on the professional front, it marked a very harmonious period in his private life. Shortly after taking the job on Merseyside, he became engaged to twenty-seven-year-old Clara Tuczek. By this stage, Bruch was forty-two years old and had

enjoyed a full and eventful personal life. Some of his letters home to Germany describe the attention he had been receiving from the young ladies of Liverpool.

> ## DID YOU KNOW?
> **Bruch can be added to that long list of precociously talented composers: by the age of 14, he had already penned his first symphony.**

Clara moved to Liverpool in January 1881. Despite Bruch's reservations about her being anything other than a housewife, she acquitted herself very well singing Verdi's *Requiem* with the Liverpool

Philharmonic in March that year. Their daughter Margarethe was born on 29 August 1882 and the register of births held by the Liverpool Record Office confirms that she was born in the Toxteth South area. So, although both Bruch and his wife were German, their daughter could claim to be a true Scouser.

Bruch left Liverpool for an American tour and subsequently a job in Germany, but he returned to work in Britain between 1898 and 1900 as the Principal Conductor of the Scottish Orchestra.

As a composer, Bruch's *Violin Concerto No. 1* dwarfed everything else that he had written, but his three operas and his choral works were moderately successful, particularly back home in Germany.

itself. It is worth noting that there is also a fifth 'interlude', a *Passacaglia*, which is often played alongside them.

RECOMMENDED RECORDING

London Symphony Orchestra; Steuart Bedford (conductor). Naxos: 8557196.

CHART POSITION 248

MAX BRUCH
(1838–1920)

Violin Concerto No. 1 in G minor

This former No. 1 in the Classic FM Hall of Fame has fallen from grace a little in the last few years, but still remains one of the most popular – and most beautiful – of all violin concertos. Bruch was a master of writing for string instruments (listen to his glorious *Kol Nidrei* for cello, or his boisterous *Scottish Fantasy* for violin, for further proof).

For violinists, one of the concerto's most obvious redeeming qualities is the degree to which it acts as a profound showcase for the instrument. The dazzling, virtuosic passages, particularly in the glorious finale, really do make the violin sing as it soars again and again, almost from within the orchestra, to ever loftier heights. The second movement, meanwhile, is pure romance: beautiful, heartbreaking themes, woven delicately within soulful orchestral accompaniment.

Often referred to as 'the Bruch Violin Concerto', it's easy to forget that the composer actually wrote three (excluding the concerto-esque *Scottish Fantasy*). The other two, though, have never equalled the *No. 1* in the popularity stakes; Bruch clearly set the bar a little too high for himself with this stunning debut. Indeed, he remained frustrated about this for most of his life, feeling pigeon-holed as something of a one-hit wonder when he had, in fact, composed much more than this one piece alone.

RECOMMENDED RECORDING

Nigel Kennedy (violin); English Chamber Orchestra; Jeffrey Tate (conductor). EMI Classics: 5574112.

CHART POSITION 3

Scottish Fantasy

Like many composers, Max Bruch was captivated by both the idea and the sound of folk music. Nowhere is this more evident than in his *Scottish Fantasy* for violin and orchestra. This work received its UK premiere while Bruch was rather grumpily in charge of the Liverpool Philharmonic in 1881, some seventeen years before he took over at the Scottish Orchestra. His time in Scotland was no more successful than his tenure in Liverpool.

Despite the fact that Bruch was a virtual stranger to Scotland at the time he wrote his *Scottish Fantasy*, there is nothing to suggest that the work is based on anything other than wholly authentic Scottish melodies. Its opening movement uses *'Auld Rob Morris'*; from there, we move on to *'Dusty Miller'*, before *'I'm down for lack of Johnnie'* in the third movement and, to conclude, the ebullient *'Scots Wha Hae'* in the finale.

Interestingly, Bruch uses a harp in the *Scottish Fantasy* – strongly suggesting he thought the instrument was a central part of authentic Scottish folk music. Whether he had actually heard a Celtic harp played at the time he wrote the piece is still very much open to debate.

RECOMMENDED RECORDING

Tasmin Little (violin); Royal Scottish National Orchestra; Vernon Handley (conductor). EMI Classics: 7243 5758022.

CHART POSITION 114

Kol Nidrei

The German composer Max Bruch was, like many of his Romantic-era contemporaries, rather keen on travelling around Europe.

Kol Nidrei, his warm and richly evocative work for cello and orchestra, was one of the first pieces he set about composing when he took up his post as Principal Conductor of the Liverpool Philharmonic Orchestra. It was composed specifically for Liverpool's Jewish community, taking as its inspiration two traditional Hebrew melodies. The first, heard at the outset, originates from the traditional Jewish service on the night of Yom Kippur; the second is an extract from a musical setting of the Byron poem 'Those that Wept on Babel's Stream'.

A common misconception about Bruch is that he was a Jewish composer. He was in fact a Protestant Christian – but he was greatly inspired by Old Testament stories and by his own modern-day friendships with a number of prominent Jewish musicians. Aside from the *Violin Concerto No. 1*, *Kol Nidrei* is Bruch's most frequently performed piece. Sumptuous, rich cello writing and gloriously assured orchestral accompaniment go a great way towards explaining its enduring popularity.

RECOMMENDED RECORDING
Jacqueline du Pré (cello); Israel Philharmonic Orchestra; Daniel Barenboim (conductor). EMI Classics: CDC 5572932.

CHART POSITION 234

Violin Concerto No. 2 in D minor

Max Bruch absolutely embodied the Romantic period of classical music. Every single one of his musical ideas is like a dictionary definition of what it meant to be a Romantic composer – extraordinary, really, given that he lived to the remarkably ripe old age of eighty-two and was still writing music alongside the likes of Schoenberg and Bartók.

Surprisingly, despite his prolific output for the instrument, Bruch was by no means an accomplished violinist himself. Hard to believe when you listen to his glorious and ever popular *Violin Concerto No. 1*. His *Violin Concerto No. 2* will always sit in its shadow.

That's not to say that *No. 2* is bereft of fine melodies, though. Far from it. The concerto, premiered in Crystal Palace in November 1877 with Pablo de Sarasate as the soloist, is powerful, expansive and deeply rewarding. Sarasate, who had premiered Bruch's *Violin Concerto No. 1*, was clearly the inspiration for this one, too. Writing to a friend in March 1877, Bruch commented 'the principal ideas of the work are products of the enthusiasm which his indescribably perfect rendering of the first concerto aroused in me'.

It's unusual because of its slow first movement and *Violin Concerto No. 2* will probably never reach the heights of the phenomenally successful *No. 1*. But that by no means suggests it's not an accomplished and hugely enjoyable work.

RECOMMENDED RECORDING
Itzhak Perlman (violin); New York Philharmonic Orchestra; Jesús López Cobos (conductor). EMI Classics: 3565232.

CHART POSITION 266

GEORGE BUTTERWORTH
(1885–1916)

The Banks of Green Willow

Butterworth was a great English composer who never fulfilled his potential because his life was cut tragically short in the First World

War. However, the prevailing view among music historians is that this was a young man who had much, much more to offer the world of classical music. He wasn't the only significant loss suffered by the world of the arts during the Great War. The composer Granados famously perished at sea, his ship torpedoed by a German U-boat in 1916. The poet Edward Thomas, a member of the same regiment as Butterworth, died in the Battle of Arras in 1917. By then, Butterworth himself was already dead; a trench named after him between Gloster and Munster Alleys. What seems to make Butterworth's case so much more tragic is the fact that he destroyed many of his existing manuscripts in 1914, before going to war.

The Banks of Green Willow was written in 1913, a short pastoral idyll. It is loosely based on the song that Vaughan Williams had lovingly recorded on one of his folk safaris in 1909. It has become almost a symbol of that long-lost halcyon Edwardian age, as if Butterworth were transcribing the disappearing world around him.

RECOMMENDED RECORDING

English String Orchestra; William Boughton (conductor). Nimbus: NI5068.

CHART POSITION 106

C

GIULIO CACCINI
(*c*.1545–1618)

Ave Maria

The very designation 'Caccini's *Ave Maria*' is one that provokes debate. Who is Caccini? And was the piece actually anything to do with him? The answer to the first question is easy: Caccini was a sixteenth-century composer, based in Florence, and a gifted singer in his own right. To answer the second question, though, is to approach something of a minefield.

No one really knows who wrote this *Ave Maria* – mainly because the setting didn't come to light until the twentieth century. Although its presence on any classical crossover singer's album is now almost guaranteed, the piece was unknown before the 1970s. One plausible reason as to why this might be is that this *Ave Maria* arguably wasn't composed until then. Many argue that its creator was, in fact, one Vladimir Vavilov, a relatively unknown Russian guitarist and composer, who recorded it in 1972 and declared it to be an anonymous song. The attribution to Caccini was then supposedly made at a later date by a musician who performed with Vavilov.

Whatever the truth, it's certain that this simple melody is beloved by many. The Lithuanian soprano Inessa Galante was the singer who captivated our hearts with her performance of it in the 1990s, and it remains a firm favourite today.

RECOMMENDED RECORDING
Inessa Galante (soprano); London Musici; Mark Stephenson (conductor). Campion: RRCD 1345.
CHART POSITION 255

MARIE JOSEPH CANTELOUBE DE MALARET (1879–1957)

Songs of the Auvergne

Canteloube is a composer whose reputation today is based on a tiny number of works. Just as, in England, Butterworth was good friends with the more prominent Vaughan Williams, with whom he shared a passion for his country's folk songs, Canteloube had fellow composer and teacher D'Indy to nourish his passion for native

French songs. Even when he was living in Paris, Canteloube founded his own offshoot of the Paris Auvergne Society which he called the *Bourée* – a group of like-minded artists keen to keep the music and arts of the Auvergne region alive. For Canteloube, however, there was the peasant's way of enjoying folk songs and then there was the artist's way. He felt that his *Songs of the Auvergne* fell very much into this latter category, with their rich orchestrations and sumptuous harmonies. They were in fact a million miles away from some of the simple 'melody and musette' settings he transcribed and published.

RECOMMENDED RECORDING

Veronique Gens (soprano); Orchestre National de Lille; Jean-Claude Casadeseus (conductor). Naxos 8557491.

CHART POSITION 175

FRÉDÉRIC CHOPIN
(1810–1849)

Piano Concerto No. 1 in E minor

The title of this glorious concerto is another example of musical cataloguing triumphing over historical fact. Far from being Chopin's first piano concerto, this is actually his second. It was published before the real No. 1, though, and therefore became forever known as the composer's *Piano Concerto No. 1*.

The issue is largely academic because Chopin's two piano concertos were composed within a year of each other. As you listen to this deeply expansive and expressive work, it has the mark of a composer who has reached full emotional and musical maturity, so it's astonishing to think that Chopin wrote it while in his late teens. At its premiere in 1830, he

played the piano part himself, and the concert marked his final public appearance in Poland. Within weeks, Chopin had left for Vienna and then Paris, where he remained for the rest of his life.

Although best known for its lyrical middle movement, this concerto also contains melodic gems throughout the two outer movements. It's unashamedly heart-on-your-sleeve stuff, with Chopin allowing the rich sounds of the piano to be cushioned by some gloriously rich string accompaniment. The majority of Chopin's output was for solo piano. But, as his two concertos for the instrument prove, he was adept at writing for piano and orchestra too.

RECOMMENDED RECORDING

Janina Fialkowska (piano); Vancouver Symphony Orchestra; Bramwell Tovey (conductor). ATMA: ACD 22643.

CHART POSITION 49

Piano Concerto No. 2 in F minor

Many great composers go through periods of significant self-doubt and introspection – particularly when embarking on a major new work. For Chopin, though, there was a sense of abandonment – naïvety, even – in much of his writing. Here was a composer who was barely out of his teens, still within education – still growing up, essentially. And yet, at the same time, he was able to tackle the form of the piano concerto for the first time and come up trumps in a quite astounding way.

Just consider the number of famous composers who had already triumphed in the genre:

Mozart composed twenty-seven; Beethoven created five, and near-contemporaries of Chopin such as Hummel and Field had also excelled when it came to writing in concerto form. Along comes Chopin, pretty much still at school, and produces two such concertos in the space of a year. Sickening, really!

If we're being really picky, we could point out that this concerto does seem to be harking back to earlier composers more than *No. 1* (which was, in fact, composed after this one). The influence of the likes of Hummel and Mozart is apparent even in the politely structured opening bars of the first movement. But, overall, this is an astonishing work for a composer so young.

RECOMMENDED RECORDING
Eldar Nebolsin (piano); Warsaw Philharmonic Orchestra; Antoni Wit (conductor).
Naxos: 8572336.

CHART POSITION 64

Nocturne in E flat major Opus 9 No. 2

Remarkably, this is the only piece of solo piano music by Chopin that has been a permanent fixture of the Classic FM Hall of Fame since its inception in 1996. Given the hundreds of not just nocturnes but polkas, mazurkas, waltzes, polonaises and plenty more besides that Chopin composed, you could arguably expect more of them to have found a place in the nation's heart.

Despite being forever associated with the nocturne – which is, quite simply, a piece of particularly wistful, dreamy music, often in-

tended to evoke images of the night – Chopin was not actually its inventor. Instead, the form was created by the Irish composer John Field, a man whose influence on Chopin can be heard clearly, not just in his solo piano music but also in his two piano concertos.

As with the concertos, this particular nocturne was composed around 1830, when Chopin was in his early twenties. It was a hugely productive time for the young composer, when his creative juices were at full spate. The simple yet beguiling melody haunts from start to finish, inviting us into an intimate world where every note matters.

RECOMMENDED RECORDING
Alexandre Tharaud (piano).
Virgin Classics: 50999 45784521.

CHART POSITION 244

AARON COPLAND
(1900–1990)

Appalachian Spring

This all-American work was written for ballet choreographer and dancer Martha Graham (indeed, the original name on the score is 'Ballet for Martha'). For an original fee of $500 (roughly the equivalent of £3,900 today) Copland wrote enough music for a 30-minute ballet, to be performed by a group of thirteen instruments. There is still footage of Graham dancing the original ballet, with a thirty-nine-year-old Merce Cunningham playing the role of the preacher alongside her.

right Frédéric Chopin: Nocturne in E flat major, Opus 9 No. 2

The ballet told the story of pioneer settlers establishing a homestead and interacting with the landscape around them. Oddly enough, the title and the ballet are unconnected, with Martha Graham opting to choose part of a poem called 'The Bridge' by the American poet Hart Crane. She deliberately misconstrued the meaning as being related to the season, rather than to the stream, which the poet had originally intended. Regardless, the ballet was a hit and Copland expanded his score for a full orchestra. Copland himself recorded the music, with the London Symphony Orchestra.

RECOMMENDED RECORDING

London Symphony Orchestra; Aaron Copland (conductor). Sony: SMK89874.

CHART POSITION 115

Fanfare for the Common Man

By the time he reached the Cincinnati Symphony Orchestra in 1931, Eugène Goossens (not to be confused with his violinist father Eugène Goossens or his conductor grandfather Eugène Goossens) had already made his name as conductor of his own orchestra and, before that, as assistant conductor to Thomas Beecham at the Queen's Hall Orchestra.

It was only natural, some years into his tenure with Cincinnati, that his thoughts should drift to his own conducting legacy with his American band. It was for the 1942 and 1943

seasons that Goossens commissioned several prominent composers to provide concert fanfares, to be played at various subscription concerts across the two years. Among others, Walter Piston, Paul Creston, Darius Milhaud, Virgil Thomson and Morton Gould all provided works, starting with Bernard Wagenaar's *A Fanfare for Airmen* in October 1942 and ending with *Fanfare for the Merchant Marine* in April 1943, which was Goossens' own effort.

The fifteenth fanfare, premiered on 12 March 1943, by Copland, is the only one still in the repertoire today. Scored originally for horns, trumpets, trombones, tuba and percussion, Copland used it just three years later as the theme for the last movement of his *Symphony No. 3*.

RECOMMENDED RECORDING

New York Philharmonic Orchestra; Leonard Bernstein (conductor). Sony: SMK63082.

CHART POSITION 139

Rodeo

Choreographer Cecil B. DeMille's niece Agnes cut her teeth with Marie Rambert's ballet company in England. It was at the American Ballet Theatre, though, that she made her big mark, both in terms of commissioning and dancing. However, she made her name from this 1942 commission from Aaron Copland – telling the story of a cowgirl who comes to realise the importance of femininity in her role – for the Ballet Russe de Monte Carlo. Indeed, luckily for her, Messrs Rodgers and Hammerstein were at the premiere of *Rodeo*, and asked her to provide the choreography for their next project, entitled *Oklahoma!*

TOP 10 STIRRING CLASSICS

1	Max Bruch	*Violin Concerto No. 1 – 3rd movement*
2	Edward Elgar	*Cello Concerto – 1st movement*
3	Ludwig van Beethoven	*Piano Concerto No. 5 (Emperor) – 3rd movement*
4	Ludwig van Beethoven	*Symphony No. 9 (Choral) – finale*
5	Camille Saint-Saëns	*Symphony No. 3 (Organ) – 3rd movement*
6	Georges Bizet	*The Pearl Fishers' Duet*
7	Gustav Holst	*The Planets – Mars and Jupiter*
8	George Frideric Handel	*Messiah – Hallelujah Chorus*
9	Jean Sibelius	*Finlandia*
10	Pyotr Ilyich Tchaikovsky	*1812 Overture*

What is less well known about the *Rodeo* score is that Copland's role was more that of arranger than composer. Here he shows his genius for orchestration, using several familiar American folk melodies, with which his 1942 audience would certainly have been more familiar, such as the railroad tune '*Sis Joe*', the cowboy song '*If He'd be a Buckaroo*' and, most notably, in the *Hoe Down* section, an instrumental classic, *McLeod's Reel*. Even less well known is the fact that Agnes DeMille had chosen a number of the folk tunes herself before Copland arrived on the scene.

RECOMMENDED RECORDING

San Francisco Symphony Orchestra; Michael Tilson Thomas (conductor). RCA: 09026635112.

CHART POSITION 270

D

PETER MAXWELL DAVIES
(B. 1934)

Farewell to Stromness

In 2004, the Salford-born composer Peter Maxwell Davies became part of musical history when he accepted the invitation to become Master of the Queen's Music. Previous holders of the post include Edward Elgar, John Stanley and Arnold Bax – so 'Max', as he is called by all who know him, found himself in illustrious company.

His solo piano work *Farewell to Stromness* isn't particularly indicative of his music overall, which is often noticeable both for its visceral sound-world and for its avant-garde structures. But *Farewell to Stromness* is certainly among his most immediately accessible and most enchantingly simple melodies. Its inspiration is unique in classical music: it was written as a protest against a proposed uranium mine on the remote Orkney Islands where the composer lives. Its first performance was in the summer of 1980 at the St Magnus Festival; the title of the piece refers to the town of Stromness, which would have been just a couple of miles from the centre of the mine should it have been constructed.

Many people were introduced to the piece when it was performed in a string arrangement by members of the Philharmonia Orchestra at the blessing of the marriage of the Prince of Wales and the Duchess of Cornwall at St George's Chapel, Windsor, in 2005. The Los Angeles Guitar Quartet has also recorded an arrangement of it – but nothing really beats the simple, quietly stated solo piano original, performed by the composer himself.

RECOMMENDED RECORDING
Peter Maxwell Davies (piano).
Unicorn Kanchana: DKPCD 9070.
CHART POSITION 208

CLAUDE DEBUSSY
(1862–1918)

Suite bergamasque

Although Debussy's *Suite bergamasque* comprises four movements, it is somehow fitting that the third, *Clair de lune*, has become by far the most well known. It was within the inspirational poem 'Clair de lune' by Debussy's friend, Paul Verlaine, that the composer found the seeds of the complete work's title. Verlaine writes of 'your souls … like landscapes, charming masks and bergamasks, playing the lute and dancing, almost sad in their fantastic disguises'. The bergamask, reputedly a clumsy dance performed originally by natives of Bergamo, becomes *bergamasque* in French.

This work was written originally in what was considered Debussy's more Bohemian period, when he was still a little in the long shadow of Wagner and struggling to make ends meet as a composer. It was revived for publication some fifteen years later. As a result, some confusion remains over what was composed originally in 1890 and what in 1905. In those intervening years, the movement *Pavane* had been retitled *Passepied* and the *Promenade sentimentale* was now the famous *Clair de lune*. Not an easy piece to play well, this work allows the most accomplished pianists to shine.

RECOMMENDED RECORDING
Pascal Rogé (piano). Onyx: ONYX4018.
CHART POSITION 66

Prélude à l'après-midi d'un faune

Debussy's *Prélude à l'après-midi d'un faune* was planned originally as merely the first part of a trilogy. The composer intended the final set of three pieces to have included an *Interlude* and a *Paraphrase finale*. In the end, for reasons best known to himself, Debussy decided to combine all his thoughts on Mallarmé's poem ('The Afternoon of a Faun' of the title) to just one single movement. The composer was thirty-two years old when he wrote it and it was eighteen years later when Nijinsky danced to it in Diaghilev's Ballets Russes production in Paris.

This piece is a big turning point in music, perhaps allowing us to hear the traditional system of keys and tonalities being stretched to their limit for the first time. Bernstein, Boulez and many more great musicians have sat to ponder the *Prélude à l'après-midi d'un faune*, coming to the conclusion that it was ten minutes that changed the musical world. Afterwards, it felt to many composers that there was nowhere else to go but a new modern style of classical music composition. All this, and it sounds sumptuously wonderful, too.

RECOMMENDED RECORDING
Cleveland Orchestra; Pierre Boulez (conductor). Deutsche Grammophon: E435766-2.
CHART POSITION 161

LÉO DELIBES
(1836–1891)

Lakmé

Most of us would be hard pressed to describe the characters, plot or musical development of Delibes's three-act opera *Lakmé*. Its resurgent popularity in the 1990s was down to one thing: the use of one particular section of the opera in a certain television commercial. *The Flower Duet* first appeared in a British Airways advert in 1989 and quickly became one of the most well-known pieces of classical music in Britain.

Up until then, the opera had lain in relative obscurity. Its only slight success had been that, unlike other operas by the composer, this one had remained in the repertoire of major opera companies worldwide and continued to be held in high esteem by the classical music cognoscenti. It's a tragic opera set in the Orient, a place known for its beautiful flowers – hence the title of this duet, sung by the principal character Lakmé and her slave Mallika. The sumptuous, exotic music is light, delicate and instantly beautiful, much like the flowers it depicts.

The *Flower Duet*'s use in popular culture isn't restricted only to those British Airways commercials. More recently, it's been heard in films such as *Meet the Parents* and *True Romance* and television shows including *The Simpsons*.

RECOMMENDED RECORDING

Natalie Dessay (soprano) as Lakmé; Delphine Haidan (soprano) as Mallika; Gregory Kunde (tenor) as Gerald; José van Dam (bass-baritone) as Nilakantha; Toulouse Capitole Choir and Orchestra; Michel Plasson (conductor). EMI Classics: CDS 5565692.

CHART POSITION 96

Coppélia

If marches and waltzes are inherently Viennese, mazurkas are intrinsically Polish and nocturnes are forever Irish at their core, much of the world's greatest ballet music will always be associated with one city: Paris. It was here that Chopin's *Les Sylphides* – seen as the first truly Romantic ballet – was premiered, and it was also the city where Stravinsky's *Rite of Spring* caused a riot at its first performance in 1913. In between these two landmark events came the world premiere of *Coppélia* in 1870.

Unusually for its time, the principal male role is danced by a woman. In terms of plot, *Coppélia* is a carbon copy of Offenbach's *The*

Tales of Hoffmann. Both take as their inspiration E. T. A. Hoffmann's story *Der Sandman* – a fantastical tale of a dancing doll being brought to life by her creator, the toymaker Dr Coppélius.

Elements of comedy run through the ballet: the doctor imagines that he has succeeded in bringing Coppélia to life when he has, in fact, been dreaming. Musically, from the dainty *Waltz* to the rousing *Mazurka*, *Coppélia* is packed full of bright, saccharine tunes. In that sense, it's a sort of French *Nutcracker* – and a delightful one at that.

RECOMMENDED RECORDING

Orchestra of the Royal Opera House; Mark Ermler (conductor). Conifer: ROH 006.

CHART POSITION 287

FREDERICK DELIUS
(1862–1934)

The Walk to the Paradise Garden

The period from the turn of the twentieth century to 1918 was a golden one for Delius. In the space of just seventeen years, he composed *Brigg Fair*, *A Mass of Life*, *Fennimore and Gerda*, *On Hearing the First Cuckoo in Spring*, *Appalachia* and more. This purple patch kicked off with an opera to his own German libretto. Although he was born in Bradford, his parents were both German and he was known as 'Fritz' at home, so the language was far from alien to him. Finished in 1901, *A Village Romeo and Juliet* became a minor hit for the composer, transferring from its original Berlin run to London (with Thomas Beecham conducting) and then to Washington. Although fairly

---

right Léo Delibes: Coppélia

rarely performed as a complete opera today, the music written to cover a large amount of scenery shifting (between scenes 5 and 6) endures. During this musical interlude, Sali and Vreli walk to the pub (The Paradise Garden) where they go to drink and dance. *The Walk to the Paradise Garden* quickly became a concert favourite.

La Calinda

Another of Delius's best-known works falls into the same category as *The Walk to the Paradise Garden*, being an interlude from an opera that is now rarely heard in full. *Koanga* predates *A Village Romeo and Juliet* by just four years and comes from the composer's Bohemian years in Paris during the 1890s. Delius himself considered it his best opera to date. It was his third after *Irmelin* and *The Magic Fountain* and it drew on his experiences in the orange groves of Florida. The hero of the opera, Koanga, is an African prince and voodoo priest, now working as a slave on a Mississippi plantation.

Delius incorporated a traditional Martinique dance from the seventeenth century into the plot, for which he wrote a small musical interlude, borrowing from something he had written earlier in his first orchestral work, the *Florida Suite*. When his trusty companion and scribe Eric Fenby arranged the interlude for orchestra in 1938 – some forty years later – it quickly became another hardy perennial on concert programmes up and down the land.

On Hearing the First Cuckoo in Spring

This is the sister piece to *Summer Night on the River*. Together, they make up *Two Small Pieces for Orchestra*, which is occasionally referred to as *Two Mood Pictures for Small Orchestra*. It was written in the year that the Titanic was making headlines for all the wrong reasons. Its first performance, just under a year later, took place in Leipzig.

At the centre of the work is an old Norwegian folk song called '*In Ola Valley*', which is stunningly beautiful in its own right. It had also attracted the attentions of the composer Grieg in his time. For Delius's sublime arrangement, we have the eccentric Australian composer Percy Grainger to thank, as he was the one who stuck it under Delius's nose in the first place.

Following its British premiere in 1914, it became a favourite, helped on its way by the never-flagging championship of the conductor and great friend of Delius, Thomas Beecham. It is just possible that Beecham and Delius were already familiar with '*In Ola Valley*' prior to Grainger's encouragement, having spent the summer of 1909 rambling in the Norwegian mountains together, no doubt ears permanently pricked for any musical titbits. Today, it feels like a Delius original.

GAETANO DONIZETTI
(1797–1848)

Lucia di Lammermoor

Australian soprano Dame Joan Sutherland made her name performing coloratura repertoire. Literally meaning 'colouring', the term refers to particularly high-octane vocal gymnastics at the top of a soprano's register, designed to challenge the performer to their limits and wow audiences in the process. Dame Joan became famous for her performances of the Mad Scene from this Donizetti opera; it remains perhaps the greatest operatic challenge for any coloratura soprano today.

While the music in *Lucia di Lammermoor* is both extraordinarily accomplished and structurally coherent, the same cannot be said of the plot. Donizetti wasn't the first composer to set a farcical, disjointed story to music – and he surely won't be the last – but this one really stretches things to the limit. The opera follows the misfortunes of two feuding Scottish families, a political mission to France, forgery, a forced marriage, utter madness and suicide.

Aside from the famous Mad Scene in the third act, the other crowning glory of *Lucia di Lammermoor* is the glorious *Sextet*, which, when performed well, cannot fail to send shivers down the listener's spine. Donizetti skilfully ensures all six characters have individual musical lines and distinct phrasing to distinguish them from the other five performers. As a result, within this heavenly blend of sound, there are also six different melodic

ideas, all woven together to create something truly magical.

ANTONÍN DVOŘÁK
(1841–1904)

Symphony No. 9 in E minor
From the New World

The subtitle of Dvořák's *Symphony No. 9* is important: it's not 'To the New World'; it's 'From'. This is very much a symphony that looks back, from the USA, to Dvořák's native Bohemia. It is almost as if he were stood atop Lady Liberty herself, hand over his forehead to shield the sun, desperately looking to see if he can make out his faraway homeland. It was the lure of an amazing fee that persuaded Dvořák to venture to New York. From his house overlooking Stuyvesant Park, he appeared to spend much of his time pining for home, rarely going out (unless contractually obliged to) and taking every opportunity to remind himself of home, particularly during the summer, which he spent with the Czech community of Spillville, Iowa.

When he premiered this work in Carnegie Hall in 1893, critics disagreed over whether

Antonín Dvořák
1841-1904

'I should be glad if something occurred to me as a main idea that occurs to Dvořák only by the way.'
JOHANNES BRAHMS

Dvořák loved his Czech homeland and was terribly homesick when he moved to the USA for three years in the 1890s. While he was there though, he discovered American folk melodies, which heavily influenced his composition. He had already developed a passion for the native tunes of his homeland and these remained with him throughout his composing career.

He travelled far and wide and was particularly popular in Britain, with major works receiving their world premieres in cities such as Birmingham, London and Leeds. Yet his heart remained in his homeland and having started off his career as a viola player in a Prague orchestra, he ended it by nurturing the talents of younger Czech composers, such as Suk and Novák.

Away from music, Dvořák was a committed train-spotter. He would practise his hobby at the Franz Josef Station in Prague; it's said he knew the train

DID YOU KNOW?
Dvořák didn't come from a particularly musical family. His father juggled two jobs: a butcher by day, a pub landlord by night!

timetable off by heart. But, he was after all, only living up to his name (remove the middle 'tonín Dv' from Antonín Dvořák). When he went to work in New York as the director of the National Conservatory of Music, he developed a passion for steam ships.

Believe it or not, he also became something of a pigeon fancier while he was in the city.

There's a steady stream of anecdotes that surround Dvořák's life. On one occasion when he was staying in London – to oversee a performance of his Piano Concerto at Crystal Palace – he was thrown out of the Athenaeum Club. He'd mistaken it for a coffee house and was immediately evicted.

It was also said that Dvořák (and Mrs Dvořák, for that matter) liked to get up very early indeed. When they stayed with the composer and organist Charles Villiers Stanford in Cambridge, he was more than a little surprised that, when he woke at 6 a.m., the Dvořáks were already to be found sitting under a tree in his garden.

it was an all-American symphony (as he'd promised) or just more of Dvořák's usual fare. What is certain is that it has lived on its myriad merits ever since, remaining one of the most popular symphonies of all.

RECOMMENDED RECORDING
Oslo Philharmonic Orchestra; Mariss Jansons (conductor). EMI Classics: 5008782.
CHART POSITION 17

Cello Concerto in B minor

This is one of the two most performed cello concertos in the world (the other being by Elgar) and with such a story to tell that it would make a great weepy all on its own. Like the *New World Symphony*, it is another work hailing from the composer's American period and is therefore infused with the same sense of homesick longing that pervades the symphony. Yet there is far more to the *Cello Concerto* than initially meets the ear. Homesickness tells only half the tale. With Dvořák in America was his wife, Anna, whom he had married only after courting and being turned down by her elder sister, Josefina. At that time, he had started but not finished an early cello concerto, an expression of his love. Now, in America, he learned that Josefina was seriously ill – and began another cello concerto. Into it, he wove Josefina's favourite of his songs, called *'Leave Me Alone'*. It is heard most achingly in the wonderful slow movement. Intended originally for his friend Hanus (who played alongside composer Suk in the Czech String Quartet) it was eventually premiered in

England by British cellist Leo Stern, whom Dvořák had befriended in Prague.
RECOMMENDED RECORDING
Mstislav Rostropovich (cello); Berlin Philharmonic Orchestra; Herbert von Karajan (conductor). Deutsche Grammophon: 4474132.
CHART POSITION 98

Rusalka

Dvořák wrote *Rusalka*, his penultimate opera, at the age of sixty, with just three years left to live. He had lost none of his compositional powers, though; it proved his biggest operatic hit. It's based on the folk tale of Undine, the water nymph (from the Latin *unda*, meaning wave) although, by the time Dvořák offered up his music, Hans Christian Andersen's 'The Little Mermaid' was already sixty-five years old, so there is the odd doff of the cap to this version, too.

The premiere took place in the National Theatre in Prague, where Dvořák himself had once played in the house band. Mahler tried but failed to get it into Vienna. Today, it is still revived, buoyed by the stand-out success of possibly its finest moment. It comes in Act I, when Rusalka (the 'little mermaid') tells her father she has fallen in love with a mortal, and wants to become human. Having been pointed in the direction of the local witch, Rusalka sings to the moon, with the wish that the moon tell her beloved all about her. This *Song to the Moon* remains the shining-hit aria of the whole work.
RECOMMENDED RECORDING
Kate Royal (soprano) as Rusalka; Orchestra of the English National Opera; Edward Gardner (conductor). EMI Classics: 2681922.
CHART POSITION 121

Symphony No. 8 in G

The younger brother to the limelight-stealing *New World Symphony*, its inclusion here represents an impressive moment in the sun for the *Symphony No. 8*. It's one of Dvořák's less expansive works – possibly something to do with not just its position before his mighty *Symphony No. 9*, but also after his *Symphony No. 7*.

Dvořák had had to go through lengthy and sometimes slightly bizarre negotiations with his publisher, Simrock, over his *Symphony No. 7*. First, an advance hadn't been forthcoming, forcing Dvořák to complain that he had endured a bad potato harvest and needed some money upfront. Simrock then refused to print Dvořák's correct first name on the cover, instead insisting on Germanising it.

The composer dedicated his *Symphony No. 8* to the music world: 'To the Bohemian Academy of Emperor Franz Joseph for the Encouragement of Arts and Literature, in thanks for my election'. Debts duly paid, he produced a fun and lively symphony, replete with folk tunes that the aforementioned academy would no doubt have loved.

It took him only two and a half months from beginning to end and the spontaneity shines through, with the whole thing played right through in little more than half an hour, making it one of his most easily programmable works.

RECOMMENDED RECORDING
Budapest Festival Orchestra; Iván Fischer (conductor). Channel Classics: CCSSA90110.
CHART POSITION 204

Slavonic Dances

In the late nineteenth century, piano-duet sheet music was the iTunes download of its day. In almost every parlour in Europe, they were the party pieces of choice, so much so that publishers would outbid each other for the piano duets of the great composers.

Dvořák's publisher, Simrock, had even threatened to call off publishing his *Symphony No.7* if the composer didn't stump up the piano-duet version ahead of the orchestral score. Simrock must have thought all his Christmases had come at once when Dvořák supplied him with eight *Slavonic Dances* in this format: perfect, folk-like tunes (although all original Dvořák compositions) in a beautifully saleable form.

Eight years later, Dvořák repeated the trick – again to his publisher's delight – providing eight more. Today, we are probably more familiar with the orchestrations provided by the composer himself as a way of maximising their potential, although the piano-duet originals remain an engaging listen.

RECOMMENDED RECORDINGS
Czech Philharmonic Orchestra; Charles Mackerras (conductor). Supraphon: SU 34222.
CHART POSITION 277

LUDOVICO EINAUDI
(B. 1955)

Le Onde

Of all the composers to have ever entered the Classic FM Hall of Fame, Ludovico Einaudi is probably the most contentious. For every person who adores his minimalist melodies, there's someone else who likens them to an A-level composition project and simply cannot fathom their appeal. But, whatever your personal views on the contemporary Italian composer's piano music, there's no doubt that he has a unique ability to reach a large audience with his brand of laid-back, repetitive tunes.

Le Onde ('The Waves') was Einaudi's first big hit, and it's also the title track from his first major album, released in 1996. It takes as its inspiration the Virginia Woolf novel *The Waves* and the undulating, hypnotic melody evokes images of the rhythms and patterns of the ocean.

In his native Italy, Einaudi is held up as an art-house composer, while in the UK his music is regarded as being 'classical crossover'. The continued popularity of *Le Onde* proves that Einaudi has succeeded in connecting with a large number of people and the uniqueness of his success should make us wary of pigeon-holing him within such vague and all-embracing terminology.

RECOMMENDED RECORDING
Ludovico Einaudi (piano).
Sony BMG: 74321 397022.
CHART POSITION 128

I Giorni

Einaudi was taught by the avant-garde Italian composer Luciano Berio, although the music for which Einaudi has become famous couldn't be more different from that of his teacher. Whereas Berio composed, in the main, very complex, challenging works, Einaudi's solo piano pieces are like classical pop songs: all lasting no more than around five minutes, all with an introduction, verse, chorus and middle eight. He is often likened to composers such as Michael Nyman, Thomas Newman and Erik Satie, and it's certainly fair to say that there's something of the *Gymnopédies* about Einaudi's most popular pieces.

Einaudi was inspired to compose *I Giorni* ('The Days') after hearing a twelfth-century folk song that originated in the country of Mali. The song describes the killing of a hippopotamus by a hunter, and the subsequent mourning in the local village. The entire album from which this song is taken (also called *I Giorni*) is one long lament, with each piece demonstrating Einaudi's ability to compose utterly simple yet beguiling melodies.

I Giorni, released in 2002, was the first solo-piano follow-up to *Le Onde*, the disc that introduced the composer to British audiences and which became an almost instant hit on Classic FM.

RECOMMENDED RECORDING
Ludovico Einaudi (piano).
Sony BMG: 74321 974622.
CHART POSITION 224

EDWARD ELGAR
(1857–1934)

Cello Concerto in E minor

Somebody once said that the way Elgar chooses to open his *Cello Concerto*, with those tortured chords sounding as if they have to be excavated from the cello face, is as if Shakespeare had started *Hamlet* at 'To be or not to be'. Most concertos take a little time to come to their main point. If they don't make you wait until the slow movement — and many do — for their crux, they at least keep the listener waiting through a short orchestral introduction. Elgar was having none of it.

Perhaps the timing of the composition explains it all. In 1918, and aged sixty-one, he had gone through the period of his life where he would have been regarded as a budding composer. In fact, he had already been acknowledged as a national treasure for some time. Now, he was seriously wondering whether some critics were right to write him off as a spent force.

He came around from the anaesthetic after an operation to remove an infected tonsil with this tune already in his head, so he wasn't going to let it go to waste. He didn't and it remains one of the most English of all pieces of English music.

RECOMMENDED RECORDING
Natalie Clein (cello); Royal Liverpool Philharmonic Orchestra; Vernon Handley (conductor). EMI Classics: 5014092.
CHART POSITION 5

Enigma Variations

One theme — endlessly talked about — and fourteen variations on it. Each variation was the result of a parlour game between Elgar and his wife, Alice. He'd played the theme to her, which he described as 'nothing much, but something might be made of it'. He then proceeded to improvise how it might sound played either in the style of — or in tribute to — their closest friends. Between then and publication in 1899, the 'Enigma' legend was added. Scholars have long since decoded the half-disguises to the various 'friends within' each movement, but the name and indeed the very nature of the central enigma itself

---

right Edward Elgar: Enigma Variations

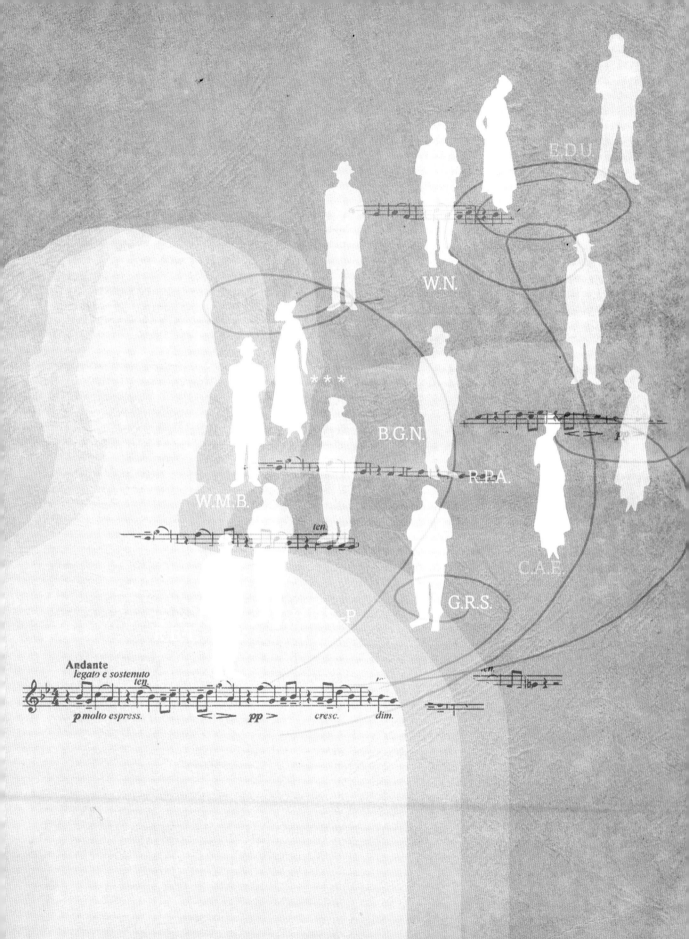

Edward Elgar
1857-1934

'There is music in the air. All you have to do is take as much as you require.' EDWARD ELGAR

One of the greatest British composers, Elgar is quite rightly regarded as a national treasure. He spent much of his life in his native Worcestershire and the beautiful surrounding English countryside inspired him to write many of the most quintessentially English tunes.

Elgar didn't receive a music education honed in Europe's finest conservatoires. Instead, he learned much from his father, who ran a music shop and travelled around Worcestershire tuning pianos. By his mid-teens, Elgar was earning money as a jobbing musician, having studied the piano and organ as a boy. His only foray into the world of work outside music, as a clerk in a solicitor's office, was short-lived. Until his success as a composer meant that he could write and conduct full-time, he continued to teach and to play the violin in local orchestras.

He made his name as the composer of large-scale choral works – there was a real need for them at the time, as England had a multitude of choral societies in most of the major cities, many of which also

DID YOU KNOW?

Elgar was a sports fanatic. His golf clubs can still be seen today at the Elgar Birthplace Museum, and he was a big fan of horse-racing, too.

regularly hosted big music festivals. By the 1900s, Elgar was also becoming known for his orchestral compositions, with each new one making him ever more famous, right across Europe. He also benefited greatly from the newly invented gramophone, which allowed him to

make recordings of his new compositions which could then be disseminated all around the world.

When Abbey Road Studios opened in London in 1931, the first recording ever made there was of Elgar's *Falstaff*, with the composer himself conducting. Elgar was a keen convert to the new technology and conducted many of the premiere recordings of his works himself. Most of these still survive today, allowing us to hear exactly how he intended them to sound – a luxury not afforded to previous generations of composers.

By the time of Elgar's death in 1934, he had become a firm part of the British classical music Establishment, having been knighted in 1904 and appointed Master of the King's Music in 1924. He left behind some of the most enduring examples of English music ever composed.

endures. Every year sees a new tune suggested as the 'hidden theme': the *Prague Symphony*, 'Rule, Britannia', *The Art of Fugue*, they're all contenders, so it would seem. Yet it is in the light of Elgar's penchant for puzzling and trickery in the first place – the very reason there is an enigma – that might suggest Elgar was having us all on. He never publicly disclosed the secret – and maybe that's the best way.

RECOMMENDED RECORDING
Royal Philharmonic Orchestra; Yehudi Menuhin (conductor). Regis: RRC1219.
CHART POSITION 8

The Dream of Gerontius

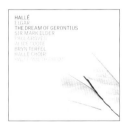

Victorian England loved its monster choral works. It wolfed them down at seemingly endless year-long seasons of festivals up and down the country. Coming just one year after the successful *Enigma Variations*, it would probably not have mattered which choral monster Elgar supplied for the Birmingham Festival. As it happened, he created a masterpiece, certainly his greatest choral work – if not the greatest by any English composer.

Elgar had planned this piece since his thirties, and possessed a copy of Cardinal Newman's original poem with annotations by General Gordon of Khartoum; Gordon's notes on the text were retrieved from his belongings after his demise and became a popular Victorian publication. Despite a near-disastrous premiere performance, the work thrived (particularly, early on, in Germany, when Richard Strauss used it to hail 'Meister' Elgar as 'the first progressive English musician'). Over here, what is less well remembered is that it was only grudgingly accepted because of its Roman Catholic themes, to the point that it was banned in some cathedrals.

RECOMMENDED RECORDING
Paul Groves, Alice Coote & Bryn Terfel. Halle, Hallé Choir, Hallé Youth Choir, Sir Mark Elder. Hallé: CDHLD7520
CHART POSITION 91

Pomp and Circumstance Marches

For someone who claimed to pride himself on not being a part of the Establishment, Elgar loved many of the trappings that came with it. He lobbied fairly furiously for his position as Master of the King's Music; he was a member of the Athenaeum Club, and he was not beyond pulling a few strings with his friends in high places, when the need arose.

When it came to the subject matter for his music, he loved all things Establishment, too. A huge fan of chivalry in all its forms, the 'pomp and circumstance' of his marches' titles comes from Shakespeare's *Othello* (the 'pride pomp and circumstance of glorious war' from Act III, scene 3). In his lifetime, there were five marches, with the first four, including the most famous first – the 'Land of Hope and Glory' march – coming between 1901 and 1907, long before the harsh realities of the First World War changed many British people's attitudes to the pomp of war. Nevertheless, a late straggler, the fifth, followed in 1930, and the composer Anthony Payne completed a sixth from Elgar's notes in 2006.

RECOMMENDED RECORDING
Royal Philharmonic Orchestra; Yehudi Menuhin (conductor). Virgin: 5614302.
CHART POSITION 104

Violin Concerto in B minor

Despite the status that Elgar's *Cello Concerto* has acquired since its premiere, there is a case to be made for proposing that it was in fact the *Violin Concerto* that was truly the composer's favourite among his own works. Many accounts suggest that he was writing for his friend and muse, Alice Stuart-Wortley, whom some claim was the great true love of his life. It is also worth noting that Elgar was writing here for his own instrument. He prided himself on the way in which he had plied his trade as a player for many years, rising up through the practical ranks of real musicians. If the festival orchestras of Victorian England were his coal face, then the violin was his pick axe.

The dedication on the work's front page reads 'Herein is enshrined the soul of ...'. This mystery figure was long thought to be Alice Stuart-Wortley, but if the five dots were not substitutes for letters, as often thought, but Morse code, they could be 'H.E.', for Helen Elgar, Elgar's sister. And Helen Elgar's nickname in her family? Only 'Dot'!

RECOMMENDED RECORDING
Nigel Kennedy (violin); City of Birmingham Symphony Orchestra; Simon Rattle (conductor). EMI Classics: 5034172.
CHART POSITION 176

Symphony No. 1 in A flat

A composer's first symphony is important. Some put it off for decades, overshadowed by other writers and their former glories. Brahms was one such, taking more than fourteen years to offer up his first. Elgar spent a full ten years ruminating on his *Symphony No. 1*, but its arrival, on 3 December 1908 in Manchester, was greeted with an unprecedented response. 'An immediate and phenomenal success,' reported the *Musical Times*. It soon went on to garner around a hundred performances over the following year.

The composer had intended to make this a 'Gordon of Khartoum' tribute symphony (see *The Dream of Gerontius*) but, on publication of the score, insisted this plan had gone by the wayside and that his *Symphony No. 1* had 'no programme beyond a wide experience of human life with a great charity (love) and a massive hope in the future'.

By way of a little aside, Elgar's is pretty much the only symphony of note written in the key of A flat. It could be that one of the reasons for this is that it is not the ideal key for playing in, particularly not for the fiddlers – something of which Elgar, as a violinist, would have been well aware.

RECOMMENDED RECORDING
London Philharmonic Orchestra; Vernon Handley (conductor). LPO: LPO0046.
CHART POSITION 192

Chanson de Matin

In the years before his first real success as a composer, Elgar relied on choral composition for much of his income. Unfortunately, these time-consuming, large-scale works were not always the most efficient of payers. Luckily for Elgar, he had been befriended by a senior figure at the music publishers Novello. August Jaeger was someone who genuinely appreciated his music and he was immortalised as 'Nimrod' in Elgar's *Enigma Variations*.

Having had a pretty unsuccessful sortie into London to make his musical fortune in the 1880s, Elgar retreated to Malvern, from where he wrote, bemoaning his fate to the ever receptive Jaeger. Complaining of lean times, he sent Jaeger a violin piece called *Evensong*, suggesting the name could be changed to *Vespers* if needed. In the end, the publisher preferred to call the piece *Chanson de Nuit*.

A couple of years later, Elgar wrote to Jaeger again, claiming to have recently rediscovered its companion piece. The two works provide a simple day-and-night contrast of styles, with *Chanson de Nuit* being very much the richer of the two. *Chanson de Matin*, as its name would suggest, is simpler and fresher.

RECOMMENDED RECORDING
Britten Sinfonia; Nicholas Cleobury (conductor). Sony Classics: 8869 7707282.
CHART POSITION 199

Introduction and Allegro for Strings

The position of Elgar's *Introduction and Allegro for Strings* in his composing life is quite striking. It was written after the *Enigma Variations*, after *Sea Pictures*, and after the *Pomp and Circumstance Marches Nos.1–3*, but before his period of self-doubt following the composition of his *Symphony No. 2*, a time of endless soul-searching about whether he was 'composed out'.

When it came actually to writing it in 1905, it involved a typically Elgarian method of composition. Elgar used numerous notebooks, which he kept with him at all times, for those moments when the muse struck. For this work, he dipped into his jottings and borrowed something that was dated four years earlier.

It had come from a rather bracing walk along the Cardiganshire coast, when he had heard a distant choir, and he had stashed it away for a possible 'Welsh Rhapsody' of some sort. In the end, the Welsh piece never came, so he borrowed the tune for this work, which features both a string quartet and a string orchestra. It was written originally for the strings section of the fledgling London Symphony Orchestra, from an original suggestion by his publisher, Jaeger.

RECOMMENDED RECORDING
Allegri String Quartet; Sinfonia of London; John Barbirolli (conductor). EMI Classics: 5672402.
CHART POSITION 202

Serenade in E minor for Strings

The *Serenade* can stake a healthy claim as one of the very first works ever written by Elgar. Even though it has a publication date putting it alongside the composer's thirty-sixth birthday, it had its own birthday long before then, back in the mists of Elgar's youth. Similarly, the *Wand of Youth Suite*, was 'written' in 1907, but featuring a tune by an Elgar possibly as young as just ten years old. The tune used in the *Serenade* is probably not quite that old, but it still relies on early notes for the music at its heart.

It was premiered, in a private performance, by the delightfully named Worcester Ladies Orchestral Class (conductor one E. Elgar) in 1892, but then heard professionally

in the UK, in one of Victorian England's favourite stomping grounds, New Brighton. For a short but golden time, New Brighton was north-west England's centre of the musical universe, with Saturday concerts timed at 3.30 p.m. 'after the banks close', attracting not just huge audiences but great conductors and composers.

RECOMMENDED RECORDING
Academy of St Martin in the Fields; Neville Marriner (conductor); Decca: 4527072.
CHART POSITION 223

Sea Pictures

Sea Pictures comes immediately after the *Enigma Variations* in the chronology of Elgar's output. It was written in October 1899, just four months behind its mysterious neighbour. But it nearly didn't happen at all; or at least certainly not with its original alto, Dame Clara Butt. When Elgar first called on her, at her home, to discuss the work, she was in the bath and refused to see him. He persevered until the piece was first performed at the Norwich Festival.

As a collection of five very different poems set to music, the critics (of today) often rail against the choice of words. One poem is by Elgar's wife of ten years, Alice, called 'In Haven (Capri)', which she had originally written as 'Love Alone Will Stay', and which was published separately a couple of years earlier. Nevertheless, it is a perennial favourite with the musical public.

RECOMMENDED RECORDING
Della Jones (mezzo-soprano); Royal Philharmonic Orchestra; Charles Mackerras (conductor). Decca: 4428277.
CHART POSITION 240

Salut d'Amour

Not content with mere rings to mark their engagement in 1888, Edward Elgar and his wife-to-be Alice exchanged artistic gifts too. She had given him a poem that she had written a few years earlier, entitled 'The Wind at Dawn', although she retitled it 'Love's Grace' for the occasion. Elgar immediately set it to music, winning himself a rather useful £5 in the process when he entered it into a composing competition. (Using a measure of average earnings, that's the equivalent today of some £2,600 − not a bad day's work for a would-be composer and his fiancée). In return, Elgar gave Alice a musical love token, entitled *Liebesgruss* − written in Settle, in Yorkshire.

Never one to look a gift piece in the mouth, Elgar sent a few versions to Schott's publishers, who gave him just two guineas for it and promptly published it as *Salut d'Amour*, calling him mysteriously 'Ed. Elgar' − the hope being that if he sounded less English, it would sell more. And it did. Sadly, Elgar received only his two guineas.

RECOMMENDED RECORDING
Itzhak Perlman (violin); Samuel Sanders (piano). EMI Classics: 4769572.
CHART POSITION 242

left Edward Elgar: Salut d'Amour

F

Requiem

In his seven-section *Requiem*, the French composer Gabriel Fauré distilled some of the most beautiful melodies he ever composed. The creation was almost certainly a musical tribute to his father, who died in 1885, three years before work on the *Requiem* began.

As with much of Western classical music, the requiem owes its roots to Christian faith. Traditionally, at its heart, it is a prayerful lament for the dead. Fauré's *Requiem* was altogether different, though, because here was a composer who, unlike many of his contemporaries, had no clear religious beliefs. By contrast, he was very much a doubter, described by his own son as 'a sceptic'. In place of the sombre nature of many requiems that had gone before, Fauré's is noted for its calm, serene and peaceful outlook. Anyone looking for morose themes is searching in the wrong place. Instead, here we find musical solace in a work that focuses not on the morbid, but on the supposedly restful and fear-free nature of death.

Of all seven sections, the *Pie Jesu*, *Agnus Dei* and *In Paradisum* emerge as the most glorious,

filled with rich, soulful melodies. The work garnered the praise of many other composers – not least Camille Saint-Saëns, who thought it divine. It was performed at Fauré's own funeral in 1924.

RECOMMENDED RECORDING Accentus (choir); members of the National Orchestra of France; Laurence Equilbey (conductor). Naïve: V 5137.
CHART POSITION 25

Cantique de Jean Racine

Fauré was a precociously brilliant composer. By his late teens, he had already developed his own unique and utterly assured musical voice. Nowhere is this better demonstrated than in his *Cantique de Jean Racine*. Composed in 1865, when Fauré was just twenty, it's very much a precursor to the *Requiem*, with similarly lush, intense choral writing layered on top of sparse organ accompaniment. As with

TOP 10 OPERAS

1	Georges Bizet	*The Pearl Fishers*
2	Pietro Mascagni	*Cavalleria rusticana*
3	Giuseppe Verdi	*Nabucco*
4	Wolfgang Amadeus Mozart	*The Marriage of Figaro*
5	Giacomo Puccini	*Madama Butterfly*
6	Wolfgang Amadeus Mozart	*The Magic Flute*
7	Giacomo Puccini	*La bohème*
8	Jules Massenet	*Thaïs*
9	Giuseppe Verdi	*La traviata*
10	Richard Wagner	*Tristan and Isolde*

the *Requiem*, it takes a religious text as its inspiration – in this case, words by the French playwright Jean Racine.

Fauré studied composition at the École Niedermeyer in Paris, and submitted this piece for the school's composition competition. He won first prize and his success spurred him on to write more religious music.

Despite coming in for some criticism during his lifetime for a failure to embrace larger-scale works, Fauré stuck to his guns and resolutely refused to move away from chamber music and elegant choral miniatures. While the *Cantique de Jean Racine* is only five minutes long, it's none the worse for that, and it confirms Fauré's status not just as an outstanding young musician but as one of France's most influential and important composers.

RECOMMENDED RECORDING
Choir of King's College, Cambridge; James Vivian (organ); Stephen Cleobury (conductor). Decca: 4600212.
CHART POSITION 42

Pavane

'Shouldn't you be at work?' Those were the words Des Lynam chose to utter at the start of BBC1's 2 p.m. broadcast of England versus Tunisia during the 1998 World Cup Finals. They were followed immediately by the haunting sounds of Fauré's *Pavane* – the channel's theme music for its coverage of the tournament that year. And although the piece had always been relatively popular, its use in such a mass-market way immediately introduced the French composer's music to a whole new audience.

Composed in 1887, it's another perfect example of Fauré refining his musical ideas into miniature form, with the result that the *Pavane* is done and dusted within six minutes. The work was written for orchestra, but the composer went on to pen an arrangement that included a choir, although only the original version remains in regular performance today. It's thought that Fauré probably added the chorus at the request of Countess Greffulhe, a wealthy patron of the arts in Paris.

The pavane began life as a sixteenth-century court dance, and is thought most likely to have originated in Italy. Fauré's take on the genre is a beautiful example, flowing gracefully and freely in a thoroughly enchanting way. Its success spurred the young composer on towards writing his *Requiem*, which he had virtually completed a year later.

RECOMMENDED RECORDING
Montreal Symphony Orchestra; Charles Dutoit (conductor). Decca: 4214402.
CHART POSITION 103

GERALD FINZI
(1901–1956)

Eclogue

Everyone should own a copy of this work, and not just so that they can say that they have the music of a composer whose first name was Gerald. It's a piece that Finzi started writing in the late 1920s, but never got round to finishing. At least, not finishing in the manner he had wanted. The idea originally was to write a grand piano concerto – it's very possible that his *Grand Fantasia and Toccata* for piano might well have been part of the original plan, too – but, for some reason, it was never to be.

This movement is based on an archaic form of poem that was originally meant to be a conversation between shepherds (although quite how interesting that might have been without music is another matter). In the end, probably knowing that other movements were never going to come, Finzi reworked it so that it could be played on its own. Even then, it didn't see the public light of day until the composer was dead and buried.

RECOMMENDED RECORDING
Peter Donohoe (piano); Northern Sinfonia; Howard Griffiths (conductor). Naxos: 8555766.
CHART POSITION 215

Clarinet Concerto

During the Second World War, Gerald Finzi started work at the Ministry of War Transport. Prior to that, he had worked tirelessly on everyone's behalf except his own: he aided the ailing English composer Ivor Gurney; he helped publish a great deal of English folk music, and, last but not least, he became a dedicated apple grower, rescuing a number of rare apple breeds from extinction. His own compositions, though, were sporadic but brilliant (the *Five Bagatelles* were premiered in the National Gallery, at a wartime concert).

After the war years, he seemed to gain fresh impetus, and it was in this period that he composed his *Clarinet Concerto*, now probably his best remembered work. It was premiered at the Three Choirs Festival in 1949, taking place that year in Hereford. Sadly, within just a couple of years, he would be told of a fatal illness, and he died in 1956, aged fifty-five. His output, though small, is revered more and more every year.

RECOMMENDED RECORDING
Emma Johnson (clarinet); Royal Philharmonic Orchestra; Charles Groves (conductor). ASV: CDDCA787.

CHART POSITION 296

CÉSAR FRANCK
(1822–1890)

Panis angelicus

The Belgian-born but ultimately French composer César Franck wrote some glorious music, brimming with inventive, intoxicating melodies. From the sunny *Violin Sonata in A* to the intricate *Variations symphoniques* for piano and orchestra, any journey through Franck's music is deeply rewarding. And yet, he's far and away remembered for this one piece of music, *Panis angelicus*, which has been recorded hundreds of times and is still performed frequently the world over.

The melodic line is sung by a solo tenor, accompanied by a relatively reserved organ and sedate string chords. Although known primarily as a stand-alone piece, *Panis angelicus* was also included by Franck within his *Mass for Three Voices*. However, *Panis angelicus* was completed in 1872 – twelve years after the *Mass* – so its inclusion was a rather belated affair.

Like his fellow French composer Gabriel Fauré, César Franck was a precociously talented child, adept not just at composition but also as a concert pianist. His particularly demanding father placed considerable pressure on the young composer, urging him to teach alongside his studies. Despite the pressure from his father, the young César wasn't dissuaded from following a musical path in later life. And for that, we can be truly thankful.

RECOMMENDED RECORDING
Choir of St John's College, Cambridge; Andrew Nethsingha (conductor). Chandos: CHSA 5085.

CHART POSITION 241

G

Rhapsody in Blue

The name Charles Hambitzer might not be familiar to you, but he is one of the hundreds of unsung musical heroes who fall into that enlightened category of teachers who not only can recognize true genius when they see it, but who also do something – plenty, in fact – about it. Hambitzer took on George Gershwin when his pupil was just fourteen years old. Immediately, he realized the level of talent he had on his hands. He made sure Gershwin went to concerts and gave him significant pieces to learn by the great composers for the piano. The effort certainly paid off. Working first as a song plugger in New York's Tin Pan Alley, and studying harmony and counterpoint for nearly ten years, Gershwin went on to compose musicals, films, jazz and classical music. Whatever he tried his hand at, he managed to turn out music that was a cut above average.

Rhapsody in Blue was premiered by Paul Whiteman's concert band in New York in 1924. Today, the work is a permanent fixture of the repertoire, with its infusion of jazz and classical music and its distinctly New York sound.

RECOMMENDED RECORDING
André Previn (piano); London Symphony Orchestra; EMI Classics: 5668912.
CHART POSITION 46

Piano Concerto in F

One year on from his *Rhapsody in Blue* and George Gershwin was at it again. Despite the knockers (and they are always there, even today) Gershwin proved that he could write a coherent piano concerto not once but twice. In an era when several composers were trying to make an assault on jazz, working from the outside in, Gershwin worked from the inside out. His increasing mastery of the classical orchestra took the classical music world by storm.

With help from tutors such as Joseph Schillinger, and prompted by some wise but possibly cruel words by fellow composer Glazunov, Gershwin erased his shortcomings just as easily as if they were slips on the manuscript. The *Concerto in F* (the proper title omits the word piano) was premiered by its commissioners, the New York Symphony Orchestra, conducted by Walter Damrosch, with the composer himself playing the piano. As Damrosch said in the concert's programme: 'George Gershwin seems to have accomplished ... [a] miracle ... He is the Prince who has taken Cinderella [jazz] by the hand and openly proclaimed her a princess to the astonished world, no doubt to the fury of her envious sisters.'

RECOMMENDED RECORDING
André Previn (piano); London Symphony Orchestra. EMI Classics: 5668912.
CHART POSITION 253

PHILIP GLASS
(B. 1937)

Violin Concerto No. 1

Nowadays, 'minimalism' is a term that's frequently bandied about when it comes to describing a particular kind of music. But in the 1970s, it was an entirely new concept, and Philip Glass was at the forefront of its definition.

The first use of the word 'minimalism' in music is ascribed to the British composer Michael Nyman. He transferred it from the visual arts and applied it to classical works that have simple, repeated melodic ideas, within a relatively small framework of pitch and harmony. The second movement of this concerto by Philip Glass sounds like a dictionary definition of the term: sparse, hypnotic and brooding, it's the one section of the piece that has guaranteed its continued appeal.

Nowadays, Glass is less keen to be tied down by the m-word, preferring instead for his music to simply be described as having 'repetitive structures'. Commenting on his *Violin Concerto*, composed in 1987 and his first major orchestral work, Glass said, 'The search for the unique can lead to strange places. Taboos – the things we're not supposed to do – are often more interesting'. The repetitive nature of the piece has its detractors, but there's no doubt that this is one of the most significant instrumental concertos to have been composed in the last thirty years.

RECOMMENDED RECORDING
Gidon Kremer (violin); Vienna Philharmonic Orchestra; Christoph von Dohnányi (conductor). Classic FM: CFM FW 056.
CHART POSITION 148

CHRISTOPH WILLIBALD
VON GLUCK (1714–1787)

Orpheus and Eurydice

A reform opera. It sounds like a place where bad composers are sentenced to hard labour. It was Gluck's attempt to make new things happen in what he considered to be the increasingly stuck-in-the-mud world of eighteenth-century French opera – or *azione teatrale* ('theatrical action'), as he would have known it. How was it stuck in the mud? Well, it was over-mannered and it was over-reliant on techniques that meant that works with the loosest of plots were being allowed to pass for operas. Gluck's idea, which was developed by composers such as Puccini years later, was to make opera much more real.

Gluck seems to have been adhering to the unwritten law of opera that appears to state that 'when new ground is to be broken, it must be to the story of Orpheus'. In his version of the story, out went the dull recitatives, replaced by fully accompanied ones; out went sheer virtuosity just for virtuosity's sake and in came singing that enhanced the plot or advanced the character. It was a revolution both in style and content, which moved the whole genre of opera into a new place. Other composers raced to embrace Gluck's trail-blazing ideas.

RECOMMENDED RECORDING

Juan Diego Flórez (tenor) as Orphée; Ainhoa Garmendia (soprano) as Eurydice; Chorus and Orchestra of the Teatro Real, Madrid; Jesús López Cobos (conductor). Label: Decca. Catalogue No.: 4782197.

CHART POSITION 177

HENRYK GÓRECKI
(1933–2010)

Symphony No. 3
Symphony of Sorrowful Songs

This work owes its mass appeal to the powerfully evocative second movement: the setting of an eighteen-year-old girl's prayer, inscribed on the wall of a Gestapo prison in 1944.

The Polish composer behind the hit, Henryk Górecki, holds a special place in the history of Classic FM. The *Symphony of Sorrowful Songs* was played in the very first week that the station began broadcasting in September 1992 and the audience response was so great that it quickly raced to the top of the classical music charts.

Górecki was almost totally unknown outside classical music circles, so in that respect the symphony was a slightly unusual selection. But it captured the British public's imagination, remaining the country's most popular classical CD for months. The original

recording of the work, featuring soprano Dawn Upshaw alongside the London Sinfonietta conducted by David Zinman, has since sold well over a million copies.

The composer's death in 2010 led to a resurgence of interest in his music.

RECOMMENDED RECORDING

Dawn Upshaw (soprano); London Sinfonietta; David Zinman (conductor). Nonesuch: 7559 792822.

CHART POSITION 101

CHARLES GOUNOD
(1818–1893)

Mors et Vita

The Victorians liked their music to be big – and, generally, the bigger the better. Their *X Factor* was the oratorio; their Wembley Stadium the local town hall. It was a throbbing, hungry beast of a society that fed on choral spectaculars and, in order to keep it sated, the work of British composers was not enough. Gounod was a long-term visitor to these shores – getting himself into a bit of a pickle with the English soprano and amateur social worker Georgina Weldon (the less said about that, the better; suffice it to say, not one of Gounod's happiest times). As a man who espoused fifteen minutes of Bible-reading every day, Gounod's thoughts were never far away from the next big brimstone-and-treacle epic that might have them cowering in the aisles. *Mors et Vita* ('Death and Life' – it doesn't get any more broad brush) was premiered in Birmingham in 1885, and featured a judge, who sits on a throne, intoning his judgments. That judge (Judex) owns possibly the most beautiful music in the whole piece. It has certainly become a firm favourite with Classic FM listeners and the *Judex* tends to eclipse the rest of the work.

RECOMMENDED RECORDING
Toulouse Capitole Orchestra; Michel Plasson (conductor). EMI Classics: CDS 7544592.
CHART POSITION 133

St Cecilia Mass

Gounod was quite the young, thrusting entrepreneur in 1854. He would have been thirty-six years old and appeared to have been keen to get himself noticed wherever it might be possible. Operas, theatre works, society music, church music, you name it: he was pitching for it. One can't help but think he might not have been totally out of place selling himself to Lord Sugar in *The Apprentice*. Despite things being a little hit and miss in his opera affairs, his concert and church work appeared to be paying dividends. A symphony had been well received and, when he penned his *Petite Messe Solonnelle de Sainte-Cécile*, it brought him to pretty much all of Paris's attention. A turning point, as they say. Having never been shy about putting himself forwards, he was now like the cat that had got the cream and it is said to have been his coming of age as a composer. Perhaps this innate appreciation of his own self-worth came about as a result of having won the famous Prix de Rome composing prize at the first attempt. After all, many great French composers had

failed after years of entering the competition.
RECOMMENDED RECORDING
Barbara Hendricks (soprano); Laurence Dale (tenor); Jean-Philippe Lafont (bass); Chorus of Radio France; New Philharmonia Orchestra; Georges Prêtre (conductor); EMI Classics: 7470942.
CHART POSITION 233

EDVARD GRIEG
(1843–1907)

Piano Concerto in A minor

How, you wonder, would Grieg feel about the fact that many of us associate this particular piece of music with Morecambe and Wise? Eric's version of the piece, conducted by André 'Andrew Preview' Previn, is one of the most memorable TV sketches of all time, frequently coming towards the top of those seemingly endless countdowns to find the nation's favourite funny moment.

The concerto itself was no laughing matter for Grieg, though. Instead, it was a pretty weighty, serious affair. At the age of twenty-five, the young Norwegian composer was determined to make his mark on the world with this, his first work to employ an orchestra. From the thunderous roll of the timpani in the opening bars, Grieg sounds totally assured and in command of his orchestral writing throughout this concerto – and yet, he was far from experienced in composing for such large forces.

The work was an instant success and many expected Grieg to replicate it soon after with a second concerto for the instrument.

Edvard Grieg
1843–1907

'I am sure my music has a taste of codfish in it.'
EDVARD GRIEG

Grieg is Norway's most famous musical son, although the Scots could lay claim to him being one of their own because his Scottish great-grandfather emigrated to Scandinavia after the Battle of Culloden.

From an early age, Grieg was a highly proficient pianist, studying first in Leipzig before moving on to Copenhagen. Grieg didn't particularly enjoy his time away, but he did gain the opportunity to hear performances from the likes of Clara Schumann and Richard Wagner. When he went back home, he concentrated his efforts on learning more about traditional folk music. Gradually, these melodies became an important part of his own compositions, with many of his works containing soaring tunes that evoke his Norwegian home.

His significance outside Norway was perhaps greater than many would credit, with his influence particularly apparent on the French composers of the early twentieth century. Ravel said that, other than Debussy, there was 'no composer to whom

DID YOU KNOW?
Grieg was adored by the people of Norway. On the day of his funeral, up to 40,000 people lined the streets to pay their respects.

I feel a closer affinity'. He was also admired greatly by the likes of Liszt, Delius and Grainger.

Throughout his life, Grieg performed as a concert pianist and he became famous for his virtuosic performances of his own *Piano Concerto* in cities across Europe.

Grieg was given an honorary degree by Cambridge University in 1894. Straight after the ceremony he rushed to the post office and sent a telegram to a friend, a physician in Bergen who shared his surname. He signed his telegram 'Doctor Grieg'.

After he died, Grieg's music quickly came to be regarded as old-fashioned, with its lyrical melodies and folk Romanticism. It didn't fit comfortable alongside Schoenberg and his new way of composing, which was very much in vogue in musical circles at the time. However, the years have been kind to Grieg and his position in classical music history is now far more secure, with his compositions today seen as the finely crafted output of a gifted tunesmith.

Intriguingly, though, he never chose to write another. The driving, anthemic outer movements, sandwiched either side of the most beautiful *Adagio*, combine to create a stunning work that's hard to beat – a fact the composer was arguably shrewd enough to realise.

RECOMMENDED RECORDING
Leif Ove Andsnes (piano); Berlin Philharmonic Orchestra; Mariss Jansons (conductor). EMI Classics: 0946 3943992.
CHART POSITION 12

Peer Gynt Suite No. 1

Many a TV advertisement (or, dare we say it, telephone on-hold service) has used the opening movement, *Morning* from Grieg's *Peer Gynt Suite No. 1* to create a musical mood. The fourth movement depicting life *In the Hall of the Mountain King*, meanwhile, will forever be remembered by thousands as the Alton Towers theme tune. Grieg, however, had very different ideas at the forefront of his mind when he composed this glorious music.

He had been asked by the playwright Henrik Ibsen to set to music his quintessentially Scandinavian play *Peer Gynt*. The composer responded by creating a collection of tableaux, some of which were later formed into two separate suites. He didn't have much faith in them, feeling under pressure from Ibsen to come up with the melodies as quickly as possible, but they were received with huge enthusiasm by the Norwegian audiences of his day.

Given that the two suites are the composer's own distillation of the best melodies from the play, it's not surprising that they quickly became more popular than the complete score for *Peer Gynt*. Indeed, that very score wasn't even published in Grieg's own lifetime, finally becoming available in 1908, the year after the composer's death.

RECOMMENDED RECORDING
Estonian National Symphony Orchestra; Paavo Järvi (conductor). Virgin Classics: 5457222.
CHART POSITION 54

Holberg Suite

Many composers have unashamedly looked to the past for musical inspiration: think of Prokofiev with his *Classical Symphony*, Stravinsky's Baroque-inspired *Pulcinella Suite* and this, Grieg's *From Holberg's Time – Suite in the Olden Style*, to give it its most accurate title. Now always referred to as the *Holberg Suite*, it eschews the Romantic conventions of its day, instead harking back to the Classical-era playwright Ludvig Holberg, who, like Grieg, was born in the city of Bergen.

Composed to mark the 200th anniversary of Holberg's birth, the work opens with a sprightly, energetic *Praeludium*, followed by a more introspective *Sarabande*, a rather polite *Gavotte*, a stately *Air* and, finally, a boisterous *Rigaudon*. It was originally composed for piano – an instrument in front of which Grieg was always at home – but was later turned into an orchestral suite by the composer. It's this arrangement that is by far the most often heard today.

First performed in its original piano version by Grieg himself at the Bergen Holberg Celebration in December 1884, the work was very well received, which probably explains Grieg's decision to transcribe it for orchestra so soon after. Although not so well known as his mighty *Piano Concerto* or the lyrical *Peer Gynt Suites*, this is supremely crafted music which drives home Grieg's status as one of Europe's most important Romantic composers.

RECOMMENDED RECORDING
Bergen Philharmonic Orchestra; Ole Kristen
Ruud (conductor). BIS: SACD 1491.
CHART POSITION 126

Lyric Pieces

When selections for the Classic FM Hall of Fame are made each year, we always subsume votes for particular sections of classical pieces into the larger work. So, opting for an individual aria means your vote counts towards the full opera, and if you were to choose a piano miniature that forms part of a larger set of pieces, your vote would be amalgamated into that set. In the case of Grieg's *Lyric Pieces*, while it's certainly true that we receive votes for a number of different compositions within the collection, the set's success is down to one particular tune: *Wedding Day at Troldhaugen*.

It's the sixth entry from Book 8 of Grieg's *Lyric Pieces*, and was written to commemorate the composer's own silver wedding anniversary. Grieg's summer villa, built just outside Bergen in 1885, was also called Troldhaugen, so this particular tune was evidently full of meaning for him.

Wedding Day at Troldhaugen remains the most popular excerpt from Grieg's *Lyric Pieces* by quite a long shot, but it would be remiss not to mention a few other descriptively titled pieces that all contribute to the music's enduring popularity. Among them, the menacing *March of the Trolls* and the beautiful *Nocturne*, both of which were included in Grieg's *Lyric Suite*, which was simply an orchestration of some his most popular *Lyric Pieces*.

RECOMMENDED RECORDING
Leif Ove Andsnes (piano).
EMI Classics: 0946 3943992.
CHART POSITION 268

GEORGE FRIDERIC HANDEL
(1685–1759)

Messiah

The love affair that British classical music audiences have with this oratorio is quite phenomenal. Since its Dublin premiere in 1742, it has been performed by choirs across the land every year since at least 1745. Handel continued to work on it after its initial performance, finally arriving at the version we know today in 1754.

The forgotten man behind the success of *Messiah* is the librettist, Charles Jennens, who adapted the words of the King James Bible, which Handel set to music. Not for him a Lennon and McCartney or Gilbert and Sullivan style writing credit.

During Victorian times, there was a phase when *Messiah* was performed by ever expanding musical forces – there almost seemed to be a competition to see just how big a chorus and orchestra could be crammed onto one stage before they fell through. Earlier, Mozart even got in on the act, with his own arrangement of *Messiah*, which was not, it has to be said, to everyone's taste. One critic remarked that it 'resembles elegant stucco work upon an old marble temple ... easily ... chipped off again by the weather'.

The rousing *Hallelujah Chorus* is by far the most widely known section of the work. Audiences used to tend to stand during performances – a tradition that began when King George II stood up during the chorus at the oratorio's debut London performance.

RECOMMENDED RECORDING

Kerstin Avemo (soprano); Patricia Bardon (mezzo-soprano); Lawrence Zazzo (counter-tenor); Kobie van Rensburg (tenor); Neal Davies (bass-baritone); Choir of Clare College; Freiburg Baroque Orchestra; René Jacobs (conductor). Harmonia Mundi: HMC901928/29.

CHART POSITION 18

Solomon

The year 1749 was a monster one for Handel. He had so many projects on the go, friends must surely have feared for his health. (After all, he was not a slip of a thing). As well as the *Music for the Royal Fireworks*, numerous anthems were written, including *How*

right George Frideric Handel: Messiah

George Frideric Handel
1685-1759

'Handel understands effect better than any of us; when he chooses, he strikes like a thunderbolt.'

WOLFGANG AMADEUS MOZART

Handel showed great talent as a youngster, but he had to suffer for his art. He was forced to sneak a small keyboard up to the loft of his house to practise on, because his father wouldn't let him go near a musical instrument.

Although he was German by birth, he came to be considered as one of Britain's great composers, after becoming a British citizen. This came to pass when the Elector of Hanover was promoted to the job of being King George I. Handel's music includes opera and instrumental works, but he's probably best known for his great big choral masterpieces, which are still regularly performed up and down the country today.

Handel was a specialist in the oratorio, a religious story set to music and performed by solo singers, a choir and an orchestra. Usually though, the story is told without scenery and costumes, so the event is more of a concert.

DID YOU KNOW?

Handel's father wasn't keen on his son becoming a musician. The only way the young composer could practice was by playing on a clavichord hidden in the attic of his home!

When he was in Italy, Handel was challenged to a duel – with a difference. The composer Domenico Scarlatti dared him to agree to a 'keyboard duel' – Handel on organ Scarlatti on harpsichord.

The result was a fudge: Handel was declared the better organist, Scarlatti the better harpsichordist.

Handel was reputedly a big chap with an enormous appetite. Indeed, you often see pictures of him with his jacket bursting at the seams. In one restaurant, he booked a table for four and ordered four meals. When the waiter arrived with four feasts and enquired after his other guests, Handel barked at him to put the food down and rapidly gobbled the lot.

Handel was an exact contemporary of Johann Sebastian Bach, both being born in the same year – 1685. In a further coincidence, both suffered from cataracts and were treated unsuccessfully by the same British optician.

Beautiful are the Feet. There must be nothing so demoralising for a composer as writing music that is not performed and Handel was no different. He wanted some of the music he had already written in the previous year to see the light of day. One work that fell into this category was his oratorio *Solomon*. He had spent precious time on it in 1748 and felt it should be out there in front of the listening public.

Solomon consists of three acts, plus an overture – sixty-two sections in all, with liberal mention for one of the lead characters, Zadok the Priest. But don't get confused. The anthem *Zadok the Priest* doesn't feature. That had already been written, twenty-two years earlier, for a coronation.

The premiere of *Solomon* was at what was then called the Theatre Royal, which is, give or take the odd destruction, what we would today call the Royal Opera House.

RECOMMENDED RECORDING

Inger Dam-Jensen (soprano); Alison Hagley (soprano); Susan Bickley (soprano); Susan Gritton (soprano); Andreas Scholl (contralto); Paul Agnew (tenor); Peter Harvey (bass); Gabrieli Consort and Players; Paul McCreesh (conductor). Deutsche Grammophon Archiv: 4596882.

CHART POSITION 53

Zadok the Priest

June 1727 was a notable date in history because of the death of King George I. However, there was something else that had set London society talking. Two sopranos, who were the leading lights of the opera world at the time, had brought their chronic rivalry to a rather public head when they came to blows on stage, in front of a very offended Princess of Wales. The sight of two cat-calling singers, writhing around on stage,

scratching and slapping, was too much for the Princess and she had the entire opera season terminated.

This gave Handel a little bit of extra time to compose, allowing him to concentrate on the music for the new king. *Zadok the Priest* is just one of four coronation anthems he wrote, but it's by far the most popular. Its adrenalin rush of an introduction, with its teasing promise of release only to start again, is one of the most spine-tingling moments in music. The moment the choir enters, Handel knows he's got you: you're on the floor and he can kick you with some of the best choral writing of all time.

RECOMMENDED RECORDING

Choir of King's College, Cambridge; Academy of Ancient Music; Stephen Cleobury (conductor). EMI Classics: 2289440.

CHART POSITION 59

Water Music Suites

It is to be hoped that you have never been caught out and turned up at a performance of *Water Music*, only to find it's the piece of the same name (but very different sounding) of the twentieth-century American composer John Cage. This work does not consist of three pleasant suites, split into minuets, bourrées, airs and hornpipes, light and florid in nature, and with beguiling catchy tune after beguiling catchy tune. John Cage's *Water Music* is written for a pianist who is instructed to pour water into pots, play cards and blow whistles under water, while an assistant displays the score on a poster. Quite a different experience altogether from Handel's piece, which is now a household favourite, easy on the ear and jauntily life-affirming. Exactly the sort of music you would like to waft you down the River Thames if you were a king with the weight of government on your shoulders. There are three suites in all: the first in F, the second in D and the third in G. It's *Suite No. 1* that is the most popular. In eleven sections, it begins with a beautiful 'French-style' *Ouverture* and ends up with the *Alla Hornpipe*.

RECOMMENDED RECORDING

Zefiro; Alfredo Bernadini (conductor). Ambroisie: AM192.

CHART POSITION 100

Xerxes

A short sortie into the plot of *Xerxes* brings home how little entertainment has changed over the centuries. Today, we can't get enough of our costume dramas replete with steamy characters, set against backdrops of ancient intrigues. It's true that these are historical in nature, but, essentially they are just soap opera plots that have been re-set in the past.

Well, *Xerxes* follows pretty much the same formula. It focuses on a particular supposedly accurate point in the life of the Persian King Xerxes I (who lived from 485 BC to 465 BC). Indeed, it contains one or two other moments that are said to be true. But, beyond them, Handel allows his librettist to suspend time, and to engage in

a largely invented gossipy plot. The music, though, is simply divine, especially if one is hearing a version using the original idea of Xerxes as a counter-tenor, rather than the female voice so often used today. In one of the stranger beginnings to an opera, Xerxes sings the famous opening aria *'Ombra mai fù'* to a shade-giving tree. It's a beautiful tune, which is known as the *Largo* in its orchestral arrangement, even though it is, in fact, marked on the score as *larghetto*.

RECOMMENDED RECORDING

Ann Murray (mezzo-soprano) as Xerxes; Lesley Garrett (soprano) as Atalanta; Valerie Masterson (soprano) as Romilda; Christopher Robson (counter-tenor) as Arsamenes; Jean Rigby (mezzo-soprano) as Amastris; Christopher Booth-Jones (baritone) as Elviro; Rodney Macann (bass-baritone) as Ariodates; Orchestra and Chorus of English National Opera; Charles Mackerras (conductor). Arthaus Musik (DVD); 100076.

CHART POSITION 150

Music for the Royal Fireworks

Famous wars are usually followed by less famous 'peaces'. Occasionally, though, a particularly important treaty will give rise to a famous peace and it was one such for which Handel wrote his *Music for the Royal Fireworks*. The Treaty of Aix-la-Chapelle was signed to mark the ending of the War of the Austrian Succession and Handel was commanded to provide the music for the state celebrations that were duly organised. The music was a roaring success, but the fireworks were something of a disaster, after they managed to set fire to the wooden staging built to house them, wreaking havoc. The popularity of the new work was plain for all to see when the stampede to get tickets to watch its dress rehearsal almost brought central London to a standstill. Against the king's express orders, the music was written to incorporate strings as well as woodwind for its premiere. Shortly afterwards, Handel rewrote the score for a full orchestra. The *Music for the Royal Fireworks* is often paired with Handel's *Water Music* on CD recordings.

RECOMMENDED RECORDING
English Concert; Trevor Pinnock (conductor). Deutsche Grammophon Archiv: E4472792.
CHART POSITION 159

Sarabande

A sarabande is a dance that originated in Central America back in the sixteenth century. It became popular in the Spanish colonies before making its way to Europe. At first, it was regarded as being rather scandalous, even being banned in Spain for its obscenity. Baroque composers, such as Handel, adopted the sarabande as one of the movements for the suites they were writing at the time.

In *Coriolanus*, Shakespeare describes 'giddy fortune's furious fickle wheel'. He might well have been talking about that infinitesimal difference between the chance discovery of one musical manuscript over another. Quite why this particular tiny fraction of Handel's output – a movement from a harpsichord suite – should have attracted almost undue attention is a good example of the 'fickle wheel'.

It was left in obscurity since its composition in the early 1700s, until the director Stanley Kubrick took a shine to it for his 1970s film, *Barry Lyndon*. At that point, it

was as if someone had lit a blue touch paper and retired as film and television directors the world over proclaimed themselves fans. Its most celebrated outing was in a wall-crunching advert for Levi Jeans.

RECOMMENDED RECORDING
(arranged by Olivier Fourés) Daniel Hope (violin). Deutsche Grammophon: 4778094.
CHART POSITION 201

PATRICK HAWES
(B. 1958)

Quanta Qualia

Former Classic FM Composer in Residence Patrick Hawes is a quintessentially English composer who prides himself on writing in the same idiom as the likes of Elgar, Vaughan Williams and Delius. The pastoral, reflective sound-world Hawes inhabits is no better demonstrated than in this, his beautiful *Quanta Qualia* for soprano, chorus and orchestra.

Quanta Qualia is taken from the 2004 album *Blue in Blue* – an instant hit in the classical charts. Within just a few weeks of its release, the piece had been voted the fastest ever new entry into the Classic FM Hall of Fame, proving that Hawes's music clearly resonated in a powerful way. Much of it is inspired by the composer's rural surroundings: he lives on the Norfolk coast and has often remarked that the beauty of nature spurs him on to write music.

Quanta Qualia is a sonorous, reflective and deeply moving work, with layers of laid-back strings and choral accompaniment supporting a soaring and incredibly high-pitched soprano line, sung impressively by Janet Coxwell on the original recording. Following on from the work's success, Hawes went on to compose the piano album *Towards the Light* for Classic FM and was commissioned by HRH The Prince of Wales to write the *Highgrove Suite*, inspired by the Prince's own gardens.

RECOMMENDED RECORDING
Janet Coxwell (soprano); Conventus (choir); English Chamber Orchestra; Patrick Hawes (conductor). Black Box: BBM 1081.
CHART POSITION 220

JOSEPH HAYDN
(1732–1809)

The Creation

Haydn's massive late oratorio *The Creation* is considered by more than a few to be his great masterpiece, despite the limitations of a rather dubious series of words; the retranslated texts are often either bizarre or forced or both.

Haydn was inspired to create *The Creation* following his trips to the UK, where he heard the oratorios of Handel still being performed with massive forces. He is quoted as saying that, once in the flow, he begged God to let him be able to finish the work – clearly knowing he was onto a corker.

At one particular performance, just a year before he died, Haydn had to be carried into the hall on a chair to hear his music. As the audience billed and cooed at various sublime sections, Haydn was forced to take the spontaneous applause. He is said to have pointed to the sky, smiled and said, 'It's not from me: everything comes from up there!'

RECOMMENDED RECORDING
Heather Harper (soprano); Pamela Bowden (mezzo-soprano); Alexander Young (tenor);

John Shirley-Quirk (bass); Choir of King's College, Cambridge; Academy of St Martin in the Fields; David Willcocks (conductor). EMI Classics: 3759292.
CHART POSITION 162

Trumpet Concerto in E flat

Despite having his own highly virtuosic orchestra, Haydn wrote his *Trumpet Concerto* for an old friend called Anton Weidinger, who was a member of the Imperial Court Orchestra in Vienna. Weidinger was also something of an inventor and Haydn composed the concerto for a brand new trumpet, which could play more notes than ever before. The particular incarnation of the instrument has since died out, in favour of the valve version that we hear today.

Haydn had an ulterior motive for writing the new work for Weidinger. He had managed to poach him from the orchestra in Vienna, persuading him to join the band of musicians, which Haydn headed, in the employ of the Austro-Hungarian Esterházy family. Weidinger premiered the work on his arrival, changing bits of the music as he did so (either with or without Haydn's consent, it's unclear).

RECOMMENDED RECORDING
Tine Thing Helseth (trumpet); Norwegian Chamber Orchestra. Simax: PSC1292.
CHART POSITION 174

Cello Concerto No. 1 in C

In the first few years after he arrived at the Esterházy Palace, when he was still in his twenties, Haydn decided he needed to raise the standards of playing in the orchestra. He employed a mixture of carrot and stick to ensure that the best players remained onside. While increasing the number of players in the band – and hence competition to play the best bits of the music – he wrote appetising concertos to ensure that the most essential members didn't consider walking away. So, in addition to brand new symphonies in which all the musicians played an important part (the *Philosopher*, the *Horn Signal* and the *Alleluia* all date from this period), there were choice concertos for the chosen ones.

One such player was the cellist Joseph Weigl. *The Cello Concerto No. 1* was his present from Haydn – and one that was subsequently lost for two hundred years. It was not until 1961 that it was rediscovered, having been salvaged from Radenin Castle in Prague. So, although it was written in the 1760s, it has become a firm favourite with audiences only in the last fifty years. Mstislav Rostropovich gave the newly discovered work its re-premiere in 1962, once it had been authenticated.

RECOMMENDED RECORDING
Mstislav Rostropovich (cello); Academy of St Martin in the Fields; Iona Brown (conductor). EMI Classics: 5672342.
CHART POSITION 300

Ladies in Lavender

The British composer Nigel Hess has written hundreds of scores for stage and screen, but it was with his music for Charles Dance's 2004 film *Ladies in Lavender* that he truly struck gold with Classic FM listeners. The film, starring Judi Dench and Maggie Smith, is set in picturesque 1930s Cornwall. The sweeping, lyrical score perfectly matches the stunning scenery and ocean vistas.

For the main theme, Hess employs a full symphony orchestra alongside a solo violin, performed on the original soundtrack by the star American fiddle player Joshua Bell. Letting the violin take the lead on a film score is nothing new – think of John Williams's haunting music for *Schindler's List* or Shostakovich's *Romance* from *The Gadfly* – but it works remarkably well here. The piece unashamedly harks back to the Romantic era, with its indulgent, wistful sound and tug-on-your-heart-strings tunes. The score also includes a stand-alone *Fantasy for Violin and Orchestra*, in which Hess turns the major melody on its head, reworking it in a minor key.

In addition to his composing talents, Hess is an accomplished pianist, as evidenced on his disc *Silent Nights*, which features him performing his own arrangements of Christmas carols alongside members of the Royal Philharmonic Orchestra.

RECOMMENDED RECORDING
Joshua Bell (violin); Royal Philharmonic Orchestra; Nigel Hess (conductor).
Sony: SK 92689.
CHART POSITION 256

GUSTAV HOLST
(1874–1934)

The Planets

It's probably an oft-made point, but it's worth making again: Holst's *The Planets* is not about the planets. That is, it's not about astronomy. Rather, it's about astrology. So we are not hearing a suite of tributes to, say, Saturn, the planet with rings around it. Instead, Holst was writing about Mars, the bringer of war; Venus, the bringer of peace; Mercury, the winged messenger; Jupiter, the bringer of jollity; Saturn the bringer of old age; Uranus, the magician; and Neptune, the mystic.

Holst had managed to finish his much pondered suite – it had been in his mind for some time – by 1916, by which time the First World War made all thoughts of a performance impractical. However, in the war's closing days, and in between his own personal war efforts, he was granted the use of the great Queen's Hall in London, as a gift from a friend. He immediately commandeered the twenty-nine-year-old Adrian Boult to conduct his new suite.

The instant success of *The Planets* encouraged a public in need of solace to explore some of the earlier works of Holst that they might otherwise have missed.

RECOMMENDED RECORDING
London Philharmonic Orchestra;
Adrian Boult (conductor).
EMI Classics: 6278982.
CHART POSITION 16

left Gustav Holst: The Planets

JAMES HORNER
(B. 1953)

Titanic

Mention the movie *Titanic* and all sorts of memories are evoked. For some, it's the sight of Kate Winslet romancing Leonardo di Caprio. For others, it's the sheer scale and cost of the movie. And, for many of us, our thoughts turn instantly to the masterful film score, composed by James Horner.

Titanic was a record breaker, in a truly titanic sense. Box office targets were smashed when, in 1998, millions of us went to see this much hyped movie. It garnered more Oscars than any other modern film, it ran on (and on ... and on ...) for over three hours, and it placed huge demands on Horner – not least because of the amount of music that such a long film was bound to require.

The composer apparently turned his back quite deliberately on the traditional idea of what a film score for a Hollywood blockbuster should sound like. Gone were the full-on fanfares and *fortissimo* scores of the likes of John Williams; instead, he focused on the Irish background of di Caprio's character, Jack Dawson, and chose music highly reminiscent of the likes of Enya and Clannad.

Titanic earned James Horner his fortune. And it also made Celine Dion, who sang the pop theme tune, a fair bit of money too.
RECOMMENDED RECORDING
original soundtrack; James Horner
(conductor). Sony: COLS 2K60797.
CHART POSITION 280

JOHANN NEPOMUK HUMMEL
(1778–1837)

Trumpet Concerto

Hummel was a prodigious talent, who toured around Europe while still in short trousers. He wowed audiences as a pianist wherever he went, but it is as the composer of a work for the trumpet that he is best known today.

He was a pupil of Haydn and ended up taking over his job. Hummel wrote his *Trumpet Concerto* for Anton Weidinger, the same player for whom Haydn had written his. Clearly Mr Weidinger was the man of the moment, with more than one of the significant composers of the time falling over themselves to write music especially for him to perform. Not only was Wiedinger a bit of an animal with his technique, but his rather shiny new trumpet could reach the parts other trumpets couldn't reach. Hummel and Weidinger premiered the work on the very day that Hummel arrived in Haydn's old job, so it might well have been a case of 'Anything you can do, I can do better'.

Although it is this work for which he is chiefly remembered, Hummel wrote all types of music, except for symphonies, out of respect for the work of Beethoven, whom he believed he couldn't better.

RECOMMENDED RECORDING

Alison Balsom (trumpet); Deutsche Kammerphilharmonie. EMI Classics: 2162130.

CHART POSITION 285

J

KARL JENKINS
(B. 1944)

The Armed Man
Mass for Peace

The Welsh composer Karl Jenkins – almost as famous for his remarkable moustache as for his music – is, quite simply, a phenomenon in contemporary music. And this, his *Mass for Peace*, is the primary explanation of his enduring popularity. It was, we're rather proud to say, given its premiere at a Classic FM Live concert in the autumn of 2000 at London's Royal Albert Hall. A year later, the work entered the Classic FM Hall of Fame – and, over the next few years, it climbed rapidly into the Top Ten, where it's remained as the nation's favourite piece of contemporary music.

Many sections of the work are worthy of close examination – not least the *Agnus Dei* and the *Sanctus* – but it's the haunting *Benedictus* that captivates listeners to the greatest extent, leaving them begging for more. Jenkins's writing for soulful cello is sublime (if you ever needed proof that the instrument is the closest in sound to the human voice, you'll find it here) and the heavenly choral accompaniment truly transports you to another place.

Never one to define himself by one set of beliefs, Jenkins uses all sorts of inspirations for the text of *The Armed Man*, including the Muslim call to prayer, the sixteenth-century *L'Homme armé* Mass tradition, and ancient religious texts.

RECOMMENDED RECORDING

Guy Johnston (cello); National Youth Choir of Great Britain; London Philharmonic Orchestra; Karl Jenkins (conductor). EMI Classics: 50999 21729621.

CHART POSITION 119

Adiemus
Songs of Sanctuary

Adiemus is, quite simply, the twentieth-century definition of 'classical crossover'. His music knows no bounds – and that is very much its virtue. In 1995, *Adiemus* ensured that this Welsh composer of advertising music would burst forth into the mainstream. As with so many pieces of classical music, *Adiemus*'s

success in the late twentieth century was initially down to its use on a television advert – in this case, a Delta Airlines commercial. But whereas with composers of the past, such use is always posthumous, in Jenkins's case the music was actually commissioned by the airline and then developed further by Jenkins into a full-blown classical work.

To say it is scored for sopranos and orchestra is to already define *Adiemus* in conventional ways that the composer would arguably resist. The female soloist (on the original recording, Miriam Stockley) performs in a fusion of styles, with Western melodic structures, world music influences and free time-signatures abounding. The second female singer (in this case, Mary Carewe) harmonises in a parallel manner, creating an equally New Age feel and non-Western classical music sound-world.

Now an established part of the music we regularly play on Classic FM, it's easy to forget how groundbreaking *Adiemus* was when it was first aired on the radio.

RECOMMENDED RECORDING
Miriam Stockley (soprano); Mary Carewe (soprano); London Philharmonic Orchestra; Karl Jenkins (conductor). Virgin: CDV 2890.
CHART POSITION 143

Requiem

Any composer attempting to write a Requiem must immediately feel very conscious of how many of history's greats have composed in this idiom. From Mozart to Verdi and Fauré to Berlioz, an illustrious list of composers have all triumphed with their moving, exquisite and often gargantuan requiems.

Step forward Welsh music master Karl Jenkins – who, in 2005, decided it was time to add his name to this collection. Jenkins's *Requiem* absolutely fits into his unique and distinctive style. As with all of his major

works, it's an unashamed melting pot of musical styles. In keeping with tradition, Jenkins chose to set the traditional Latin text of the Requiem Mass. He makes a nod in the direction of the conventional, while still including a few surprises along the way. In the case of his *Requiem*, it's the use of Japanese haiku poems, which, just like the Latin text, focus on the subject of death. The line-up of musicians also includes a shakuhachi (a Japanese flute).

RECOMMENDED RECORDING
Nicole Tibbels (soprano); Sam Landman (treble); Catrin Finch (harp); Serendipity (choir); Côr Caerdydd (choir); Cytgan (choir); West Kazakhstan Philharmonic Orchestra; Karl Jenkins (conductor). EMI Classics: 7243 5579662.
CHART POSITION 252

Palladio

Many of Karl Jenkins's compositions are fairly straightforward in title: *Requiem* is certainly a conservative name for a piece, and *A Mass for Peace* is a descriptive subtitle for his famous work *The Armed Man*. But *Palladio*? What does that one-word title allude to in describing this three-movement work for string orchestra?

Jenkins's inspiration was Andrea Palladio, a sixteenth-century Italian architect commissioned by the wealthy families of his day to build beautiful villas, as well as a substantial number of churches. The existence of aesthetic beauty within a very defined architectural

Karl Jenkins

b.1944

'From this quiet, gentle human being, comes the most amazing, haunting music, that is instantly recognizable, and loved across the world.'

DAME KIRI TE KANAWA

Karl Jenkins is among Britain's most performed living classical composers. Born in Swansea and educated at Cardiff University and the Royal Academy of Music in London, he made his mark initially on the jazz world, performing at Ronnie Scott's in London, and playing oboe in the ground-breaking jazz group Nucleus at venues such as the Montreux Jazz Festival and the Newport Jazz Festival in Rhode Island. Jenkins then joined Soft Machine, one of the leading proponents of the 'Canterbury Sound' of the 1970s.

There then followed an incredibly successful period composing music for television advertisements. Among the brands advertised alongside his music: Levi's, British Airways, Renault, Volvo, Cheltenham & Gloucester Building Society, Tag Heuer, Pepsi, De Beers and Delta Airlines.

DID YOU KNOW?

In November 2010, the Queen awarded Karl Jenkins the CBE for services to music, in a ceremony at Windsor Castle.

Jenkins then turned his hand to more mainstream classical music composition, with *Adiemus* topping classical charts around the world. His output since has included classical commissions by HRH The Prince of Wales, the London Symphony Orchestra and the Wales Millennium Centre, as well as the soundtrack to the film *River Queen*.

In 2004, Jenkins achieved the highest ever chart position for a living composer in the Classic FM Hall of Fame – an achievement that he has repeated every year since. He has also been among the most consistently popular British composers of all time in the annual top 300 chart.

Possibly less well known is the fact that one of Jenkins's middle names is the wonderfully individual 'Pamp', which has its origins in the German 'pfampf' (or the Swedish 'pamper') meaning thick set. It may even hark back to Pamphilus, the Greek king of the Dorians, after whom the Dorian mode is named.

framework surely inspired Jenkins: indeed, in the opening movement of *Palladio*, the rigid, repetitive string lines exist as the building blocks for an ever developing sense of drama, driven home by the *staccato* cellos.

Palladio harks back to Italian Baroque composers such as Albinoni, who, like Jenkins, could happily let a multiple-movement work last no more than a quarter of an hour. It's an interesting work in comparison with the rest of Jenkins's most popular pieces in that it's inherently conventional, conservative and unchallenging. Whereas his other big hits mould different musical styles, *Palladio* stays well within an eighteenth-century comfort zone throughout.

RECOMMENDED RECORDING

Smith Quartet; London Philharmonic Strings; Karl Jenkins (conductor). Sony: SK 62276.

CHART POSITION 269

left Karl Jenkins: Palladio

ARAM KHACHATURIAN
(1903–1978)

Spartacus

Khachaturian was just hitting his fiftieth birthday when he produced his music to the ballet *Spartacus*. The plot of the ballet had been around for some fifteen years and was suggested to him by a critic called Volkov. The composer finally got to work 'with a feeling of enormous creative excitement', but his preparation had been nothing if not extensive. He'd had a blast of a trip around Italy, visiting the very places at the centre of the famous story of a slave rebellion.

Despite taking a fair few liberties with the plot, the ballet score won Khachaturian the Lenin Prize in 1954, and was premiered in what is now the Mariinsky Theatre, in St Petersburg, just two years later.

By far the most captivating moment comes in Act II when Spartacus manages to free his wife Phrygia and the lovers celebrate with the heart-rending *Adagio of Spartacus and Phrygia*. It's a popular moment, made only all the more popular by this particular tune's starring role in the 1970s and 1980s television drama *The Onedin Line*, where its

waves of pleasure suited perfectly the waves of the ocean.

RECOMMENDED RECORDING

Armenian Philharmonic Orchestra; Loris Tjeknavorian (conductor). ASV: CDDCA772.

CHART POSITION 79

Masquerade Suite

Khachaturian was enjoying a good period in 1941, musically speaking at least. He had not long written his music for the ballet *Happiness* and his *Violin Concerto*. So when he was asked to provide incidental music for the revival of a play by Lermontov – and feeling he was on a roll – he quickly agreed. Soon, however, he was beginning to regret his decision as the theme for a central waltz in the production eluded him.

There is a section of the plot where Lermontov has the play's principal character, Nina, say, 'How beautiful the new waltz is!' She goes on to describe a work somewhere between sorrow and joy. Perhaps it was the pressure of so naked a line, the plaudit weighing heavily on his shoulders that caused him the sleepless

TOP 10 CHORAL WORKS

1	Ludwig van Beethoven	*Symphony No. 9 (Choral)*
2	George Frideric Handel	*Messiah*
3	Wolfgang Amadeus Mozart	*Requiem*
4	Gregorio Allegri	*Miserere*
5	Gabriel Fauré	*Requiem*
6	Gabriel Fauré	*Cantique de Jean Racine*
7	Carl Orff	*Carmina Burana*
8	George Frideric Handel	*Solomon*
9	Giuseppe Verdi	*Requiem*
10	George Frideric Handel	*Zadok the Priest*

nights. Soon, with a little help from a friendly teacher, he had his theme – and its exuberant place at the heart of this suite is probably the biggest single reason for its success. Loris Tjeknavorian, conducting the Armenian Philharmonic Orchestra, gives not only a nationalistically authentic performance, but a simply stunning one, too.

RECOMMENDED RECORDING

Armenian Philharmonic Orchestra; Loris Tjeknavorian (conductor). ASV: CDDCA772.

CHART POSITION 259

MORTEN LAURIDSEN
(B. 1943)

O Magnum Mysterium

During the first decade of the twenty-first century, one of the most exciting trends to emerge in classical music was the rediscovery of the relevance of choral music. From Eric Whitacre to Howard Goodall, Rihards Dubra to Gabriel Jackson, a wealth of contemporary composers have broken new ground in creating ethereal harmonies that are regularly described as 'heavenly'. And nowhere is this more obvious than in the glorious music of the American composer Morten Lauridsen.

Although composed in 1994, *O Magnum Mysterium* took a good few years before garnering such widespread praise. And while it is performed all year round, the piece is, at its heart, all about Christmas. The text tells the story of the birth of Jesus, and Lauridsen's music is as sensitive and spiritual as you could possibly wish for. Dense layers of sustained choral lines placed one on top of the other blend to create indulgent yet deceptively simple harmonies – a hallmark of the composer's consistently moving output.

Lauridsen has, for a number of years, been one of the most performed composers in America – but the emergence of *O Magnum Mysterium* spread his music much further afield. As the composer himself has said, 'I wanted this piece to resonate immediately and deeply into the core of the listener, to illumine through sound.' He certainly achieved just that.

RECOMMENDED RECORDING
Polyphony (choir); Stephen Layton (conductor). Classic FM: CFM CD 44.
CHART POSITION 294

FRANZ LEHÁR
(1870–1948)

The Merry Widow

Lehár was thirty-five years old when, quite by chance, he was given the opportunity to set to music a libretto by Viktor Leon and Leo Stein. The pair had already had successes with operettas by Johann Strauss II. Originally, their new work was intended for Richard Heuberger, but Lehár took his chance in auditioning for the job by playing a song over the telephone. Once he was given the opportunity, he set about producing his finest operetta – and the one that afforded him the biggest success of his career.

The Merry Widow was to become the most performed operetta of its generation, transferring to virtually every territory that had an opera house. When it came to England, in 1907, two years after the premiere, the stage identities of the central characters had to be changed when British high society decided it didn't want to risk upsetting the royal family of Montenegro, who shared a name with the major protagonists.

The operetta is replete with great, inventive tunes and it is easy to see why, more than a hundred years later, it is still a firm fixture in many opera houses around the world. In 1975, Robert Helpmann (who played the child catcher in the 1968 film *Chitty Chitty Bang Bang*) set parts of the music for a ballet, with the agreement of the Lehár estate.

RECOMMENDED RECORDING
Cheryl Studer (soprano) as Hanna; Bryn Terfel (bass-baritone) as Zeta; Barbara Bonney (soprano) as Valencienne; Boje Skovhus (baritone) as Danilo, Rainer Trost (tenor) as Camille; Heinz Zednik (tenor) as Njegus; Monteverdi Choir; Vienna Philharmonic Orchestra; John Eliot Gardiner (conductor). Label: Deutsche Grammophon. Catalogue No.: 4399112.
CHART POSITION 283

FRANZ LISZT
(1811–1886)

Hungarian Rhapsody No. 2 in C sharp minor

If Liszt were around today, he would surely have made it to the final of *Britain's Got Talent* (or *Hungary's Got Talent* if we're being pedantic). Aside from being an acclaimed composer,

Liszt was a phenomenally accomplished pianist. His ability to play the sheer number of notes that he did, at such speed and with such precision, amazed all who heard him. So it's not surprising that in his solo piano repertoire, Liszt stretches the capabilities of both the instrument and the soloist to their limits.

Nowhere is there a better example of this than in his famous *Hungarian Rhapsody No. 2*. It was *Tom and Jerry* who demonstrated the musical acrobatics of the piece to many of us for the first time. Do you remember the episode where Jerry's hiding inside the piano, only to be bounced into the air every time Tom hits one of the keys?

This particular rhapsody actually comes from a set of twenty such pieces, all composed for solo piano, although some were later orchestrated. As well as being a vehicle for demonstrating the performer's virtuosity, they also convey some of the greatest elements of Hungarian folk music, which Liszt painstakingly researched before lovingly composing this set.

RECOMMENDED RECORDING
Leslie Howard (piano). Hyperion: CDA 674189.
CHART POSITION 243

HENRY LITOLFF
(1818–1891)

Concerto Symphonique No. 4 in D minor

Contemporaneous pictures of Henry Litolff make him look more like a minor character from a Harry Potter novel than a world-famous piano virtuoso and composer. His talent was first spotted by the Bohemian composer and pianist Ignaz Moscheles, who was highly regarded during his lifetime, but whose fame has sadly not stood the test of time. Litolff left audiences spellbound with his magical performances on the piano from the age of fourteen – admittedly, quite late by the prodigy standards of some classical composers in this book.

In order that he might continue to enchant concert-goers across Europe, Litolff wrote himself a series of symphonies with a solo piano part. They were not quite concertos – and they weren't quite symphonies either. Instead, they were pieces that were specifically designed to make him sound great when he played them. The first of these *concertos symphoniques* is sadly now lost and the remaining ones number from 2 to 5 (so don't be caught out if anyone asks if you like his first). The fourth is just a joy of a work and is said to have inspired Liszt. So much so, in fact, that he dedicated his own piano concerto to the half-Scots, half-Alsatian master of the piano keyboard.

RECOMMENDED RECORDING

Peter Donohoe (piano); Bournemouth Symphony Orchestra; Andrew Litton (conductor). Hyperion: CDA66889.

CHART POSITION 165

JON LORD
(B. 1941)

Durham Concerto

The transfer from pop or rock musician to classical music supremo is a path many have attempted to tread, with only limited success. In the case of the former Deep Purple keyboard player Jon Lord, though, the traversal from one genre to another has been triumphant.

Lord's *Durham Concerto* was his first solely classical piece, commissioned by Durham University to celebrate its 175th anniversary. The work was five years in the making, finally premiered in the city's cathedral on 20 October 2007 and featuring the Royal Liverpool Philharmonic Orchestra, Northumbrian pipes player Kathryn Tickell, cellist Matthew Barley, violinist Ruth Palmer, and Lord himself at his beloved Hammond organ.

It's a deeply evocative work: not for Lord such dry descriptions as 'first movement' or 'finale' – instead, we have *Durham Awakes*, *The Cathedral at Dawn* and *The Road to Lindisfarne*. There are hues of folk music running throughout and brilliant uses of orchestral colour as Lord employs the woodwind to particularly quirky effect.

The *Durham Concerto* has been described as being reminiscent of the music of Vaughan Williams and Thomas Tallis, among others. For a proudly British composer, whose route to classical music was certainly less conventional than your average musician's, that's something about which Jon Lord can be very happy.

RECOMMENDED RECORDING

Kathryn Tickell (Northumbrian pipes); Ruth Palmer (violin); Matthew Barley (cello); Jon Lord (Hammond organ); Royal Liverpool Philharmonic Orchestra; Mischa Damev (conductor). Avie: 2145.

CHART POSITION 292

PAUL MCCARTNEY
(B. 1942)

Standing Stone

It says much about the incredible range of Paul McCartney's music that, hot on the heels of his *Flaming Pie* album (featuring guests Steve Miller and Ringo Starr) and just prior to *Run Devil Run* (with guests including Pink Floyd's Dave Gilmour) he produced his second major modern classical work. *Standing Stone* is a large-scale symphonic work (with choir) based on an extended poem, which McCartney wrote himself. In the CD liner notes, McCartney said that he was attempting to 'describe the way Celtic man might have wondered about the origins of life and the mystery of existence'.

It is in four movements and was inspired by the mysterious stone circles that feature on the CD's front cover, in an image by his late wife, Linda. The premiere took place in the Royal Albert Hall in London in October 1997. Immediately, *Standing Stone* was a big hit, reaching No. 1 in the classical charts. Poignantly, for a work that would prove to be his last before Linda died from breast cancer in 1998, it culminates in the beautifully lyrical 'Celebration'.

RECOMMENDED RECORDING
London Symphony Orchestra and Chorus;
Lawrence Foster (conductor).
EMI Classics: 5564842.
CHART POSITION 282

HAMISH MACCUNN
(1868–1916)

The Land of the Mountain and the Flood

'O Caledonia! Stern and wild,
Meet nurse for a poetic child!
Land of brown heath and shaggy wood,
Land of the mountain and the flood.'

These words from Walter Scott's *Lay of the Last Minstrel* had been written for a full eighty-two years when they moved the Scottish composer Hamish MacCunn to music.

As a boy of eight, MacCunn had been taken to his first season of concerts, one of the

famous August Manns series at Crystal Palace in London. So it was apt that, as a prodigious nineteen-year-old, he should have gone back there to hear the premiere performance of his major new work.

Although the music critic George Bernard Shaw was withering in his review – attacking the perceived formulaic nature of its middle section – *The Land of the Mountain and the Flood* has stood the test of time, remaining by far the composer's most popular work. Sadly, MacCunn, who lived in London, rather than the beloved Scottish countryside of his music, died from an illness at the tragically young age of forty-eight.

RECOMMENDED RECORDING
Royal Scottish National Orchestra; Alexander Gibson (conductor). Chandos: CHAN10412X.

CHART POSITION 203

GUSTAV MAHLER
(1860–1911)

Symphony No. 5 in C sharp minor

Mahler is famous for the way in which he stretched classical music to its limits. Principally, this happened through his huge symphonies, which nearly all require a very large orchestra and often last for over an hour. Indeed, in the case of this work, Mahler even adds a fifth movement, not content with any convention that dictated the fourth movement to be the finale. And yet, despite all this grandness of scale and depth, the main reason for the enduring popularity of his *Symphony*

left Hamish MacCunn: The Land of the Mountain and the Flood

No. 5 is the exquisite, ten-minute *Adagietto* that forms the fourth movement and which, more presciently, was put to such powerful use in the film *Death in Venice*.

Luchino Visconti's 1971 film tells the story of a composer; thus, Mahler's *Symphony No. 5* becomes, for the purpose of the movie, a composition by the main character Gustav von Aschenbach. The critical success of *Death in Venice* and its widespread audience over a forty-year period have ensured that, more than any concert hall performance, it's this film that has introduced more people to Mahler than anything else.

RECOMMENDED RECORDING
San Francisco Symphony Orchestra; Michael Tilson Thomas (conductor). San Francisco Symphony: 821936 00122.

CHART POSITION 29

Symphony No. 2 in C minor
Resurrection

Not content with stretching the orchestra to its limit, Mahler clearly fancied a challenge when composing his *Symphony No. 2* in the late 1800s. His triumphant symphonic debut, the 'Titan', had called for many more instruments than was the norm, so for his follow-up he decided to go one step further. The gargantuan symphony orchestra would remain, but alongside it was placed an organ, an offstage brass ensemble, and some church bells. And a choir. A very large choir. And, to round things off, some soloists. It's little wonder that, whenever the *Resurrection Symphony* is performed, it's the only work on the programme.

But if the roll-call of performers sounds indulgent and overpowering, the actual effect is spine-tingling. Mahler was a master at writing for such large forces. Far from feeling overwhelmed by a mass of noise, the very best performances of his *Symphony No. 2* convey its many different musical ideas, all woven together to create the most thrilling and joyous sound.

Written across a six-year period, the *Resurrection Symphony* was Mahler's most loved work during his own lifetime. The premiere performance in March 1895 featured the Berlin Philharmonic Orchestra (plus a bus load of singers, bell-ringers and the like) with the composer himself conducting. It was, quite simply, a triumph.

RECOMMENDED RECORDING
Eteri Gvazava (soprano); Anna Larsson (contralto); Orfeón Donostiarra (choir); Lucerne Festival Orchestra; Claudio Abbado (conductor). Deutsche Grammophon: DG 477 0582.

CHART POSITION 76

Symphony No. 1 in D
Titan

Composing at the end of the Romantic era, as Mahler found himself doing, must have been something of a challenge. Many Classical conventions had not just been questioned, but had been completely overthrown. Composers' emotions had been expressed in music in the most heartfelt of ways and everyone from Beethoven to Berlioz, via Brahms and Bizet, had composed masterpieces. So, along comes Mahler, inevitably a product of his day, but also a composer who was determined to break new ground. How did he do it? By applying a whole new meaning to the word 'orchestra'.

Despite the changes that had already occurred to orchestras in terms of the music they played, very few composers were yet to tamper with how this group of musicians was actually constructed. Mahler, however, decided to challenge the status quo. He called for a much larger orchestra than would have been expected. Orchestral sections were introduced, extra players were added, and the result was a symphony that very much lives up to its nickname.

Composed when Mahler was twenty-eight, *Titan* exudes youthful exuberance and joy, though it then gives way to melancholy and introspection. The composer was ultimately to shape the history of the symphony – and the clues to his long-term intentions were there for all to see in his first attempt at the genre.

RECOMMENDED RECORDING
Tonhalle Orchestra, Zurich; David Zinman (conductor). RCA: 82876 871562.

CHART POSITION 178

Symphony No. 8 in E flat
Symphony of a Thousand

There's a supreme confidence in much of Mahler's music – a sense that here was a composer who was utterly at home and assured of his own position in the world. The very nicknames of his symphonies (*Titan, Resurrection* and here the *Symphony of a Thousand*) only serve to highlight the point. And yet, when it came to his *Symphony No. 8*, Mahler was troubled. Here was a composer who had triumphed many times before but who was wondering whether he could truly come up with the goods again.

So, while on holiday in the summer of 1906, Mahler wrestled with this barren future, this wasteland of musical ideas. He simply did not know what to compose next. And then, as

Gustav Mahler
1860–1911

*'The symphony must be like the world.
It must embrace everything.'*

GUSTAV MAHLER

A renowned conductor during his lifetime, particularly of opera, Mahler rose to real popularity as a composer only during the latter half of the twentieth century. He was a tortured soul, who was analysed by Freud. His biggest hit is the *Adagietto* from Symphony No. 5. In total, he wrote nine symphonies, which seems to be the number to write – with Beethoven and Dvořák both clocking up nine apiece. Mahler once remarked to the composer Sibelius that 'the symphony is a world'.

Mahler's talent was first recognised not by another great classical music luminary, but by a farm manager in his native Bohemia, who heard the youngster playing and recommended that he attend the Vienna Conservatoire. There, he took lessons in composition and studied piano performance.

DID YOU KNOW?
Mahler's agent nicknamed Symphony No.8 the 'Symphony of a Thousand', because he thought it was a catchy title. Mahler hated it, though!

He was quite the international jetsetter, wowing audiences in the concert halls in all the major classical music centres across Europe, including Prague, Leipzig, Budapest and Vienna, where he was appointed Conductor of the Vienna Court Opera and of the Vienna Philharmonic Orchestra (the two big jobs in the city tended to go hand in hand). In 1907, he made the move across the pond, becoming Chief Conductor of the New York Metropolitan Opera for just one year, although he was to return to the USA shortly afterwards to become Music Director of the New York Philharmonic Orchestra. Not long after he took that job, his health began to suffer, not least because of the huge number of rehearsals and concert performances that he took on; he died of pneumonia back in Vienna at the age of fifty.

It was not until the end of the Second World War, more than thirty years after his death, that his genius as a composer was recognised. Today, it is for his masterful symphonies that he is chiefly held in the highest regard.

he powerfully recalled, 'on the threshold of my old workshop, the Spiritus Creator took hold of me and shook me and drove me on for the next eight weeks until my greatest work was done'. Within two months, Mahler had composed this mighty choral symphony. An astonishing piece of music, it encompasses settings of the Latin text 'Veni, creator spiritus', a message to the world about the nature of redemption, references to the Holy Spirit, and a deep expression of love from the composer to his wife, Alma, and a large section of Goethe's *Faust*.

RECOMMENDED RECORDING
Twyla Robinson (soprano); Adriane Queiroz (soprano); Erin Wall (soprano); Michelle DeYoung (mezzo-soprano); Simone Schroder (contralto); Johan Botha (tenor); Hanno Muller-Brachmann (bass-baritone); Robert Holl (bass-baritone) Staatskapelle Berlin; Pierre Boulez (conductor). Deutsche Grammophon: 4776597.

CHART POSITION 229

Symphony No. 4 in G

Mahler will always be remembered for his huge orchestral works – and his *Symphony No. 4* fits perfectly into that mould. It's interesting, then, that the symphony also exists in pared-down form. At the end of the First World War, the composer Arnold Schoenberg set up the Society for Private Musical Performances; an arrangement of Mahler's *Symphony No. 4* was constructed for the Society by the Austrian musician Erwin Stein in the early 1920s, featuring one soprano and only twelve accompanying musicians.

The majority of Mahler's work on constructing the original symphony took place during 1899 and 1900. There is, however, evidence of a slightly earlier influence: the final movement is an orchestral setting of the song *'Das himmlische Leben'*, which translates as 'The heavenly life'. Despite the reference to things eternal, though, the majority of his *Symphony No. 4* does not focus on making grand gestures or statements about the meaning of life, the idea of conflict, or any other big philosophical concept. Instead, it is first and foremost an ebullient, colourful symphony, full of expressive orchestral detail and glorious melody.

Symphony No. 4 was premiered in Munich on 25 November 1901, with the composer himself conducting. It was by no means embraced by the public, many of whom were expecting more from Mahler – both in terms of the scale of the sound and the ideological inspirations. But today it is a perfect entry point to the music of this most soulful of composers.

RECOMMENDED RECORDING
Sarah Fox (soprano); Philharmonia Orchestra; Charles Mackerras (conductor). Signum: SIGCD 219.

CHART POSITION 247

PIETRO MASCAGNI
(1863–1945)

Cavalleria rusticana

The thing we tend to forget, in these days of iTunes and *The X Factor* is that the seemingly rarefied thing that is opera today was itself once a great money-making scheme. A successful opera, with rave reviews in one country, could immediately transfer to opera houses around the globe, netting their composers and promoters massive financial rewards.

This was how it was for Mascagni, who was twenty-seven years old when his one-act opera *Cavalleria rusticana* (which translates as 'Rustic Chivalry') won the Sonzogno publisher prize for the best opera of 1890. Mascagni was soon a name on the lips of those in the know in the drawing rooms and salons of Europe. Today, his opera is still there, a fixed part of many opera companies' repertoires.

If only Mascagni could have repeated the feat, he might not have died almost penniless in liberated Italy in 1945. Nevertheless, his hit opera does contain one of the single most attractive tunes in operatic history – the *Intermezzo*. There are no words to accompany this part of the opera; instead it is a short piece of orchestral music used by the composer to denote the passage of time.

RECOMMENDED RECORDING

Julia Varady (soprano) as Santuzza; Carmen Gonzales (mezzo-soprano) as Lola; Luciano Pavarotti (tenor) as Turiddu; London Opera Chorus; National Philharmonic Orchestra; Gianandrea Gavazzeni (conductor). Decca: E4443912.

CHART POSITION 22

JULES MASSENET
(1842–1912)

Thaïs

Even among a group of classical music experts, you'd be hard pushed to find anyone who could instantly tell you the plot of French composer Jules Massenet's relatively unknown opera *Thaïs*. Instead, the work's popularity, longevity and wide appeal are down not to anything particularly operatic, but to a six-minute instrumental section that is heard during a scene change. In that sense, the beautiful *Meditation* for solo violin and

orchestra is officially an intermezzo in opera-speak; but far from being filler music, it's a captivating and pure performance piece in its own right.

French Romantic music is often distinctive for its particularly delicate qualities and nowhere is this more evident than here. The indulgent violin solo, cushioned by dream-like harmonies from the harps and, later, a sweeping orchestra, perfectly embodies the sound of French music at the time.

Given the innocent and predominantly optimistic sound-world the *Meditation* inhabits, it's something of a shock when heard in the context of the full opera. Rather than signifying a happy conclusion, it precedes the final, tragic section culminating in the death of Thaïs. But then, this wouldn't be opera if it all ended happily ever after!

RECOMMENDED RECORDING

(*Meditation* only) Maxim Vengerov (violin); Virtuosi (orchestra); Vag Papian (conductor). EMI Classics: CDC 5571642.

CHART POSITION 70

FELIX MENDELSSOHN
(1809–1847)

Violin Concerto in E minor

Anyone aspiring to be a concert violinist simply has to have this one in his or her repertoire. Nearly 150 years after its composition, Mendelssohn's *Violin Concerto* remains one of the most regularly performed and most loved of all instrumental concertos. And ever since its birth, the work has had a rather strange affinity with very young soloists.

When Mendelssohn was a teenager, he forged a very strong friendship with fellow composer Ferdinand David. As well as being a fine writer of music in his own right, David was also one of the most accomplished violinists of his day, so Mendelssohn composed this concerto for him. It took Mendelssohn five years from start to finish, during which time he would regularly seek David's advice on revisions, themes and structure.

Its premiere in 1844 featured David at the fiddle and another composer, the Dane Neils Gade, conducting. The second performance of the work, meanwhile, saw another teen star take to the stage: the fourteen-year-old Joseph Joachim, who would go on to become Europe's finest violinist of his time.

More recently, the work was one of the first to be recorded by the young Scottish violin star, Nicola Benedetti. The teenage Mendelssohn, who was inspired to compose this piece, would surely have been proud that, centuries on, it is still the first choice for budding young soloists today.

RECOMMENDED RECORDING
James Ehnes (violin); Philharmonia Orchestra; Vladimir Ashkenazy (conductor). Onyx: 4060.
CHART POSITION 27

Hebrides Overture
Fingal's Cave

How do you conjure up the sounds and sights of Scotland in a single piece of music? That was the challenge facing Mendelssohn when, in 1829, he travelled home from a memorable trip to the Scottish island of Staffa and its famous Fingal's Cave. The journey had evidently made an immediate impression on the composer: just hours later, he had written the first few bars of this piece and sent them off to his sister, Fanny, along with a note that described 'how

extraordinarily the Hebrides affected me'.

His travels to Scotland were part of a wider tour of Europe for Mendelssohn during his early twenties, and it's not hard to see why he was particularly captivated by what he encountered on Staffa. Fingal's Cave is over sixty metres deep and in stormy tides the cacophonous sounds of the waves inside it rumble out for miles. The intense and rolling melodies within the music perfectly capture this sense of both drama and awe; calmer passages, meanwhile, convey stiller waters and more tranquil surroundings. But it's never long before the return of that stormy scene.

On completing the score, Mendelssohn triumphantly wrote 'Fingal's Cave' on the front page, leaving no room for doubt that his *Hebrides Overture* was wholly inspired by this awesome Scottish landscape.

RECOMMENDED RECORDING
Vienna Philharmonic Orchestra; Christian Thielemann (conductor). Deutsche Grammophon: 4745022.
CHART POSITION 62

Symphony No. 4 in A
Italian

While the nicknames of many musical works were added after their creation (and often not even by the composers themselves), in the case of Mendelssohn the subtitles given to particular pieces of music were both wholly intentional and immediately revealing. Two of his earlier works – the *Scottish Symphony* and the *Hebrides Overture* – were both directly inspired by scenes north of the border, and his *Symphony No. 4* is a musical postcard home from Italy.

right Felix Mendelssohn: Hebrides Overture

Felix Mendelssohn

1809-1847

'A romantic who felt as ease within the mould of classicism.'

PABLO CASALS

This German-born composer was a frighteningly clever child, excelling as a painter, poet, athlete, linguist and musician. He made his public debut as a pianist at the age of nine and by the time he was sixteen he had composed his *Octet for Strings*.

Mendelssohn wasn't one of those composers who had to struggle with poverty all his life, scratching a living performing and writing music wherever he could, at the mercy of avaricious publishers or tempestuous patrons. Instead, he was born into a wealthy family who were friendly with many of Berlin's leading artists and musicians. His stable family background quite probably contributed to his own very happy marriage, which gave him five children.

As well as composing, Mendelssohn was a highly proficient conductor, being given the plum job of music director of the

> ## DID YOU KNOW?
>
> **Mendelssohn came from a very talented family. His grandfather, Moses, was one of the most respected scholars of his day on everything from theology to metaphysics.**

Leipzig Gewandhaus Orchestra in 1835, when he was just twenty-six. He retained the role until his tragically young death only a dozen years later.

Mendelssohn was a great lover of Britain – and the people of Britain loved

him and his music back in equal measure. He travelled widely around the country, with trips to Scotland sparking two of his best-loved works: his *Scottish Symphony* and his *Hebrides Overture*. His oratorio *Elijah* was given its premiere in Birmingham in 1846. Queen Victoria and Prince Albert were both fans of Mendelssohn's music and he performed for them both in public concerts and in private.

Mendelssohn was commissioned by the Liverpool Philharmonic Society to compose the opening work for their new concert hall. It was to be a cantata, setting to music the words to Milton's *Comus*. However, Mendelssohn died suddenly before the hall was built. Any plans that he had for *Comus* died with him, without a note being written down.

Soon after the young composer's first visit to Britain, he headed off to Italy as part of the same European tour. The buoyant and optimistic mood within which the work immediately begins bears all the hallmarks of a happy man, eager to make his mark on the world and express his travels through music.

On one level, however, the *Italian Symphony* is not particularly Italian. Not for Mendelssohn the continuous use of local folk songs or musical traditions; instead, the work is much more an expression of how Italy made him feel. Indeed, it's not until the final movement – some twenty minutes into the symphony – that we first hear a genuinely Italian music motif, in this case the sound of a national peasant dance.

RECOMMENDED RECORDING
Vienna Philharmonic Orchestra; John Eliot Gardiner (conductor). Deutsche Grammophon: 4591562.
CHART POSITION 136

A Midsummer Night's Dream

Many commentaries on this work tend to focus on the fact that Mendelssohn wrote his *Overture* to *A Midsummer Night's Dream* when he was only seventeen, in contrast to the rest of the incidental music, composed many years after. And while that's certainly true, it's easy to marvel only at that one fact instead on focusing on how exquisite the rest of the work actually is.

Aside from the *Overture*, *A Midsummer Night's Dream* was written in 1842. Mendelssohn's challenge was, essentially, the nineteenth-century equivalent of composing a film score: to write music that reflected, enhanced and enlightened the acting, while never detracting from it. His was initially inspired to compose music for the play because it was a childhood

favourite; to quote Mendelssohn's sister, Fanny, 'We were entwined with *A Midsummer Night's Dream* and Felix particularly made it his own. He identified with all of the characters. He recreated them, so to speak, every one of them whom Shakespeare produced in the immensity of his genius'.

From the triumphant *Wedding March* to the impish *Scherzo*, via the shimmering *Intermezzo* and the enchanting *Nocturne*, this is music of which Shakespeare would surely have approved.

RECOMMENDED RECORDING
Leipzig Gewandhaus Orchestra; Riccardo Chailly (conductor). Decca: 4756939.
CHART POSITION 153

Elijah

Mendelssohn was evidently bursting to write his glorious oratorio *Elijah* quite some time before he actually composed the music. Soon after the premiere of his first oratorio, *St Paul*, in 1836, his thoughts turned to the subject of this Old Testament prophet – a person who intrigued the young Mendelssohn and who would, he thought, be a perfect musical subject. Frustratingly, though, no librettist could be convinced of this. So, the work remained on the back-burner for a good ten years, during which time Mendelssohn cracked on with writing his *Piano Concerto No. 2* instead.

In the end, the composer penned most of the libretto himself, spurred on by a commission from the Birmingham Festival to write an oratorio for performance in the city in 1846. It was very much the *Messiah* of its day: a hugely popular work that absolutely cemented

TOP 10 FILM SOUNDTRACKS		
1	Dmitri Shostakovich	*The Gadfly*
2	John Williams	*Schindler's List*
3	Ennio Morricone	*The Mission*
4	John Williams	*Harry Potter*
5	Hans Zimmer	*Gladiator*
6	Dmitri Shostakovich	*The Unforgettable Year 1919*
7	John Williams	*Saving Private Ryan*
8	Nigel Hess	*Ladies in Lavender*
9	John Barry	*Dances with Wolves*
10	James Horner	*Titanic*

Mendelssohn's position as one of the greatest composers of sacred music. Two thousand people attended the premiere performance of *Elijah*, which saw Mendelssohn himself take to the podium at Birmingham Town Hall.

To quote a review published in *The Times* shortly afterwards, 'The last note of *Elijah* was drowned in a long-continued unanimous volley of plaudits, vociferous and deafening ... Never was there a more complete triumph; never a more thorough and speedy recognition of a great work of art.'

RECOMMENDED RECORDING
Renée Fleming (soprano); John Mark Ainsley (tenor); Bryn Terfel (bass-baritone); Edinburgh Festival Chorus; Orchestra of the Age of Enlightenment; Paul Daniel (conductor). Decca: 4556882.

CHART POSITION 271

<hr>

CLAUDIO MONTEVERDI
(1567–1643)

Vespers

For music to survive four hundred years and to remain popular is not only quite remarkable but also testament to its innate quality. By 1610, Monteverdi was a married forty-something working very successfully at the court of Vincenzo I in Mantua. He was a singer, a viol player (or gambist to give it its slightly more attractive epithet) and, for the previous eight years, had been a court composer, too.

Three years earlier Monteverdi had composed what is acknowledged to be one of the first ever operas, *L'Orfeo*. There is roughly an hour and a half of evening hymns in the

Vespers of the Blessed Virgin 1610 (to give them their full name) and, as such, they are probably the biggest thing in sacred music the other side of Bach. It's very possible that the whole ambitious work was written as a sort of audition piece for another court, because Monteverdi was keen to move on. If that was the case, then it might have worked; he transferred to a prestigious new job at St Mark's in Venice less than three years later.

RECOMMENDED RECORDING

Michael Chance (alto); Mark Tucker (tenor); Nigel Robson (tenor); Bryn Terfel (baritone); Monteverdi Choir; London Oratory Junior Choir; English Baroque Soloists; His Majesties Sagbutts and Cornetts; John Eliot Gardiner (conductor). Deutsche Grammophon: 4295652.

CHART POSITION 219

music is an eclectic mix of styles. Within the broadly symphonic sound-world, there's also space for liturgical chorales and indigenous drumming. It was deliberately intended to reflect the mission of Spanish Jesuits in their attempt to protect a South American tribe from exploitation.

Morricone was honoured with both a Golden Globe and a BAFTA for *The Mission* – although it wasn't this film score alone that won him an Oscar. Indeed, no one film garnered him that particular success; instead, the bestowment of an honorary Academy Award in 2007 ensured a well-earned gong found its way onto the composer's trophy shelf.

RECOMMENDED RECORDING

City of Prague Philharmonic Orchestra; Paul Bateman (conductor). Classic FM: CFMCD 46.

CHART POSITION 170

ENNIO MORRICONE
(B. 1928)

Gabriel's Oboe

Given the number of transcriptions of this piece of music that exist, it could very well have been called *Gabriel's Cello*, *Gabriel's Organ* or even *Gabriel's arrangement for four-piece boy band*. The contemporary Italian composer's music for the 1986 movie *The Mission* includes this beautiful two-minute piece, which manages simultaneously to be both lyrical and stately. No surprise, then, that over the last decade it's become an increasingly popular wedding processional.

The Academy Award-winning composer Ennio Morricone is an undisputed movie-music master, having written the scores for hundreds of films. Beginning his career in the 'Spaghetti Westerns' genre, it was Morricone's music for *The Mission* that really brought him worldwide fame. The

WOLFGANG AMADEUS
MOZART (1756–1791)

Clarinet Concerto in A

The first of Mozart's twenty entries here is from the final year of his life. The autumnal *Clarinet Concerto* was born out of respect and friendship. The man for whom Mozart wrote the music, Anton Stadler, was one of two clarinet players in his family, with Anton's brother Johann arguably the better, which must be saying something. Reports from the time describe Anton's playing as being 'so delicate in tone that no one who has a heart can resist it'.

Mozart gave him one of his most enduring works, albeit creating some confusion in the process. Stadler was a big champion of the

Wolfgang Amadeus Mozart
1756-1791

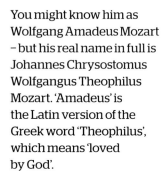

'If I were a dictator, I should make it compulsory for every member of the population between the ages of four and eighty to listen to Mozart for at least a quarter of an hour daily for the coming five years.'

SIR THOMAS BEECHAM

You might know him as Wolfgang Amadeus Mozart – but his real name in full is Johannes Chrysostomus Wolfgangus Theophilus Mozart. 'Amadeus' is the Latin version of the Greek word 'Theophilus', which means 'loved by God'.

When those in the know sit down to debate 'Who's the greatest of them all?' Mozart and Beethoven usually end up coming first and second, although the top spot changes hands as often as a magician's playing card. Probably the best-known child prodigy, Mozart could play the keyboard by the age of three and could compose from five. He went on his first European tour when he was six and by the time he had reached the grand old age of twelve, he had finished two operas.

Mozart's father, Leopold, loved to show off his son's talents as a way of making money. When the prodigy was just seven years old, his party trick was to cover the piano keyboard with a cloth and then to play fiendishly difficult pieces without being able to see any of the notes.

DID YOU KNOW?

Mozart's burial in a pauper's grave wasn't actually due to poverty. Rather, it was commonplace for anyone other than the very richest in society to be buried in this way.

As an adult, Mozart could knock out a new piece of music in a matter of minutes. Once when he was walking along the street, a beggar asked him for some money. Mozart was, as usual, a bit short of cash at the time, so he wrote out a tune on a piece of manuscript paper. He told the beggar to take it to a music publisher, who would exchange it for cash.

Mozart's music is an excellent choice if you're planning to take someone to a live classical concert for the first time. It's nice to know that he did have some faults though – he was said to be very arrogant, had a strange obsession with his rear end and was hopeless at managing his money. He was buried in an unmarked pauper's grave.

basset clarinet, an instrument possessing a few extra low notes than your average clarinet. Because of the publishers' general desire to print only a standard clarinet version – and the fact that Stadler allegedly pawned the basset version – confusion over how Mozart originally intended it to be played was rife until recent times. The original version featuring the lower notes is now making something of a comeback.

RECOMMENDED RECORDING
Sabine Meyer (clarinet); Berlin Philharmonic Orchestra; Claudio Abbado (conductor).
EMI Classics: 5568322.

CHART POSITION 2

Requiem

When Count von Walsegg's wife Anna died on Valentine's Day 1791, it set in motion a series of events that, one could argue, has never stopped. Walsegg approached Mozart for a requiem, through a third party, totally spooking an already unstable Mozart in the process. Walsegg was probably intending to pass off the work as his own once Mozart had completed writing it – he had form in this area.

The work was never delivered by Mozart, who died before he had finished composing it. It was brushed into some sort of shape by Mozart's only composition pupil, Sussmayr, but to the complete lack of satisfaction of scholars down the centuries. As a result, the world and his wife have tried to complete

it after him. Regardless, the *Requiem* still sounds wonderful to most ears.

To add further intrigue, when the unfinished manuscript was displayed in Brussels in the 1950s, a section was torn from the last page and never retrieved. As Mozart worked on the *Requiem* on his deathbed, it's highly likely that someone stole the last notes ever written by Mozart.

RECOMMENDED RECORDING
Felicity Lott (soprano); Willard White (bass); London Philharmonic Orchestra and Choir; Franz Welser-Möst (conductor).
EMI Classics: 5209492.

CHART POSITION 19

Piano Concerto No. 21 in C

There are composers who can only dream of playing the music they write for their own instruments. Elgar and Sibelius come to mind: both would have cut off their bow hands to have been able to play their own violin concertos to a virtuosic standard. Mozart was a fiddler, too, but was also lucky enough to write pretty much all his piano concertos to play himself. Indeed, the economics of his freelance, almost at times itinerant life as a composer and performer meant he was not just lucky to play them, but financially compelled to do so. The famous *Piano Concerto No. 21* (a staggering figure in itself: 21 piano concertos!) is one such, written when he was only twenty-nine, just six years before his early death. It is sometimes referred to as the *Elvira Madigan*, after a now otherwise long-forgotten film that featured the work.

When he had finished writing the piece, an unprecedented busy and successful time followed for Mozart. He premiered the concerto himself at a benefit concert in the National Court Theatre at which he also, according to the adverts, did some of his famous improvisations. So great was Mozart's memory for music, that he was said to be able to store at least two complete new symphonies in his head before he needed to write them down.

RECOMMENDED RECORDING
Murray Perahia (piano); English Chamber Orchestra. Sony: SMK898.
CHART POSITION 28

The Marriage of Figaro

Mozart wrote forty-one symphonies and twenty-seven piano concertos. And yet the work which said everything for him, the genre of music he truly thought to be the crucial currency of a composer, was the opera. Mozart considered opera to be the supreme musical language, where everything was perfectly possible and, with a genius such as Mozart's, possibly perfect. Mozart would have just hit thirty and had been enjoying one of his most successful periods when *The Marriage of Figaro* received its premiere. He was in Vienna, at the centre of the musical world and away from what he considered the parochial restrictions of his native Salzburg.

One contemporary reporter, who was lucky enough to witness Mozart himself directing the entire opera from the keyboard, said, 'Mozart directed the orchestra, playing his fortepiano; the joy which this music causes is so far removed from all sensuality that one cannot speak of it. Where could words be found that are worthy to describe such joy?' Apart from the wonderful *Overture*, vocal highlights include the divine *'Sull'aria'* duet, and the aria *'Porgi'*.

RECOMMENDED RECORDING
Carol Vaness; Nuccia Focile; Alessandro Corbelli; Alastair Miles; Susanne Mentzer; Scottish Chamber Orchestra and Chorus; Charles Mackerras (conductor). Telarc: 3CD80725.
CHART POSITION 51

The Magic Flute

Often referred to by many as Mozart's only pantomime, *The Magic Flute* is a riot of life, lust and ludicrous plot that somehow belies its portentous position in Mozart's output. It was premiered in his beloved Vienna just three months before his death. It had a libretto by the tenor who premiered the role of Papageno, Emmanuel Schickaneder, who was also said to have exerted considerable musical influence over Mozart at several points in the opera.

Mozart wrote much of the music with more than a passing reference to all things Masonic (he was a serving Freemason himself). Three becomes a magic number, as a result, with ladies, spirits, gates, trials, even chords all coming in the Masonically significant trios. The *Queen of the Night*'s Aria was written for Mozart's sister-in-law, Josepha, and her striking, naturally high coloratura. Other highlights, such as the the *Birdcatcher's Aria* and the *Overture*, make it a perennial favourite.

RECOMMENDED RECORDING
Barbara Hendricks (soprano); June Anderson (soprano); Thomas Allen (baritone); Robert Lloyd (bass); Alastair Miles (bass); Scottish Chamber Orchestra and Chorus; Charles Mackerras (conductor). Telarc: 2CD80727.
CHART POSITION 63

right Wolfgang Amadeus Mozart: The Magic Flute

Concerto in C for flute and harp

There is a wonderful scene – one of many – in the 1984 Milos Forman film adaptation of Peter Schaffer's play *Amadeus*, in which the jealous Salieri sees the score of Mozart's *Flute and Harp Concerto* and is simply bowled over, incredulous at how divine the melody and orchestration are. And he's right.

The central slow movement must surely be one of the most glorious melodies not just in Mozart's output but, possibly, in all music. Written as it was for a father and daughter combination to play (Mozart was trying, yet seemingly failing by all accounts, to teach composition to the daughter of the Duc de Guines), it represents the only time Mozart ventured to write for the unwieldy harp.

Some music historians have even suggested that Mozart was, pretty much, writing for piano and flute in his head. It was probably an attempt to get more money out of the Duc but, despite a good reception – 'the Duc plays the flute incomparably, and she magnificently on the harp' according to the composer – it was not to be.

RECOMMENDED RECORDING
Emmanuel Pahud (flute); Marie-Pierre Langlamet (harp); Berlin Philharmonic Orchestra; Claudio Abbado (conductor). EMI Classics: 5571282.
CHART POSITION 67

Ave verum corpus

Just forty-six bars containing around three minutes of music. And yet they are capable of leaving the listener just as moved as might an entire five-day long cycle of Wagner's *The Ring*. And certainly less tired.

Ave verum corpus is another work that Mozart composed in the final year of his life. It was written almost as a payment to a friend – in much the same way that Picasso would give away sketches. Anton Stoll was a chorus master at a small church in Baden, and had often helped Mozart by making travel arrangements for his wife, Constanze. Despite having his money worries, Mozart still liked to make sure his wife had her restorative periods at Baden.

Writing very simply, Mozart was perhaps conscious of the limitations of a small-town choir, although, as the Austrian pianist Artur Schnabel once said of the work, it is 'too simple for children, and too difficult for adults'. It was written to be performed on the Feast of Corpus Christi and contains the words *sotto voce* (meaning 'subdued') in Mozart's hand on the score.

RECOMMENDED RECORDING
The Sixteen; Academy of St Martin in the Fields; Harry Christophers (conductor). Coro: COR 16057.
CHART POSITION 71

Solemn Vespers

It is perfectly possible to hear the music of a composer and simply to take it on the musical merits it presents. One need not know the background to the work, the circumstance in which it was written, nor, indeed, in some extreme cases such as Wagner's, the potentially unsavoury views of its composer. Mozart's *Solemn Vespers* from 1780 sound simply divine, on a sheer musical level. Six movements of wonderful, religious music, culminating in, surely, one of Mozart's finest tunes in the *Laudate Dominum* (imagine how delighted the soprano must have been to see she had been given such a corker).

Mozart himself, however, felt restricted in these works. They were written for performance in Salzburg where his employer, the Archbishop Colleredo, insisted on a very conservative style in comparison with, say, the Italian manner of the day. No matter for Mozart, though: soon enough, he was to be booted out of the Salzburg court, enabling him to seek his fortune in Vienna.

These Vespers are one of a pair. They come alongside the *Solemn Vespers for Sunday* and were written a year apart.

RECOMMENDED RECORDING
Winchester Cathedral Choir; Academy of Ancient Music; Christopher Hogwood (conductor). Warner: 2564601912.
CHART POSITION 72

Eine Kleine Nachtmusik

The real title for this perennial favourite is *Serenade No. 13 in G*, although it's the informal title that has stuck. The more common name comes courtesy of Mozart's obsessively organised side, a character trait about which we rarely hear. Despite possessing a brain that could remember music with 100 per cent precision, Mozart kept a detailed log of everything he'd written, just in case. The title 'Eine Kleine Nacht-Musik' is what he jotted next to the entry for this particular serenade written for a string quartet with an added double-bass. It's another piece from his great purple patch. He was thirty-one years old.

One frustrating by-product of Mozart's personal catalogue of all his works is that we also know that there were originally five movements of this work, rather than the four that now survive. Oddly enough, Mozart never published *Eine Kleine Nachtmusik* in his lifetime. It was left up to his widow, Constanze, to sell it in a job lot of his music to a publisher in 1799, presumably to raise much needed cash. It saw public light of day only in 1827, some forty years after it was written.

RECOMMENDED RECORDING
Orpheus Chamber Orchestra.
Classic FM: CFM FW 025.
CHART POSITION 74

Così fan tutte

Translated as 'All Women Do the Same', *Così fan tutte* is admittedly not the most politically correct title in all opera, although there are plenty of other contenders, including Verdi's *'La donna è mobile'* ('Women are fickle') from his opera *Rigoletto*.

For Mozart, though, it signalled an external expression of faith in him as a composer, at a time when he needed a boost. The one-time boy wonder had realized, from early on, that music generated further music. If he could have a piano concerto ready by the time he hit town, to play when he got there, he might very well impress enough people to get a commission for, perhaps, another piano concerto.

So it proved with the opera *The Marriage of Figaro*. It was down to a revival of *Figaro* that Mozart was commissioned to write *Così* in 1789, ready for a 1790 premiere, on the day after his birthday.

Mozart's diaries reveal that he rehearsed it, with singers, in his apartment before Christmas. On one occasion he even invited Haydn along to hear it.

RECOMMENDED RECORDING
(highlights) Leila Cuberli (soprano) as Fiordiligi; Cecilia Bartoli (mezzo-soprano) as Dorabella; Joan Rodgers (soprano) as Despina; Kurt Streit (tenor) as Ferrando; Ferruccio Furlanetto (baritone) as Guglielmo; John Tomlinson (bass) as Don Alfonso; Berlin Philharmonic Orchestra; RIAS Chamber Chorus of Berlin; Daniel Barenboim (conductor). Erato: 94821.
CHART POSITION 108

Clarinet Quintet in A

One hopes that the people around and about Mozart realised just how remarkable a composer and performer he really was, although much of the evidence from the time suggests that many failed to spot it. While composers such as Sibelius or Grieg were honoured and supported by their own governments, Mozart was left to get by as a jobbing, freelance musician, constantly resorting to borrowing from friends.

Hopefully though, Anton Stadler valued Mozart's work more than most. As the recipient both of this glorious work and of Mozart's *Clarinet Concerto*, he was truly blessed. Mozart refers to this quintet in his letters as 'the Stadler quintet'. Written when the composer was thirty-three, it pairs Stadler's new basset clarinet (see the *Clarinet Concerto* entry earlier) with a standard string quartet. It was considered by many to be almost a dummy run for the great concerto. Mozart's effortless writing, combined with some simply inspired tunes, means it is still one of the most widely played works in the repertoire today.

RECOMMENDED RECORDING
Thea King (clarinet); Gabrieli String Quartet. Hyperion: CDA30010.
CHART POSITION 116

Symphony No. 40 in G minor

All but two of Mozart's forty-one symphonies are composed in what we would call 'happy' or major keys. The exceptions are known as *The Little G Minor Symphony* and *The Great G Minor Symphony*; or *Nos. 25* and *40* respectively. *No. 25* was effectively used in Milos Forman's 1984 film *Amadeus* at the very opening of the movie, to establish that brown, foreboding eighteenth-century atmosphere.

No. 40 is arguably the most popular of all of Mozart's forty-one symphonies, despite the fact that its first movement became one of the most annoying ringtones of the mobile phones of the 1990s. It was probably quite popular in Mozart's lifetime, too. Although scholars can't be absolutely certain, it would appear Mozart performed it more than once, going on to rescore it for slightly different musical forces. It has one of the catchiest opening movements of any symphony. The work was said to have soon come to the attention of Beethoven. As well as paying homage to its composition by writing out passages in his own hand, he is thought to have been inspired by the last movement when he wrote his own *Symphony No. 5*.

RECOMMENDED RECORDING
Les Musiciens du Louvre; Marc Minkowski (conductor). Archiv: 4775798.
CHART POSITION 129

Piano Concerto No. 23 in A

The piano concertos of Mozart are one of the greatest examples of the blending of practical musicianship with sheer musical genius. They run from mere childhood offerings, which are themselves still wonders to behold, via the great masterpieces of Mozart's Viennese years, right through to his final years, when his concertos were marked out as coming from the pen of a genius. He composed his *Piano Concerto No. 1* when he was eleven years old and *Piano Concerto No. 27* when he was near death at the age of thirty-five. *Piano Concerto No. 23* comes right smack-bang in that Viennese masterpiece period. It was probably written around the same time as his opera *The Marriage of Figaro* was premiered, and was almost certainly included in one of Mozart's numerous but necessary subscription concerts. Indeed, around twelve of the twenty-seven concertos were composed across a two-year period from 1784 to 1786, when Mozart would have been between twenty-eight and thirty. As with many of his piano concertos, it is a very positive-sounding work, nearly always trying to look on the bright side.

RECOMMENDED RECORDING
Mitsuko Uchida (piano); English Chamber Orchestra; Jeffrey Tate (conductor). Philips: 4685402.
CHART POSITION 146

Piano Concerto No. 20 in D minor

Written just before the massive hit *Piano Concerto No. 21*, this one was premiered in a casino of all places. It should be noted that casinos in Mozart's day were venues where one often heard concerts, so probably it would not have proved too much of a problem for the players to be heard above the blackjack.

Correspondence from the time suggests that Mozart went up to the wire when it came to putting in the composition work on this piece. The ink was, literally, still wet on the page when he gave it its first public performance. His father Leopold wrote in a letter to Mozart's sister Nannerl '... an excellent new piano concerto by Wolfgang, on which the copyist was still at work when we got there, and your brother didn't even have time to play through the rondo because he had to oversee the copying operation'. Mozart often kept the piano parts to his concerto totally in his head, so this would have been nothing untoward for him.

RECOMMENDED RECORDING
Mitsuko Uchida (piano); English Chamber Orchestra; Jeffrey Tate (conductor). Philips: 4685402.
CHART POSITION 152

Don Giovanni

First of all, let's get that full title down: *Il Dissoluto Punito, ossia il Don Giovanni*. Translated, that's 'The Rake, Punished, or Don Giovanni'. As a title, it does exactly what it says on the tin and for many it is Mozart's operatic masterpiece.

The opera's Prague premiere came when Mozart was thirty-one and perhaps at the pinnacle of his popularity. It is easy to see why many music lovers cite *Don Giovanni* as their favourite opera of all time. Tchaikovsky, one of those who placed it above all others, once visited a friend who owned the original manuscript, remarking that he was 'in the presence of divinity'. As well as its imposing *Overture*, highlights include the *Catalogue Aria* in which Don Giovanni's servant, Leporello, lovingly lists his master's lovers. In addition, the *Champagne Aria* (precursing a party) and lovely arias such as *'Dalla sua pace'* make this among opera's finest few hours. It must also count as one of the most quoted operas by other composers, featuring in works by Offenbach, Rossini and Liszt.

RECOMMENDED RECORDING
Johannes Weisser (baritone) as Don Giovanni; Lorenzo Regazzo (bass) as Leporello; Alexandrina Pendatchanska (soprano) as Donna Elvira; Freiburg Baroque Orchestra and Chorus; René Jacobs (conductor). Harmonia Mundi: HMC 90196466.
CHART POSITION 160

Horn Concerto No. 4 in E flat

Blessed are the cheese-makers, for they shall have Mozart horn concertos. At least, if your name was Leutgeb. After a good run as Europe's most sought-after horn player – Joseph Haydn, Hoffman, Dittersdorf and Michael Haydn all wrote works for him – Joseph Leutgeb settled in Vienna where he inherited a cheese shop and would have been content to hang up his mouthpiece. Would have, that is, were it not for the presence in Vienna of Mozart, who

duly engaged the clearly rather talented chap to play his brand new concertos.

This one, the fourth, comes with a multicoloured score – and that's no joke. It's thought Mozart was either having a little fun with Leutgeb by writing the score in red, green, blue and black, or concealing some sort of Da Vinci code. Before you devote years of your life to the answer, it was almost certainly the former.

RECOMMENDED RECORDING
David Pyatt (horn); Academy of St Martin in the Fields; Neville Marriner (conductor). Apex: 2564681619.
CHART POSITION 168

Symphony No. 41 in C
Jupiter

First of all, the nickname. Unlike the *Eine Kleine Nachtmusik* epithet, which stems from Mozart's own description in his personal notebook, the word 'Jupiter' probably has nothing to do with Mozart. Unfortunately, it appears to be marketing hype, coined by the same chap who promoted Haydn concerts in England, one Johann Peter Salomon. If true, then the name came from London, first used in a concert programme for the Philharmonic Society of London (now the Royal Philharmonic Society) and that was a full twenty-six years after Mozart died.

Staggeringly, this very popular symphony was written within days of both Mozart's *Symphony No. 39* and *Symphony No. 40*. It could be that Mozart had at least a couple of symphonies buzzing around in his head before

right Wolfgang Amadeus Mozart: Don Giovanni

committing them almost whole to paper. But to have three fully formed works committed to memory is truly astonishing. More proof, if it were needed, of the correct use of the word 'genius' when applied to Mozart.

RECOMMENDED RECORDING
Scottish Chamber Orchestra; Charles Mackerras (conductor). Linn: CKD 308.

CHART POSITION 172

Sinfonia Concertante in E flat for violin and viola

Aged twenty-three and travelling around Europe, Mozart was no longer the 'boy wonder'. For someone who had been touring, on and off, since he was in single figures, twenty-three represented almost the autumn of his touring career. And despite the pitfalls of no longer being the cute child star, the benefits of his touring years did occasionally pay off. This is one such example.

With his *Sinfonia Concertante*, Mozart delivers a veritable masterclass in the then modern-day techniques of the European ensemble – as witnessed, first hand, by the travelling Wolfgang. Mozart had heard the highly respected Mannheim court orchestra play on a number of occasions and he gained a huge amount of knowledge and understanding of orchestras and their players from working with them. Most composers would know of this sort of orchestra only by reputation, but Mozart had

gained intimate knowledge by sitting right next to the string section when he had performed with them.

A musical note to add to this entry: when this work was originally performed, the viola player would have needed to detune his instrument by one note to play the music that Mozart had written. Today, it doesn't happen so often.

RECOMMENDED RECORDING
Rachel Podger (violin); Pavlo Beznosiuk (viola); Orchestra of the Age of Enlightenment. Channel Classics: CCSSA29309.

CHART POSITION 239

Exsultate, jubilate

When you realize that this work came from the pen of someone who was, as Rodgers and Hammerstein might say, 'sixteen going on seventeen', it is truly amazing. The sheer combination of youth involved in the composition and premiere of *Exsultate, jubilate* completely belies the sound of the work. To many, it's the sound of a genius at the peak of his powers, harnessing some of the finest slices of his imagination with aplomb and wisdom.

The man – yes, man – for whom Mozart wrote it, Venanzio Rauzzini, had a good ten years on the composer. He was the Italian soprano castrato of choice for the musical chattering classes of Milan. The composer and performer had been flung together to produce Mozart's early opera, *Lucio Silla*, in which Rauzzini starred. The singer would eventually, after a couple more adulatory years wowing them in Italy, move permanently to the unlikely destination of Bath, living largely off his reputation by teaching and mounting subscription concerts.

Today, *Exsultate, jubilate* is rarely (if ever) sung by a castrato, but is a favourite of female sopranos the world over, especially its final-movement *Alleluia* in which Mozart sets to music just that one word.

RECOMMENDED RECORDING

Kiri Te Kanawa (soprano); London Symphony Orchestra and Chorus; Colin Davis (conductor). Philips: 4128732.

CHART POSITION 250

Mass in C Minor
Great

Despite Mozart sometimes being portrayed as being rather juvenile and as keen on smutty humour as he was on music, his letters and diaries do also point to a man of greater depth. The story of the *Great Mass*, for example, reveals a person with strong spiritual feelings.

At the time he composed it, Mozart would have been just twenty-two years old. He was engaged to Constanze Weber. It's true to say that he had pursued her sister, Aloysia, first, and then switched camps when rebuffed, but no matter. Suddenly, though, Constanze became ill. Illness, it need not be said, was a far greater issue back then and all was done to bring her to health again.

When she finally did recover, Mozart vowed to write a Mass in thanks for her life. This he did, despite history having deprived us of a couple of major chunks of it − parts of the *Credo* and *Sanctus* are not intact. The story of its premiere, at the Salzburg Court of Archbishop Colleredo (Mozart's boss) seems romantic, if not least for one aspect: singing the female solo was Constanze Weber herself.

RECOMMENDED RECORDING

Felicity Lott (soprano); Willard White (bass); London Philharmonic Orchestra and Choir;

Franz Welser-Möst (conductor). EMI Classics: 5209492.

CHART POSITION 278

MODEST MUSSORGSKY
(1839–1881)

Pictures at an Exhibition

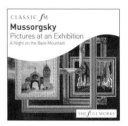

For composers, the death of a close friend or family member tends to have one of two effects: they either retreat into their own world, devoid of inspiration and unable to compose, or this life experience results in a creative surge forwards. In the case of Mussorgsky, the latter was true.

The Russian composer was good friends with a painter called Vladimir Hartmann. Tragically, Hartmann died at the peak of his career, aged just thirty-nine, and the loss of not just a close friend but an artistic inspiration had a deep effect on Mussorgsky. By way of a tribute to Hartmann, he decided to compose his set of piano pieces *Pictures at an Exhibition*, inspired by an exhibition of the artist's work, which Mussorgsky had visited after his friend's death.

Nowadays, however, *Pictures at an Exhibition* is most often heard not in its original piano version but in orchestrated form. Many musicians, from Henry Wood to Leopold Stokowski, have arranged the work for full orchestra, but it's far and away the 1922 version by Maurice Ravel that receives the most regular performance and praise today.

RECOMMENDED RECORDING

(orch. Rimsky-Korsakov) Vienna Philharmonic Orchestra; Valery Gergiev (conductor). Classic FM: CFM FW 060.

CHART POSITION 90

A Night on the Bare Mountain

It was as a teenager that the Russian composer Modest Mussorgsky was first inspired to write his orchestral poem *A Night on the Bare Mountain*. He was an ambitious young man with dreams to compose a full-scale opera called *St John's Eve*, which he said would include the scene of a witches' sabbath. Like so many of Mussorgsky's musical plans, though, this one never fully came to fruition. In later life, his failure to see ideas through to conclusion was sadly due to his alcoholism; in his youth it was mere exuberance and naive optimism, which could never quite be translated into reality.

One work that did survive this particular grand plan, though, was *A Night on the Bare Mountain*. It wasn't completed until nine years after his initial inspiration for *St John's Eve* and, despite its great popularity today, Mussorgsky really struggled to convince anyone to perform it. He even went back to the work several times, revising and refining it – to the point of adding a full choir – in an attempt to make it more performance-friendly. Sadly, the work never gained any semblance of a following in Mussorgsky's lifetime. It was only when Rimsky-Korsakov produced his own re-orchestrated version (five years after Mussorgsky's death) that the piece began to receive an appreciative audience. It's this version that we enjoy today.

RECOMMENDED RECORDING

(orch. Rimsky-Korsakov) Vienna Philharmonic Orchestra; Valery Gergiev (conductor). Classic FM: CFM FW 060.

CHART POSITION 236

JACQUES OFFENBACH
(1819–1880)

The Tales of Hoffmann

Read the short stories? Seen the play? Now experience the opera. That's how it might have been for nineteenth-century Parisians and *Les Contes d'Hoffmann*, which Offenbach himself had seen as a play at the Odeon Theatre called *The Fantastic Tales of Hoffmann*.

In the play (by Jules Barbier and Michael Carré), the writer E. T. A. Hoffmann is seen as a participant in some of his own short stories; 're-imagined', they might say today. It was this play that Offenbach then transformed into an opera, using just five of Hoffmann's original tales, including *Der Sandmann*, which Delibes had used as the basis for his *Coppélia*, eleven years earlier in 1870.

Offenbach spent a massive tranche of the autumn of his years on *The Tales of Hoffmann*, only to die while it was in rehearsals. Although it was more-or-less all ready, the promoters brought in composer Ernest Guiraud, who had made a minor name for himself just a few years earlier with his reworkings of the recitative sections of Bizet's *Carmen*.

RECOMMENDED RECORDING
Plácido Domingo (tenor) as Hoffmann; Edita Gruberova (soprano) as Olympia, Giulietta and Antonia; James Morris (bass) as Miracle; Christa Ludwig (mezzo-soprano) as Antonia's mother; Chorus of Radio France; French National Orchestra; Seiji Ozawa (conductor). Deutsche Grammophon: 4276822.
CHART POSITION 254

CARL ORFF
(1895–1982)

Carmina Burana

If you're a child of the 1970s, it may well have been the Old Spice advert. If you hail from a younger generation, it will almost certainly be *The X Factor*. Or maybe you remember its regular comical use in *Only Fools and Horses*. Perhaps you even know it as the accompaniment to which Gillingham Football Club players run onto the pitch at home games at the Priestfield Stadium. One thing's for sure, though: the vast majority of people who know and love the famous *'O Fortuna'* that opens Carl Orff's *Carmina Burana* have first come across it not through a performance of the work, but via its use in countless television shows, commercials and films.

At less than three minutes, *'O Fortuna'* is only one very small part of this mammoth, secular cantata. Orff was at pains to point out the non-religious nature of the work in its title: *Carmina Burana* is subtitled *Cantiones profanæ cantoribus et choris cantandæ comitantibus instrumentis atque imaginibus magicis*, translating as 'secular songs for singers and choruses to be sung together with instruments and magic images'.

Composed in the 1930s and inspired by a set of medieval poems, *Carmina Burana* was first performed in Frankfurt in June 1937, to great acclaim. Orff knew he had a hit on his hands, and he was fortunate enough to see the work's rapid rise in popularity during the course of his own lifetime. By the time of his death in 1982, it was indisputably established as a twentieth-century classic.

RECOMMENDED RECORDING

Saint Louis Symphony Orchestra and Chorus; Leonard Slatkin (conductor). RCA: 09026 616732.

CHART POSITION 52

JOHANN PACHELBEL
(1653–1706)

Canon in D

If you're ever doing the tourist trail in the deep south of America, pay lots of attention when you get to Charleston, South Carolina. If you see the words 'Charles Patchable', or even 'Carl Perchival', well, it's probably worth taking a second look. The Pachelbel we know and love today – principally for this work, originally called the *Kanon und Gigue für 3 Violinen mit Generalbaß* in his native Nuremberg German – gave birth to two composer sons. One ended his days in Charleston, still composing, where his name appears to have been somewhat Americanised.

In Charles's lifetime, his father would not yet have been famous for this one jaunty work, as it was rediscovered by the masses and raised onto a pedestal only in the twentieth century, after being published by a German scholar in an article about Pachelbel. Its huge popularity at weddings may originally stem from one unsupported theory that it was originally written for the nuptials of Johann Sebastian Bach's brother, Johann Christoph. It's hard to pick one recording because there are seemingly

more versions committed to disc than there are stars in the sky.

RECOMMENDED RECORDING

Il Giardino Armonico (ensemble); Giovanni Antonini (conductor). Warner: 2564632642.

CHART POSITION 10

NICCOLÒ PAGANINI
(1782–1840)

Violin Concerto No. 1 in D major

Some of the greatest pieces of classical music ever written for instrumental soloists were, unsurprisingly, composed by people who could play that very instrument themselves. Rachmaninov and Brahms, for example, were outstanding pianists in their own right, which goes a great way towards explaining their masterful works for the keyboard. And when it comes to the violin, there was one man who trumped them all in the composer–performer stakes: the Italian musical genius Niccolò Paganini.

The premieres of many works are often described as having wowed the audience of the day, but this simply does not do justice to the response Paganini received when his *Violin Concerto No. 1* was performed for the first time. Those who heard it were absolutely blown away – not just by the technical feats and showmanship Paganini had demanded of the instrument, but by the fact that he was actually able to play every single note. And these weren't just notes: there were giant leaps, packed with all sorts of complex musical wizardry, the like of which no one had ever heard before.

So inhuman was Paganini's playing, some even thought him to be the son of the Devil. But as you listen to this concerto, it's hard to believe it's anything other than heavenly.

RECOMMENDED RECORDING
Sarah Chang (violin); Philadelphia Orchestra; Wolfgang Sawallisch (conductor). EMI Classics: CDC 5550262.

CHART POSITION 190

HUBERT PARRY
(1848–1918)

I Was Glad

Settings of Psalm 122 have abounded in churches for hundreds of years. Purcell composed one. So did Boyce. Charles Hubert Hastings Parry's setting known by the 'incipit' (the first line) of the text as published in the 1662 Book of Common Prayer has become one of the most celebrated. Perhaps this is for the simple reason that it sets out to achieve musically exactly what the opening words say. From the moment it begins, it

is throbbing with energy, and the first choral cloudburst of the words 'I was glad' still sends a tingle down the spine, even on the hundredth hearing.

Parry took a couple of coronations to get it exactly right, though. He originally wrote it to accompany the crowning of Edward VII, and then, nine years later, offered it up again, for the coronation of George V. This time, he added all manner of further pomp to his original to make it into the version we know and love. When Parry's obituary was published in 1918, it was remarked that his job as Professor of Music at the University of Oxford had eaten up too much of his valuable composing time. Perhaps that was the reason it took him two goes to get *I Was Glad* absolutely spot on.

RECOMMENDED RECORDING
The Sixteen; Robert Quinney (organ); Harry Christophers (conductor). UCJ: 1795732.

CHART POSITION 249

Jerusalem

Although now far more widely known, William Blake's poem, 'And Did Those Feet in Ancient Times' (he didn't call it 'Jerusalem'), was originally included only in a short preface to a much longer one (called 'Milton, A Poem'). The text concerns the legend that Jesus might have travelled, with Joseph of Arimathea, to England – in fact, to be precise, to Glastonbury. When it was included as a patriotic poem in a 1916 collection for a country at war, it immediately caught Parry's eye. Parry was more than happy, at the suggestion of the Poet Laureate, Robert Bridges, to set it to music, calling it simply *Jerusalem*. And it's still there, rousing successive generations, usually in its 1922 re-orchestration by Elgar

---

right Hubert Parry: Jerusalem

for the Leeds Festival. Despite representing the Establishment that Elgar claimed to dislike, both he and Parry had a form of mutual appreciation society in operation: the 1922 orchestration was pretty much an epitaph for his fellow composer, who had died just four years earlier.

Jerusalem has become an unofficial second national anthem and is often used by England at sporting fixtures, such as the 2010 Commonwealth Games, where each of the home nations is represented separately. It has become the official hymn of the English Cricket Board and is usually sung at both the Rugby League Challenge Cup Final and the Super League final.

RECOMMENDED RECORDING

The Sixteen; Robert Quinney (organ); Harry Christophers (conductor). UCJ: 1795732.

CHART POSITION 274

ARVO PÄRT
(B. 1935)

Spiegel im Spiegel

The Estonian composer Arvo Pärt is an extraordinarily reclusive yet successful musician. Worldwide, his music is among the most frequently performed of all contemporary composers – and yet he rarely, if ever, seeks any kind of limelight or recognition. In many ways, Pärt's serene work for violin and piano *Spiegel im Spiegel* is a perfect musical reflection of the composer's own character.

Pärt started out as a composer by embracing many of the popular avant-garde musical approaches of the day. His works weren't particularly melodious in the traditional sense; instead, they were both complex and challenging. But in the late 1970s, Pärt completely abandoned this approach. *Spiegel im Spiegel* was one of his first musical demonstrations of his change of heart. From this point on, his music would be 'Tinntinabular' in style – a term coined by Pärt himself to describe his minimalist, meditative compositions.

Translated as 'Mirror in the Mirror', *Spiegel im Spiegel* is enduringly popular for the calm, still environment it inhabits, in a world that is so often much more noisy and frantic.

RECOMMENDED RECORDING

Nicola Benedetti (violin); Alexei Grynyuk (piano). Deutsche Grammophon: 476 3399.

CHART POSITION 135

GIOVANNI BATTISTA
PERGOLESI (1710–1736)

Stabat Mater

Pergolesi, Palestrina and Offenbach are all composers with names adopted from their home towns. In Offenbach's case, it was his father who took the name of the small city near Frankfurt. For Pergolesi, born in Iesi in the Italy's wonderful Le Marche, the name had been his family's for at least two generations. It was acquired from the small and beautiful commune of Pergola, almost equidistant from Iesi and Urbino.

Just before the end of his extremely successful yet tragically short life, Pergolesi was commissioned by a band of artistic gentlemen to provide music for an annual Good Friday service in honour of the Virgin Mary. His *Stabat Mater* was the response. Its famous plaintive introduction, in which two singers sing so close to each other in pitch as to cause temporary dissonances, was meant to portray the pain of the subjects: each time the two singers come just one note apart, it creates a piercing sound, with each occasion representing the hammering of a nail into the body of Jesus. Poignantly, Pergolesi wrote these notes while in the throes of the tuberculosis that claimed his life.

RECOMMENDED RECORDING
Emma Kirkby (soprano); James Bowman (alto); Academy of Ancient Music; Christopher Hogwood (conductor). Decca: 4256922.

CHART POSITION 245

ZBIGNIEW PREISNER
(B. 1955)

Requiem for My Friend

The soprano Sumi Jo is famed for her ability to sing very high notes in a pure, angelic way. Nowhere is this gift put to better use than in her landmark recording of the famous *Lacrimosa* from Preisner's *Requiem for My Friend*. The Polish composer wrote the piece, his first large-scale classical work, in 1996. Until that point, Preisner had been known either for his piano miniatures or for his considerable film music output.

The friend alluded to in the title is the film director Krzysztof Kieslowski, with whom Preisner had collaborated many times. Among the most famous of Kieslowski's movies for which Preisner wrote the score were *The Double Life of Veronique* and the *Three Colours* trilogy. Although modern in sound, *Requiem for My Friend* is entirely traditional in its text, using the liturgy of the Catholic Mass for the Dead. The focus during Part I is rather broad, but in Part II, Preisner looks very personally on the loss of Kieslowski, with the inclusion of Polish texts in tribute to the director.

Preisner's choice of instrumentation is certainly quirky. There's a saxophone, an organ and a couple of counter-tenors alongside the sixty-piece orchestra, but the effect is absolutely spine-tingling. It remains the composer's most popular and most moving work, by a long shot.

RECOMMENDED RECORDING
Various soloists; Varsov Chamber Choir; Sinfonia Varsovia. Erato 3984 241462.

CHART POSITION 246

SERGEI PROKOFIEV
(1891–1953)

Romeo and Juliet

There are many things a composer can do to upset the general equilibrium of the play or text they're setting. These include excising huge chunks of text or leaving entire characters on the cutting-room floor, unable to do them musical justice. However, Prokofiev's first big idea for his ballet music for Shakespeare's *Romeo and Juliet* was probably just a little beyond the pale: he was going to change it to a happy ending. In the end, he considered, almost certainly correctly, that this would have been a step too far. He wrote the work for the Kirov Ballet, but the huge demands it placed on the dancers meant it wasn't performed for a few

TOP 10 RELAXING CLASSICS		
1	Sergei Rachmaninov	*Piano Concerto No. 2* - 2nd movement
2	Wolfgang Amadeus Mozart	*Clarinet Concerto* - 2nd movement
3	Vaughan Williams	*The Lark Ascending*
4	Edward Elgar	*Enigma Variations - Nimrod*
5	Johann Pachelbel	*Canon in D*
6	Samuel Barber	*Adagio for Strings*
7	Ralph Vaughan Williams	*Fantasia on a theme of Thomas Tallis*
8	Antonín Dvořák	*Symphony No. 9 (From the New World)* - 2nd movement
9	Sergei Rachmaninov	*Symphony No. 2* - 3rd movement
10	Gregorio Allegri	*Miserere*

years, receiving its premiere in Brno in 1938. Prokofiev wrote new sections for a 1940 production and it was then that the music really took off, eventually forming the basis of three popular suites.

The centrepiece of the work, musically, must be *The Montagues and Capulets* (sometimes known as *The Dance of the Knights*), music that has possibly not been matched for sheer drama since it was written. It has gained notoriety as the theme tune to the television programme *The Apprentice* and is also the music to which the players from Sunderland Athletic Football Club run onto the pitch at home games.

RECOMMENDED RECORDING

Royal Philharmonic Orchestra; Vladimir Ashkenazy (conductor). Decca: 4360782.

CHART POSITION 47

Symphony No. 1 in D
Classical

Prokofiev was twenty-six when he composed his First Symphony, chiefly on holiday in the countryside. It received its premiere in St Petersburg in 1918 and Prokofiev had a very clear plan when it came to writing the work: 'I thought that if Haydn were alive today he would compose just as he did before, but at the same time would include something new in his manner of composition. I wanted to compose such a symphony: a symphony in the Classical style'.

Many musical historians cite Prokofiev's *Symphony No. 1* as evidence that he, rather than Stravinsky, is the true father of the movement known as 'neo-Classicalism':

namely, the twentieth-century modernists who wrote their own version of the music of the Classical period.

And yet Prokofiev seems to be showing his neo-Classical colours more as an exercise than because of any true belief in a movement; Stravinsky was writing 'Classical' music with the benefit of the hindsight of his position in the twentieth century. Prokofiev was more imagining himself back in the eighteenth century, and imagining what he would have produced then. The resulting blend of the styles of two eras has gained the work a lasting place in the repertoire, proving to be one of the most popular symphonies, for listeners and players alike.

RECOMMENDED RECORDING
St Paul Chamber Orchestra; Hugh Wolff (conductor). Warner: 2564694520.

CHART POSITION 195

Lieutenant Kijé

Not long before Prokofiev started the lengthy negotiations that were the precursor to his writing *Romeo and Juliet*, he had taken on a job composing the music for a new film. It was directed by Aleksandr Faintsimmer (who would go on to direct *The Gadfly*) and represented an early break for the future 'People's Artist of the USSR, 1977', the comic actor Erast Garin. Nowadays, the film, which is known in the USA as *The Czar Wants to Sleep*, rarely troubles the silver screen. However, its score – and the subsequently rescued suite – have become firm favourites. The most notable success has been for the *Troika* (4th movement), which has become a seasonal favourite. So much so, in fact, that it was borrowed by rocker Greg Lake (he of Emerson, Lake and Palmer) for his Christmas classic *'I Believe in Father Christmas'*. Prokofiev produced two different versions of the suite,

one with baritone soloist, the other with saxophone. It was to prove to be one of the composer's last Paris premieres before his return to the USSR in 1936.

RECOMMENDED RECORDING
Berlin Philharmonic Orchestra; Seiji Ozawa (conductor). Deutsche Grammophon: 4637612.

CHART POSITION 293

GIACOMO PUCCINI
(1858–1924)

Madama Butterfly

Hundreds of operas have tragedy at their core, but you would be hard pushed to find a more perfect example of this theme expressed in music than Puccini's masterful opera *Madama Butterfly*. It was a personal favourite of the composer, too; he once described it as 'the most felt and most expressive opera that I have conceived'.

Madama Butterfly was both written at, and set during, the start of the twentieth century. But while Puccini wrote the opera in Italy, the location for the action is Japan. The opera tells the tale of the teenage geisha Cio-Cio San and her doomed marriage to Pinkerton, an American naval lieutenant. Puccini skilfully imbues the score with a mix of East and West. Highlights include the glorious love duet that falls at the end of Act I and the ravishing and pathos-filled soprano solo *'Un Bel Di'* ('One Fine Day'), in which Butterfly steadfastly sings of her belief that Pinkerton will return to her.

Pinkerton does indeed return – but not to Butterfly. Instead, he is cruelly found to be in the company of his new, American wife. From this point on, Puccini focuses ever deeper on heartache, culminating in Butterfly committing suicide. *Madama Butterfly*: a tragic, troubling and pain-filled opera – but a glorious one at that.

RECOMMENDED RECORDING

Angela Gheorghiu (soprano) as Cio-Cio San; Jonas Kaufmann (tenor) as Pinkerton; Orchestra and Chorus of the National Academy of St Cecilia; Antonio Pappano (conductor). EMI Classics: 26418728.

CHART POSITION 61

La bohème

It's Christmas Eve in Paris. A bunch of friends are hanging out together in their flat – among them, a young poet, Rodolfo, and his friend Marcello, a painter. Everyone is laid-back and happy; even their landlord is willing to join them for a glass of something fruity. In this most blissful of settings, what could possibly go wrong? Quite a lot, as it happens. After all, this is opera – a genre of regular fairy-tale beginnings but of all-too-frequent nightmare endings.

La bohème tells the story of Rodolfo and his love for Mimi, a young seamstress whom he meets that Christmas Eve night. Over the course of a couple of hours, Puccini treats us to some of the most ravishing and famous opera arias in the world: among them, the tenor solo *'Che gelida manina'* ('Your tiny hand is frozen') and *'Sì, mi chiamano Mimì'* ('Yes, they call me Mimi'). The highlight for many, though, is the sumptuous Act I duet *'O soave fanciulla'* ('O lovely maid in the moonlight') – a shimmering

concoction of lush orchestration and enrapturing vocal melodies.

Unsurprisingly, *La bohème* doesn't end well. Marcello gets together with his old flame Musetta, only then to discover that Mimi is dying. She passes away in Rodolfo's arms and he is left utterly inconsolable. Romantic opera is certainly never very cheerful; but in the hands of Puccini, it's always exquisitely beautiful.

RECOMMENDED RECORDING

Anna Netrebko (soprano) as Mimì; Rolando Villazón (tenor) as Rodolfo; Boaz Daniel (baritone) as Schaunard; Bavarian Radio Symphony Orchestra and Chorus; Children's Choir of the Gartnerplatz State Theatre; Bertrand de Billy (conductor). Deutsche Grammophon: 4776600.

CHART POSITION 68

Tosca

Puccini's approach to opera was, almost overwhelmingly, to focus on the tragic, the forsaken and the painful. And while we should therefore never expect to experience a kind of light relief through the subject matter he chooses, it's fair to say that in nearly all of his operas, there are moments of jollity or even farce.

The one exception, though, is *Tosca*. Here is an opera that is almost universally dark and brooding, with tragedy not just dealt with at its conclusion but running like a thread throughout. Right from the start, Puccini makes this abundantly clear: three invasive, arresting chords herald the arrival of the evil Scarpia, the man who seeks sexual gratification with our hero, Tosca, above all else.

Tosca's real love is Cavaradossi, who sings of her complete beauty in the wonderful tenor aria *'Recondita armonia'* ('O hidden harmony'). Tosca's heartbreaking aria *'Vissi d'arte'* ('I have lived for art') is similarly exquisite – and all the more moving when heard in the context of the whole opera. It is at this point that she has just volunteered to give up her own life for the sake of saving Cavaradossi.

The opera ends with the unnecessary death of both lovers, and the beauty of the music seems to belie the horror of what is taking place on the stage. It is surely impossible to experience *Tosca* and yet not be greatly moved.

RECOMMENDED RECORDING

Plácido Domingo (tenor) as Cavaradossi; Leontyne Price (soprano) as Tosca; Sherrill Milnes (baritone) as Scarpia; John Alldis Choir; New Philharmonia Orchestra; Zubin Mehta (conductor). RCA: 82876 707832.

CHART POSITION 138

Turandot

Puccini and Italia 90 are forever subliminally linked in the minds of millions of football fans. It was in Rome that year that Luciano Pavarotti, José Carreras and Plácido Domingo gathered for what was to become one of the most influential classical music concerts of the twentieth century. All sorts of opera arias and Neapolitan songs were performed, but it was Puccini's *'Nessun dorma'* from his opera *Turandot*, sung by the terrific trio, that really captured people's hearts. The commercial success of The Three Tenors – and of Pavarotti in particular – paved the way for a resurgence of interest in classical music in the UK.

Turandot was an absolutely serious opera, dealing with such themes as love, loss and tragedy. It's somewhat surprising that it was composed as late as 1926, given that the opera inhabits an altogether Romantic sound-

world. The plot is bizarre, even by operatic standards, focusing on the compulsory execution of any potential husbands of Princess Turandot who fail to answer three riddles correctly. Nowadays, very few people remember the intricacies of *Turandot*'s storyline. But ask pretty much any man or woman in the street, and they will be able to sing a few bars from *'Nessun dorma'*.

RECOMMENDED RECORDING

Luciano Pavarotti (tenor) as Calaf; Joan Sutherland (soprano) as Turandot; Peter Pears (tenor) as Altoum; John Alldis Choir; Wandsworth Boys Choir; London Philharmonic Orchestra; Zubin Mehta (conductor). Decca: 4739972.

CHART POSITION 156

Gianni Schicchi

As with all Puccini, passions run high in *Gianni Schicchi*. This 1918 opera depicts the life of a scheming yet ingenious peasant, who tries to cash in on an old man's vulnerability by changing his will and securing a pay-off for his daughter's wedding. And, while it would be easy to blame the peasant entirely, Puccini uses the opera's most famous aria to make it abundantly clear that his daughter should arguably shoulder some of the responsibility, too.

The glorious *'O mio babbino caro'* ('O my beloved papa') is sung by the young Lauretta as she pleads with her father to enable her to get hitched to Rinuccio, the love of her life. This isn't just any old request, though: Lauretta makes it perfectly clear that if Dad doesn't come up trumps, she'll commit suicide.

Unlike earlier operas – most notably, *Madama Butterfly* – Puccini chose not to set Gianni Schicchi in contemporary society but instead to base it in Florence at the turn of the thirteenth century. It's also a one-act

Giacomo Puccini
1858-1924

'I shall feel the story as an Italian, with desperate passion.'

GIACOMO PUCCINI

Puccini took the opera baton from Verdi and ran with it, writing hit aria after hit aria. *La bohème*, *Tosca* and *Madama Butterfly* are among the most performed operas today. He also penned the aria that, for many people, simply is opera – *'Nessun dorma'* from *Turandot*. This aria, made famous by The Three Tenors at the 1990 World Cup Finals in Italy, brought classical music into millions of people's lives.

The Puccini family was a musical one, with the three generations before Giacomo on his father's side all working in music. After a spell as a church organist, he became enthralled by opera when he saw a performance of Verdi's *Aida*. He is regarded as being one of the finest proponents of *verismo* opera, where the subject matter is both gritty and realistic – often causing a scandal at the time.

DID YOU KNOW?

Although we know him as Giacomo Puccini, this Italian composer had no less than five middle names. Just imagine being called Giacomo Antonio Domenico Michele Secondo Maria Puccini!

Whenever Puccini came to London, he always liked to stay at the Savoy, savouring the luxury. On one occasion, in the summer of 1911, he availed himself of the in-house barber, only to find himself sitting in a chair next to Guglielmo Marconi, a fellow Italian and the pioneer of radio broadcasting.

Right at the end of *Tosca*, the eponymous heroine meets a rather sudden end by jumping from the parapet of a prison, moments after her lover Mario has met his death at the hands of a firing squad. Usually, there's a mattress back stage to lessen the impact of the singer's fall. On more than one occasion, the tragedy has turned to hilarity as the heroine hurls herself off the parapet, only to bounce back into the audience's view.

Puccini himself died before he could finish writing his opera *Turandot*. Another composer wrote the ending. At the premiere, the conductor Arturo Toscanini stopped the orchestra playing exactly at the point where Puccini stopped composing, turned to the audience and said: 'Here, death triumphed over art.'

opera, a form that was quite the rage at the time, Pietro Mascagni having received great critical acclaim for his *Cavalleria rusticana*.

RECOMMENDED RECORDING

Angela Gheorghiu (soprano) as Lauretta; José van Dam (bass-baritone) as Gianni Schicchi; Roberto Alagna (tenor) as Rinuccio; London Symphony Orchestra; Antonio Pappano (conductor). EMI Classics: CDS 5565872.

CHART POSITION 185

HENRY PURCELL
(1659–1695)

Dido and Aeneas

The English composer John Blow produced his opera *Venus and Adonis*, which was partly based on Ovid's *Metamorphoses*, with a text by Aphra Behn, at the court of Charles II. Henry Purcell was almost certainly sitting in the audience taking it all in and he was clearly inspired by the work. He substituted Virgil for Ovid and the *Aeneid* for *Metamorphoses*. Nahum Tate, rather than Aphra Behn, wrote the text. And over the court of Charles II, he favoured the unlikely venue of Josias Priest's Boarding School for Girls, in Chelsea.

Despite its seemingly inauspicious start in life, Purcell's opera *Dido and Aeneas* has come to be seen as the first great English opera, indeed arguably the greatest English opera of all time.

As well as a corking overture and some great operatic moments, only slightly dulled by Tate's occasionally ditty-esque words, Purcell hits the operatic jackpot in terms of a tune at the moment Dido dies. '*When I am laid in earth*', is an aria of melancholic beauty perhaps unsurpassed in all opera, let alone those written by English composers.

RECOMMENDED RECORDING

Emma Kirkby (soprano) as Dido; David Thomas (tenor) as Aeneas; Judith Nelson (mezzo-soprano) as Sorceress; Taverner Choir and Players; Andrew Parrott (conductor). Chandos: CHAN0521.

CHART POSITION 210

R

SERGEI RACHMANINOV
(1873–1943)

Piano Concerto No. 2 in C minor

Rachmaninov's *Piano Concerto No. 2* is often described as the greatest piano concerto ever written. It's certainly the most popular, judging by the thousands of votes it receives every year in the Classic FM Hall of Fame – enough to make it a regular No. 1 since 1996 in our annual charts and the overall No. 1 in the aggregated chart on which we've based this book. So it's easy to presume that this was the work of an assured, confident composer, whereas the truth was very different.

The premiere of Rachmaninov's *Symphony No. 1* in 1897 was an absolute, unmitigated disaster. The critics tore the work apart and left Rachmaninov feeling personally bruised and dejected. So bad was the work's reception that the composer retreated into an abyss of depression, apparently needing to undergo hypnosis to conquer the problem. It was in

the shadow of this experience that he wrote his *Piano Concerto No. 2* in 1900. This time, the critics were enthralled. Glorious melody after glorious melody flowed from the keyboard; the dialogue between orchestra and soloist was divine; and Rachmaninov undoubtedly had a hit on his hands.

If, when listening to the sublime second movement, you think you might have heard the tune somewhere else before, take a listen to the power ballad *'All By Myself'*. The song was based on Rachmaninov's melody.

RECOMMENDED RECORDING
Stephen Hough (piano); Dallas Symphony Orchestra; Andrew Litton (conductor). Hyperion: CDA 675012.
CHART POSITION 1

Symphony No. 2 in E minor

The immediacy of the romance in Rachmaninov's music is probably the greatest reason for its widespread and continued appeal. Very few composers manage so instantly to grab the attention of their listeners, transporting them to another place in the space of a few bars of music. And in Rachmaninov's

Sergei Rachmaninov

1873-1943

'I feel like a ghost wandering in a world grown alien. I cannot cast out the old way of writing and I cannot acquire the new.'

SERGEI RACHMANINOV

Rachmaninov was one of those annoying people who wasn't brilliant at just one thing – he was top of the pile in three different areas. Today, we remember him as a composer, but in his day he was a fine conductor and magnificent concert pianist. He was already well known as a performer when he moved to America, but once he had made the United States his home, his international superstardom became truly stratospheric. He made enough money to build a house in Los Angeles that was an exact replica of his original home back in Moscow.

Rachmaninov's *Piano Concerto No. 2* was voted No. 1 in the Classic FM Hall of Fame for five years running. When we combined together the chart positions for the first fifteen years of the chart, the work came out on top overall as the nation's favourite piece of classical music.

DID YOU KNOW?

Rachmaninov was a musical giant, and something of a physical one, too. He stood at over six feet tall and had enormous hands – very useful for performing his own music.

He's known for having one of the largest pairs of hands in classical music, which is why some of his piano pieces are fiendishly difficult for less well-endowed performers. He could stretch over twelve piano keys from the tip of his little finger to the tip of his thumb. That's around four keys more than average.

Rachmaninov was once giving a recital in New York with fellow composer Fritz Kreisler. The former was on the piano and the latter on the violin. Kreisler was in a muddle about where he'd got to in the music. Panic-stricken, he whispered to Rachmaninov, 'Where are we?' The whispered reply came back from Rachmaninov: 'Carnegie Hall'.

Despite his success, Rachmaninov seldom smiled in the photographs he left behind. Tall and severe, he was once dubbed a 'six-foot scowl'. He did, however, have a passion for cars (and later speedboats). He was the first in his neighbourhood to have an automobile.

case, nowhere is this better demonstrated than in the third movement of this, his *Symphony No. 2*.

The work was composed not in Russia but in Dresden, where Rachmaninov and his family lived for the best part of four years from 1906. Dating from 1908, writing his *Symphony No. 2* was a daunting affair for the composer. Despite critical acclaim for a number of recently premiered works, the wounds caused by the critical mauling of his *Symphony No. 1* at the turn of the century had far from healed completely. Would the follow-up, Rachmaninov wondered, be treated with equal derision?

Thankfully, the answer was a resounding 'no!' The work is evidently not a simple or easy listen, not least because, at an hour in length, it requires considerable concentration. It also has a sombre, even fatalistic tone in its opening movement. But the unbridled romance of that third movement, combined with a thrilling finale, confirms the work as one of the most popular Rachmaninov ever composed.

RECOMMENDED RECORDING
London Symphony Orchestra; Valery Gergiev (conductor). LSO Live: LSO0677.
CHART POSITION 20

Rhapsody on a Theme of Paganini

This piano concerto-like work was the 1934 equivalent of sampling a pop song. Had he lived to hear it, the nineteenth-century Italian composer Niccolò Paganini would surely have been flattered to discover that Rachmaninov, of all people, had chosen his *Caprice No. 24* for solo violin as the inspiration for an ingenious theme and variations for piano and orchestra.

Rachmaninov wasn't the first composer to have written something new in response to

the famous caprice: Brahms had done the same thing in the 1860s with his *Variations on a Theme of Paganini* for solo piano. But today it's Rachmaninov's take on this sprightly melody that is far and away the favourite.

To appreciate the inventiveness of the work, it needs to be listened to from start to finish. Across a twenty-minute period, Rachmaninov moulds the main theme into all sorts of musical styles and formations. And of all the variations, it's *No. 18* (the *Andante cantabile*) that sings and soars above any other.

Rachmaninov was himself an outstanding pianist, as is borne out by his very own recording of the *Rhapsody on a Theme of Paganini*, which is still available today.

RECOMMENDED RECORDING
Nikolai Lugansky (piano); City of Birmingham Symphony Orchestra; Sakari Oramo (conductor). Warner: 2564 636752.
CHART POSITION 31

Piano Concerto No. 3 in D minor

Rachmaninov's very large hands certainly came in useful when performing this, the most technically challenging of all the composer's four piano concertos. Until 1996, the concerto was largely eclipsed by its older sibling, the famous *Piano Concerto No. 2* – but the gap between the two narrowed with the release of the film *Shine*. The movie told the true story of the Australian concert pianist David Helfgott, who suffered a mental breakdown and abandoned his career for many years. 'Rach 3', as it's often referred to by pianists, is used powerfully on the soundtrack and the Oscar-winning success of the film ensured a new audience for this muscular, Romantic work.

Rachmaninov composed the concerto in 1909 – a full nine years after the premiere of his *Piano Concerto No. 2*. The Third is grander, fuller, and more expansive in tone and style – with the soloist stretched to the very limits of his or her ability. The soloist whom Rachmaninov intended to premiere the piece was his friend Josef Hofmann; curiously, though, Hofmann never actually performed it, apparently declaring that the work was not right for him.

This three-movement masterpiece sits alongside Brahms's *Piano Concerto No. 2* as the most demanding of all Romantic concertos. It's also one of the most electrifying.

RECOMMENDED RECORDING

Simon Trpčeski (piano); Royal Liverpool Philharmonic Orchestra; Vasily Petrenko (conductor). Avie: 2192.

CHART POSITION 36

Piano Concerto No. 1 in F sharp minor

Rachmaninov said of himself, 'I am a Russian composer and the land of my birth has influenced my temperament and outlook.' He wrote his *Piano Concerto No. 1* when he was still a teenager. It's been criticised by some as too derivative, borrowing from the likes of Grieg and Tchaikovsky but, considering that the young Russian had barely reached adulthood when he composed it, it seems churlish to become overly critical.

The work begins with unabashed showmanship, as a vehicle for Rachmaninov's own accomplished skill at the piano. The young

composer seems only too keen to dazzle with virtuoso passages in the outer movements, while the introspective *Andante cantabile* remains one of his most beautiful yet relatively unappreciated melodies.

As you listen to the concerto, you can't help but hear the emergence of all the musical skills that were truly to come to fruition in the *Piano Concerto No. 2*. Fiery keyboard passages, heart-wrenching tunes, and sumptuous orchestral accompaniment are all present here, yet came to the fore only some ten years later when work began on Rachmaninov's second and most famous concerto.

This is a relatively playful work, sowing the seeds of a passionate musical intensity that was to burst forth over the years to come. It may be a slightly immature work – but it's still an astonishingly accomplished one at that.

RECOMMENDED RECORDING

Leif Ove Andsnes (piano); Berlin Philharmonic Orchestra; Antonio Pappano (conductor). EMI Classics: 4748132.

CHART POSITION 225

Vespers
All-Night Vigil

Any mention of Rachmaninov and thoughts tend to turn either to his extravagant, virtuosic piano concertos or to the Romantic lyricism of his symphonies. It's somewhat surprising, then, that this most heart-on-your-sleeve of composers decided to turn to the liturgy of the Russian Orthodox Church to compose a quiet, reflective and deeply moving set of vespers.

His *All-Night Vigil*, to give it its official title, was composed and premiered in 1915.

right Sergei Rachmaninov: Vespers: All-Night Vigil

Russia was in political turmoil at the time. The First World War had begun the previous year, Russia was committed to securing the eastern front of behalf of the Allies, and internally the country was still in a mess as a result of the Russian Revolution of 1905. It's not surprising that Rachmaninov was looking to write something more introspective than usual.

The composer had a deep and very personal religious faith, which he expresses beautifully through this unaccompanied set of choral vespers. They are separated into two parts: the evening Vespers and the morning Matins, both full of exquisitely rich harmonies. Rachmaninov followed the Church's tradition of basing ten of the fifteen sections on Russian chants, with the remaining five being more free-form. Those five were so similar to the other ten, though, that Rachmaninov himself described them as 'conscious counterfeits'.

RECOMMENDED RECORDING

Estonian Philharmonic Chamber Choir; Paul Hillier (conductor). Harmonia Mundi: HMU 807504.

CHART POSITION 263

JEAN-PHILIPPE RAMEAU
(1683–1764)

Les Indes galantes

Les Indes galantes is very much a product of its time. 'The Amorous Indies' of the title is thought to refer, in a 1730s context, to exotic lands: not specifically the Indies, but anywhere suitably remote and alien to its intended audience.

Rameau was fifty-three at the time of writing and not long engaged on his course to change the face of French opera. As a result, he was willing to tinker and tweak his works, to get them exactly right. First presented in 1735 with the help of his new found patron, the wonderfully named Alexandre Le Riche de La Poupelinière, it was reworked numerous times, with something changed or added on each occasion, in an attempt to get it just right. Taken alongside the operas that followed behind, *Castor et Pollux* and *Dardanus*, this was the making of Rameau, sealing his reputation.

The narrative for the opera seems rather strange now, with various smaller stories presented, one in each act (or *entrée*) all on the theme of love in unfamiliar climes.

RECOMMENDED RECORDING

Les Arts Florissants; William Christie (conductor). Harmonia Mundi: HMC901367/69.

CHART POSITION 284

MAURICE RAVEL
(1875–1937)

Boléro

On Valentine's Day in 1984, Jayne Torvill and Christopher Dean became the highest-scoring ice skaters of all time when they gained maximum points at the Winter Olympics in Sarajevo. Ravel's orchestral work *Boléro* will forever be synonymous with their gold-medal-winning victory. The same generation might also have observed its starring role in the Dudley Moore and Bo Derrick film *10*.

The history of this piece dates from 1928. Just before embarking on a tour of America, Ravel was commissioned by the Russian ballerina and dance impresario Ida Rubinstein to compose the music for a ballet, provisionally called *Fandango*. It was while on holiday in the French resort of Saint-Jean-de-Luz that Ravel first developed a Spanish-sounding melody that he couldn't get out of his head. And as anyone who's ever heard *Boléro* will know, Ravel certainly succeeded in ensuring that the insistent, repeated tune and undulating snare-drum rhythms are almost impossible to forget.

The composer was absolutely insistent that the tempo of *Boléro* should remain constant throughout its fifteen minutes. When the great conductor Arturo Toscanini sped the work up during a performance of it in 1930, Ravel took him to task about it afterwards.

RECOMMENDED RECORDING
Boston Symphony Orchestra; Seiji Ozawa (conductor). Deutsche Grammophon: 4158452.
CHART POSITION 80

Pavane pour une infante défunte

Ravel was a master of orchestration, as is borne out by his ever popular arrangement of Mussorgsky's famous set of piano pieces, *Pictures at an Exhibition*. But as his *Pavane pour une infante défunte* proves, the French composer was also a dab hand at reworking his own solo piano works for full orchestra.

The original piano version of the *Pavane* was composed in 1899 and dedicated to the Princesse Edmond de Polignac (otherwise known as Winnaretta Singer), a French-American musical patron who was also the daughter of the nineteenth-century sewing-machine magnate, Isaac Singer. The orchestral arrangement wasn't premiered for another eleven years.

The strikingly morose title of the work belies its actual inspiration: far from being about death, Ravel stated that 'when I put together the words that make up this title, my only thought was the pleasure of alliteration'. While it's literally true that the French should be translated as 'Pavane for a Dead Princess', Ravel was at pains to point out that it 'is not a funeral lament for a dead child, but rather an evocation of the pavane that might have been danced by such a little princess as painted by Velázquez'. His comments went largely unheard, though; even today, many believe the piece to have a quite different meaning from the one the composer intended.

RECOMMENDED RECORDING (ORIGINAL VERSION)
Angela Hewitt (piano). Hyperion: CDA 673412.
CHART POSITION 209

Piano Concerto in G

Ravel's *Piano Concerto in G* was always intended to be a frivolous work. In contrast to many of the concertos of his day, what Ravel was aiming to write was something light, fanciful and not inherently serious: 'in the spirit', as he said, 'of Mozart and Saint-Saëns'. It certainly wasn't composed in a throwaway manner, though. On the contrary, Ravel mulled over his ideas for the concerto for a full three years.

In 1928, the composer returned from his tour of America and visited Oxford, where he began to consider writing a piano concerto.

The process was rather stop–start: after the initial idea, it went on the back-burner in 1929, only for Ravel to then become distracted by the composition of his ingenious *Piano Concerto for the Left Hand*. In 1930, work on the G major Concerto resumed again – but he didn't finish it until 1931.

The light-hearted nature of the concerto is confirmed from the first sound we hear in the opening movement: a playful, percussive whip-crack. The work is jazz-tinged in the outer movements. In between, a slow movement of serene beauty confirms Ravel's status as a master of melody. 'That flowing phrase!' he apparently commented. 'How I worked over it bar by bar! It nearly killed me!'

RECOMMENDED RECORDING

Krystian Zimmerman (piano); London Symphony Orchestra; Pierre Boulez (conductor). Deutsche Grammophon: DG 4492132.

CHART POSITION 258

NIKOLAI RIMSKY-KORSAKOV
(1844–1908)

Scheherazade

The composer Rimsky-Korsakov, the fashion designer Katherine Hamnett and the American Indian chief's daughter Pocahontas all share a link to the Kent town of Gravesend. Hamnett was born there; Pocahontas died there (you can still see the statue), and Rimsky-Korsakov was stationed in the Thames estuary just off the town's coast. He was an officer in the Russian Navy, and it became his posting while he wrote part of his *Symphony No. 1*.

The anecdote is a good one, but Gravesend has no connection to this particular work, which dates from much later in Rimsky-Korsakov's life. By the time he came to write *Scheherazade*, he was out of the Navy in the conventional sense. Although, once his musical reputation had grown, officials created a special job for him – Inspector of Naval Bands – in order to keep him happy. He spent a good deal of time writing for a series of symphony concerts promoted by the musical philanthropist and publisher, Belyayev.

Despite there being 1001 nights in the original stories, Rimsky-Korsakov's *Scheherazade* has just four movements: *The Sea and Sinbad's Ship*; *The Tale of the Prince Kalender*; *The Young Prince and the Young Princess* (this is the big hit), and *The Festival at Baghdad – The Sea – The Shipwreck*.

RECOMMENDED RECORDING

Sergei Levitin (violin); Kirov Orchestra; Valery Gergiev (conductor). Philips: 4708402.

CHART POSITION 35

JOAQUÍN RODRIGO
(1902–1999)

Concierto de Aranjuez

For a work as seemingly Spanish as Rodrigo's *Concierto de Aranjuez*, it initially seems bizarre that many people's first encounter with it is forever linked to the fictional Yorkshire town of Grimley. But the concerto's use in the 1996 film *Brassed Off!* ensured that the love for this ever popular work became even more widespread. The miners affectionately referred

right Joaquín Rodrigo: Concierto de Aranjuez

to it as 'Orange Juice', after finding it rather challenging to pronounce 'Aranjuez'. Miles Davis had also been inspired by the *Concierto de Aranjuez*, adapting it for his 1960 album *Sketches of Spain*.

For the original root of the work, we need to take a journey to Madrid. As Rodrigo himself explained about this beautiful piece for guitar and orchestra, 'The *Concierto de Aranjuez* is named after the famous royal site on the shore of the River Tagus, not far from Madrid, along the road to Andalusia, and some perceive Goya's shadow in the notes of its music, full of melancholic emotion. Its music seems to bring to life the essence of an eighteenth-century court, where aristocratic distinction blends with popular culture. In its melody the perfume of magnolias lingers, the singing of birds and the gushing of fountains.'

RECOMMENDED RECORDING
Julian Bream (guitar); City of Birmingham Symphony Orchestra; Simon Rattle (conductor). EMI Classics: CDC 7546612.

CHART POSITION 24

Fantasia para un gentilhombre

Rodrigo was the twentieth century's most skilful exponent of writing for the guitar, as is amply proved by both the *Concierto de Aranjuez* and this, his *Fantasia para un gentilhombre*. It was, however, another composer to whom he looked for inspiration when composing

this particular piece. The seventeenth-century Spanish priest and musician Gaspar Sanz, who was also a fine guitar player, put together a sort of guitarists' manual in 1674. Given the not-so-catchy title of *Instrucción de música sobre la guitarra española*, it set out various dos and don'ts for guitar composition. Rodrigo was very open about the fact that Sanz's tome had inspired him to write his *Fantasia*.

This zesty, dance-filled concerto owes its success not just to Sanz, but to the inclusion of all sorts of Baroque forms, which many other composers of Rodrigo's day were disregarding. The Spanish dances of the *villano*, the *españoleta* and the *tarantella* all feature here, in a vividly depicted portrayal of musical sunshine. Rodrigo himself went blind at the age of three, but that never prevented him from composing intrinsically colourful music. On the contrary, he once commented, 'The loss of vision was the vehicle that took me down the road to music.'

RECOMMENDED RECORDING
John Williams (guitar); Philharmonia Orchestra; Louis Frémaux (conductor). Sony: M2K 44791.

CHART POSITION 299

GIOACHINO ROSSINI
(1792–1868)

The Thieving Magpie

Rossini's 1817 opera *The Thieving Magpie* received a rare boost in the British tabloid press when a judge claimed not to have heard of the footballer Paul 'Gazza' Gascoigne, musing, 'Is there not an opera called *Gazza Ladra?*' Well, this is that very work. It was a welcome, if fleeting, popular acknowledgement for what was allegedly the quickest stage work Rossini had ever produced. He was already legendary

TOP 10 BRITISH COMPOSERS		
1	Edward Elgar	*11 entries*
2	Ralph Vaughan Williams	*9 entries*
3	George Frideric Handel	*7 entries*
4	Karl Jenkins	*4 entries*
5	Frederick Delius	*3 entries*
6=	John Barry	*2 entries*
6=	Gerald Finzi	*2 entries*
6=	Hubert Parry	*2 entries*
6=	John Rutter	*2 entries*
6=	William Walton	*2 entries*

for the speed at which he could write an opera, once saying, 'Give me a laundry list, and I will set it to music.'

Quick, he may have been. But that didn't always mean that he delivered everything on time. The *Overture* to *The Thieving Magpie* was overdue and the opera's promoter reportedly had to lock Rossini in a room to force him to get it done. He is said to have thrown each sheet out of the window as it was finished in order that the copyists might get it to the orchestra on time. This overture is a perennial highlight, featuring a startling opening snare drum just to make sure that everyone is awake.

RECOMMENDED RECORDING

(Overture only) Atlanta Symphony Orchestra; Yoel Levi (conductor); Telarc: CD80334.

CHART POSITION 147

William Tell

After *William Tell* was premiered in 1829, Rossini decided to shut up shop. He didn't write any more opera for another thirty-nine years. That's one almighty long hush. Various reasons have been proffered for the silence: writer's block, fear of the younger generation of composers, even a love of cooking. In the end, it might all just have stemmed from the fact that he was the most successful opera composer in history and he wanted to enjoy life. And, luckily for him, he did.

Written as a part of his contract with the French government, *William Tell* went round the world. Just two months before Rossini died, he was able to be there when it celebrated its 500th performance at the Paris Opéra. Quite some achievement. Many have been blinded by the incredible *Overture*, allowing wonderful arias, such as *'Sombre forêt'* or the wily *'Sur la rive étrangère'*, to be overlooked. Both of these show Rossini's writing at its peak.

RECOMMENDED RECORDING
(Overture only) Philharmonia Orchestra; Carlo Maria Giulini (conductor).
EMI Classics: 2282812.
CHART POSITION 154

The Barber of Seville

It took a composer of singular confidence to agree to turn the Beaumarchais play *The Barber of Seville* into an opera in 1816. By then, opera audiences were very used to a setting by the Italian composer Paisiello. It's probably fair to say that his version was a much loved favourite with the famously loyal audience of the time.

When Rossini agreed to take on the project, he knew that he had to come up with something wonderful. By the end of the cold February night in Rome, where Rossini's work was premiered, it wasn't looking good. The composer had even taken care to call the opera something different – it premiered as *Almaviva, or the Useless Precaution*.

The evening had ended with the audience baying, 'Pai-si-ell-o, Pai-si-ell-o!' to a closed curtain. Somehow, though, Rossini turned it around. It's even possible that the audience reaction wasn't genuine and the first-nighters were a hired claque (a group of paid applauders prevalent in French opera houses at the time). Eventually retitled, Rossini's *Barber of Seville* saw Paisiello's version relegated to the dusty top shelves of the library of history. As well as possessing a simply stunning overture, the opera is a sheer delight throughout, with hit after hit, including *'Una voce poco fa'* and the *'Largo al factotum'*.

RECOMMENDED RECORDING
Maria Callas (soprano) as Rosina; Tito Gobbi (tenor) as Figaro; Philharmonia Orchestra and Chorus; Alceo Galliera (conductor).
EMI Classics: 4564442.
CHART POSITION 251

JOHN RUTTER
(B. 1945)

Requiem

John Rutter unashamedly composes instantly memorable tunes. In a world where so many composers believe music is no longer primarily about melody, Rutter stands out as someone who defiantly bucks that trend. Nowhere is it more evident than in his glorious *Requiem*. Composed in 1985, the work is reminiscent of the *Requiem* of Fauré for its simplicity, brevity and rich choral writing.

Rutter's music is popular around the world, particularly with choral societies. On both sides of the Atlantic, performances of his music can be heard week in, week out.

This seven-movement *Requiem* is traditional in its inspiration, using texts from the Requiem Mass and the Book of Common Prayer. The gloriously pure *Pie Jesu* is a real highlight – as is the *Requiem aeternam*, which opens the work. Still performed regularly across the world, Rutter's *Requiem* thoroughly earns its status as one of the most popular compositions of the last thirty years.

RECOMMENDED RECORDING
Caroline Ashton (soprano); Donna Dean (soprano); Patricia Forbes (soprano);

Cambridge Singers; City of London Sinfonia; John Rutter (conductor). Collegium: CSCD 504.

CHART POSITION 182

A Gaelic Blessing

Musicians are a mischievous lot – as evidenced by the nickname ascribed to John Rutter's *A Gaelic Blessing*. No sooner had it been composed in 1978 than it was being referred to as 'A Garlic Dressing'.

Rutter is known for his beautiful simplistic choral miniatures – and this is the finest example of them all. Commissioned by an American Methodist church, the lush string accompaniment perfectly matches the serene text Rutter chooses to set. Although the words are filled with religious significance, it would be fair to expect the composer himself to hold deep religious beliefs. Rutter, however, describes himself as 'an agnostic supporter of the Christian faith'.

Lasting under two minutes, *A Gaelic Blessing* is an enduring popular choice at weddings, christenings and funerals – not only for the deeply comforting words but for the equally tranquil and sensitive music Rutter sets them to.

RECOMMENDED RECORDING

Polyphony (choir); Bournemouth Sinfonietta; Stephen Layton (conductor). Classic FM: CFMCD 53

CHART POSITION 267

Symphony No. 3 in C minor
Organ Symphony

Perhaps history has misted over the pathway to a true understanding of Camille Saint-Saëns. To most of us, now, he is but a composer. In his day, however, he was so much more. Indeed, so much more that even his contemporaries found him hard to categorise. Liszt, for example, once called him 'the greatest organist in the world', but Saint-Saëns himself knew this side of him had to compete with the conducting, composing, mathematics, philosophy and astronomy. Whatever the subject, it seemed that Saint-Saëns was an expert at it.

His *Symphony No. 3* is probably best understood as a 'symphony with added organ', because only two of its four movements feature the instrument. It's a magnificent work, with the composer saying he was writing to his limits: 'I gave everything to it I was able to give. What I have accomplished here, I will never achieve again.' Strong stuff, but you can see what he means. The Royal Philharmonic Society, here in the UK, commissioned the work and Saint-Saëns came over to conduct its premiere at the old St James's Hall (now the site of the Le Meridien Hotel, in London's Piccadilly).

RECOMMENDED RECORDING

Michael Matthes (organ); Bastille Opera Orchestra; Myung-Whun Chung (conductor). Deutsche Grammophon: 4358542.

CHART POSITION 13

Carnival of the Animals

As far as Saint-Saëns is concerned, the two big works of 1886 were the *Organ Symphony* and the *Carnival of the Animals*. However, at the time, the public would have known only of the one. Saint-Saëns premiered his 'grand zoological fantasy' privately. It was written as a bit of fun for friends, around carnival time, which was early in the year in 1880s Paris. One of the surviving traditions from that time is the *promenade du boeuf gras* ('the procession of

Camille Saint-Saëns
1835-1921

'There is nothing more difficult than talking about music.'

CAMILLE SAINT-SAËNS

To say that Saint-Saëns was a clever boy is an understatement. This book is full of child stars, but he was probably the most prodigious of the lot, being hailed as France's answer to none other than Wolfgang Amadeus Mozart.

The young Saint-Saëns could read, write and play tunes on the piano at the age of just two. By the time he was seven years old, he was something of an expert on lepidoptera (butterflies to us mere mortals).

After studying at the Paris Conservatoire, Saint-Saëns grew into a fine pianist and organist and became a highly influential figure in the world of the arts in France. He composed elegant, tuneful music and did a good deal to promote the interests of French composers as a whole, founding the country's National School of Music in 1871. He could count the young Fauré

DID YOU KNOW?

Saint-Saëns was a proudly nationalistic composer. Together with Fauré, he established the Société Nationale de Musique, which existed solely to promote French music.

as a pupil and the likes of Gounod, Rossini, Berlioz and Liszt among the big-name composers who admired his writing and his playing.

His output included symphonies, concertos, organ music, operas and songs. He was also something of a specialist in writing chamber music for unorthodox groupings of instruments.

Towards the end of his life, Saint-Saëns undertook a triumphant tour of America, but gradually he found that his style of composition was no longer regarded as being en vogue by the Parisian chattering classes. In some ways this was unsurprising because Saint-Saëns lived to such a ripe old age that he saw classical music develop from the Romantic period into its far more modern-sounding incarnation after the First World War. He is buried in the same Paris cemetery as his fellow French composers Chabrier and Auric, as well as the Belgian-born and then French-nationalised César Franck.

the fat ox'), which signals the beginning of the end of the whole party season.

So it's easy to understand where Saint-Saëns found his inspiration for his *Carnival of the Animals*. His great friend Liszt, by then pretty ill, begged him to perform the new work again, which he did, but thereafter issued strict instructions that only *The Swan* could see the light of day again until he was dead and gone.

So, it was another thirty-five years until it was heard again, receiving its first premiere just two months after he died.

RECOMMENDED RECORDING
Soloists of the Orchestral Ensemble of Paris. Mirare: MIR 108.
CHART POSITION 109

Danse Macabre

Just like a philosopher, a composer usually, at some point, tackles the big philosophical issues in his music. Death is up there on most composers' radars as a worthy inspiration. Saint-Saëns happened on the subject in the early 1870s, originally setting to music a strange, art-house poem by Henri Cazalis, which has the first line 'Zig, zig, zig, Death in Cadence'. Originally it was for voice and piano but, thankfully, Saint-Saëns reworked it a couple of years later, substituting a violin for the voice and adding the full orchestra. When it was premiered at one of the Parisian Châtelet concerts (these took place in the Théâtre du Châtelet) it was immediately encored in full. Since then, it has remained one of Saint-Saëns's most popular pieces, with television providing endless opportunities to hear it again in theme tunes.

There is a complete programmatic story to the *Danse Macabre*, with the violin playing

---

left Camille Saint-Saëns: Danse Macabre

Death himself and the music starting at midnight – hence the twelve opening notes. However, it also very easy to simply listen to the music and to enjoy it in its own right.

RECOMMENDED RECORDING
Orchestre de Paris; Daniel Barenboim (conductor). Deutsche Grammophon: DG 4158472.
CHART POSITION 113

Samson and Delilah

It's easy to forget the problems there might have been in bringing an opera such as *Samson and Delilah* to the stage. First, there were the various challenges of matching the composer and librettist. Then, there was the need to find a suitable theatre (Saint-Saëns's good friend Liszt was instrumental in this instance, leaning on old colleagues in Weimar). Next, you needed to think about quite how you depict the destruction of the holy temple without actually destroying the opera house. And after all that, there was the little matter of censorship, because the subject is biblical and the powers-that-be were very nervy about letting it on stage at all.

When it was due to transfer to London's Covent Garden, the Lord Chamberlain slapped a ban on the whole opera, stopping all but concert performances until 1909 – some thirty years after its original Weimar run. So, English audiences were deprived of seeing, in their fully staged glory, some of the most beautiful moments in French opera and, indeed, Saint-Saëns's only regularly performed stage work.

This opera contains the sumptuous *Bacchanale* and arguably the most beautiful tune ever written for a mezzo, '*Mon cœur s'ouvre à ta Voix*' ('Softly awakes my heart').

RECOMMENDED RECORDING
José Cura (tenor) as Samson; Olga Borodina

(mezzo-soprano) as Delilah; London Symphony Orchestra and Chorus; Colin Davis (conductor). Erato: 3984247562.
CHART POSITION 157

ERIK SATIE
(1866–1925)

Gymnopédies

Satie would, without doubt, come top of any list of eccentric composers. After all, can you imagine anyone else writing a set of *Flabby Preludes for a Dog* or *Three Pieces in the Shape of a Pear*?

His three dream-like, sparse *Gymnopédies* were composed in 1888 and named after an ancient Greek rite enacted by groups of naked youths. Consequently, the set's publication only served to cement Satie's status as the musical pin-up boy of Bohemian Paris in the late nineteenth century.

Piano music was Satie's first love: he started his compositional career by writing for the instrument, and would return to it again and again. In the *Gymnopédies*, there's a wonderful sense of musical distillation: no note is extraneous; nothing is rushed; and it's almost impossible to hear them and not feel relaxed afterwards. Satie was ahead of his time with his attitudes towards the way in which classical music should be used: he coined the term 'furniture music' for pieces that could be played amid the general hubbub of everyday life, in restaurants and homes, without the need for sole concentration on the music itself.

Well over a century later, the *Gymnopédies* are frequently used in this way. They were a labour of love – but one that was supremely worthwhile.

RECOMMENDED RECORDING
Pascal Rogé (piano). Decca: 4102202.
CHART POSITION 122

FRANZ SCHUBERT
(1797–1828)

Piano Quintet in A
Trout

Now, this one gets a little complicated. Tracing the development of this piece can feel like being in a scene from the film *Airplane!*, where one character is called 'Over', another 'Roger' and someone else 'Victor'. Schubert wrote the original 'Trout' song (*'Die Forelle'*). Schubart (Christian Schubart, a German poet) wrote the original lyrics. Then Schubert wrote a *Trout Quintet*, without Schubart's help, different from the song, using the Schubert tune but not the Schubart lyrics. Clear?

The song was the work of the composer as a twenty-year-old; the quintet is from five years later. The fourth of the quintet's five moments is essentially a set of variations on the composer's own tune and has become one of the favourite moments in Schubert's output. We have one Sylvester Paumgartner to thank for this. He was an amateur cellist whom Schubert met while on his travels with a friend in the Steyr region of Austria (not far from Linz). Paumgartner not only suggested the quintet, but he also suggested that one of the movements might be based on *The Trout*.

RECOMMENDED RECORDING
Renaud Capuçon (violin); Gautier Capuçon (cello); Gerard Caussé (viola); Alois Posch (double-bass); Frank Braley (piano).
Virgin: 5455632.
CHART POSITION 65

---

right Franz Schubert: Piano Quintet in A, Trout

Franz Schubert
1797-1828

'Schubert's life was one of inner, spiritual thought, and was seldom expressed in words but almost entirely in music.'

FRANZ ECKEL

The son of a Viennese schoolmaster, the young Franz learned the musical basics from his father. The composer Salieri (he of not actually murdering Mozart fame) talent-spotted Schubert when he was just seven; he was packed off to boarding school soon after. There he sang in the choir, played violin in the orchestra and learned musical theory from Mr Salieri himself.

On leaving school, Schubert became a teacher, but by the time he was twenty years old, he took up composing as a full-time job. His work rate was simply astounding. Despite dying at the age of thirty-one, he composed more than six hundred different songs (or, as he would have said, *Lieder*).

Schubert also found time for more or less nine symphonies (one of them was unfinished), eleven operas and around four hundred other pieces. All of this was completed in a composing career that

DID YOU KNOW?

Schubert was greatly influenced by the life and the music of Beethoven. At the great German composer's funeral, Schubert was one of the torch-bearers.

lasted for just eighteen years. In 1815 alone, he wrote 140 songs – including eight in one day in October – along with a symphony, two Masses and assorted other works. He also liked to have fun and, in his day, he was famous for his musical parties known as *Schubertiads*.

Schubert stood only five foot one in his stockinged feet. This diminutive frame, added to his rather plump body, earned him the nickname *Schwammerl* among his friends. This translates as 'little mushroom'. He was also a notoriously bad timekeeper. His friends' letters are strewn with references to him being late or not showing up at all.

He contracted syphilis in 1822 and became seriously ill, although he carried on composing with the same unrelenting rate of output, writing his beautiful song-cycle *Die Winterreise* ('The Winter Journey') towards the end of his life.

String Quintet in C

Not everything a great composer writes is always great music. Everyone has a hit rate and these vary from genius to genius. Even by Schubert's own standards, though, the *Adagio* from the String Quintet in C must have made him realise he had a corker on his hands.

His attempts to pitch it to his publisher were, nevertheless, gentle to say the least: 'Finally I have written a quintet for 2 violins, 1 viola, and 2 violoncello ... The quintet rehearsal will only begin in the next few days. Should any of these compositions by any chance commend themselves to you, please let me know.'

Within a couple of months, Schubert was dead – and this posthumously published work was revealed for the masterpiece it was. As his entreaty revealed, Schubert had tinkered with the standard setting of a string quintet to include an extra cello.

Although it had been done before, it's a wonderful way of adding extra richness to proceedings. Match this with some of Schubert's most profound and restrained writing and it was a recipe for a sure-fire hit.

With the extra cello, you tend to get nice pairings featuring an extra 'celebrity' cellist, or ensembles that come together specifically to perform this piece.

RECOMMENDED RECORDING
Mstislav Rostropovich (cello); Melos Quartet. Deutsche Grammophon: 4776357.
CHART POSITION 93

Symphony No. 9 in C
Great

Few Schubert fiends will disagree with this symphony's nickname. Nevertheless, it was applied originally in order simply to distinguish it from another of his symphonies, which was also in the key of C major. As a result, the other one *(Symphony No. 6)* is landed with the epithet *The Little C*, something that must have occasionally led to confusion of a maritime nature.

Schubert's *Symphony No. 9* was referred to in his own letters as 'a grand symphony', and concert-goers tend to agree that it is almost an hour of pure musical majesty. It was written just three years before the composer died, sketched over what must have felt like almost a born-again summer. His ill-health had suddenly and unexpectedly gone into remission; throughout 1825, when the *Great* was written, Schubert appeared to be completely well. Cue the huge, grand symphony, full of fresh life – arguably more powerful than any of his others. Here was a man who, sadly wrongly, thought he was cured. The fourth movement *Allegro vivace* is simply breathtaking, in the right hands.

RECOMMENDED RECORDING
Berlin Philharmonic Orchestra; Simon Rattle (conductor). EMI Classics: 3393822.
CHART POSITION 132

Symphony No. 5 in B flat

Schubert began both a law degree and his *Symphony No. 5* in the same year. In this instance at least, it was the degree rather than the music that would remain unfinished. Once he had dropped out of studying and taken his washing back home, he fell in with the 'right' set: a chap called Schober, who was a one-man larger-than-life walking arts movement. And so it was that we came to have Schubert the composer, not the legal pen-pusher. Thank goodness.

This is the perfect entry level for anyone to whom you want to introduce Schubert with the intention of making sure that they want to hear more. It's fresh, it's fairly light and it's just bursting with tunes, in every nook and cranny. And that fits with exactly where Schubert was in life when he wrote it. At nineteen, this might well have been the piece that caused him to break off from his planned law degree. This symphony is a real product of its time – it could almost be by Mozart, given its youthful exuberance.

RECOMMENDED RECORDING
Royal Concertgebouw Orchestra; Nikolaus Harnoncourt (conductor). Teldec: 2564688316.
CHART POSITION 167

Symphony No. 8 in B minor
Unfinished

Known to Schubert's fellow Austrians as the *Unvollendete* ('Unfinished'), it might easily have been the *Unbekannt* ('Unknown') were it not for fate. A full thirty-seven years after Schubert's death, the world counted Schubert's symphonies on just eight fingers, rather than nine.

Then, in a case reminiscent of a rediscovered Picasso, a seventy-six-year-old man, possibly in the belief that he was on his way out, came forward to a Viennese conductor with the astonishing news that he had a Schubert symphony. Well, part of one. Schubert had sent it to him, some forty-three years earlier.

Why had he not come forward before? Was it anything to do with the fact that the music was incomplete with evidence of pages simply having been ripped out? It is still as much of an enigma as anything Elgar ever came up with. Schubert had some six years of his life remaining after he started working on the piece, but he never completed it. One theory, still argued over today, is that the missing fourth movement is alive and well – known now as the *Entr'acte* from Schubert's incidental music to the play *Rosamunde*. Who knows?

RECOMMENDED RECORDING
Royal Concertgebouw Orchestra; Nikolaus Harnoncourt (conductor). Teldec: 2564688316.
CHART POSITION 181

Ave Maria

It's a beautiful irony that the nation's favourite settings of the *Ave Maria* are composed by Bach and Schubert. And yet neither of them actually wrote an *Ave Maria*. The version we think of as being by Bach was assembled by Gounod 109 years after Johann Sebastian had begun pushing up the daisies. Schubert's music was actually written to the words of *The Lady of the Lake*, by Sir Walter Scott but translated into German and called 'Ellen's Third Song'. It was written as part of a set of Scott songs when the composer was twenty-eight and contains the words 'Ave Maria', but only in reference to the prayer itself.

Schubert himself did at least write about the Maria references: 'My new songs from Scott's *Lady of the Lake* especially had much success. They also wondered greatly at my piety, which I expressed in a hymn to the Holy Virgin and which, it appears, grips every soul and turns it to devotion.' So, with its new words, Schubert's tune became a perennial favourite, recorded by everyone from Pavarotti to Perry Como. Renée Fleming sings a definitive version on her Schubert *Lieder* album. Bryn Terfel has an interesting arrangement on his album *Bryn*, alongside the Norwegian soprano Sissel.

RECOMMENDED RECORDING
Renée Fleming (soprano); Royal Philharmonic Orchestra; Andreas Delfs (conductor). Decca: 4756925.

CHART POSITION 261

Impromptu No. 3 in G flat

Just after he wrote *'Fly Me to the Moon'*, Schubert wrote his *Impromptu No. 3*. Absolute nonsense, of course. Although if you listen to the chords of Schubert's *Impromptu No. 2*, you'll hear that they follow the same progression – admittedly a fairly common one – as those from the classic 1950s song. They were both part of a set of four written just a year before Schubert died – and at around the same time as he was composing his masterpiece *Die Winterreise* ('The Winter Journey').

Letters from around the time show that Schubert's music was being infused with ever more melancholia, sometimes to his friends' distaste. He was forced to write to one colleague, 'I like these songs more than all the others and you will get to like them too.' Good for him. It was remarkable that, knowing the extent of his illness, he was able to write at all, let alone continue to lead his life in the way he did. One of his companions, Franz von

Hartmann, commented at this time in his notes that 'every Wednesday and Saturday evening we go to the alehouse, where Enk, Schober, Schubert and Spaun can be found'.

RECOMMENDED RECORDING
Murray Perahia (piano). Sony: SK94732.

CHART POSITION 286

ROBERT SCHUMANN
(1810–1856)

Piano Concerto in A minor

Schumann's only piano concerto was a very long time in the making. Its success was undoubtedly down to his passionate relationship with Clara Wieck, who was to become his wife.

In 1837, some three years before they would marry, Schumann penned a letter to Clara in which he outlined his thoughts for a grand work for piano. It would, he said, be 'a compromise between a symphony, a concerto and a huge sonata'. The ambition of the young composer was evident – but little did he know that it would take a further eight years before the concerto was ready to be premiered.

The work first existed as a single-movement fantasia for piano and orchestra – and both the Schumanns, who were married by the time this fantasia was written in 1841, were pleased with the result. Robert's publishers, however, were not. And, try as they might, neither he nor Clara could convince anyone to champion the work. It lay rejected for a further four years until, in 1845, he started adding to the original fantasia. The work became what we now know as the *Piano Concerto*, which is brimming with joy and melody from start to finish. It was premiered on 1 January 1846, with Clara at the keyboard.

HOWARD SHORE
(B. 1946)

Lord of the Rings

Shore is a graduate of Berklee College of Music in Boston, where he was taught by the notable American choral composer, John Bavicchi. After cutting his teeth as a saxophone player, he moved across into arranging music for television and before long was the musical director of the legendary American television series *Saturday Night Live*. So it was that the man responsible for one of the most loved film scores of recent times was also the man who came up with the name for the Blues Brothers, who first appeared on the programme.

As well as winning Oscars for both the first and third of the *Rings* trilogy, Shore reworked his music into the 2004 *Lord of the Rings Symphony*, a format that has proved incredibly popular around the world. In this travelling concert, the work has six movements, two from each of the three films, performed by a large symphony orchestra and a choir, set against on-screen images. The original film music appears on several recordings, performed by the excellent London Philharmonic Orchestra (set up by Sir Thomas Beecham in 1932) as well as London Voices, with some material

recorded by the New Zealand Symphony Orchestra. Perfect music for the 'rider of Rohan' in your life, young or old.

DMITRI SHOSTAKOVICH
(1906–1975)

Piano Concerto No. 2 in F

For the majority of his composing career, Shostakovich wrote his music in the shadow of the oppressive Communist regime of his day. Many of the Russian composer's works are taut, angst-ridden and defiant in tone. However, his *Piano Concerto No. 2* is a gloriously free, wistful creation – particularly in the famous second movement, which guarantees the whole work's enduring popularity.

The piece was written as a birthday present for Shostakovich's nineteen-year-old son Maxim – himself an accomplished pianist. Either side of the soulful, heart-wrenching *Andante* are two vivacious movements, both full of style and an overwhelming sense of fun. Shostakovich apparently hid all sorts of family references within the music – jokes that only he and Maxim would truly understand. The concerto stands miles apart from many of his other works in its sense of freedom and abandon. It was by no means the first piece the composer had written for his children. Ever since his eldest daughter, Galina, had started playing the piano, Shostakovich would compose pieces for her – many of them published together in his *Children's Notebook*.

Written in 1957, four years after the death of Stalin, the Second Piano Concerto is an

Dmitri Shostakovich
1906-1975

'To me he seemed like a trapped man, whose only wish was to be left alone, to the peace of his own art and to the tragic destiny to which he had been forced to resign himself.' **NICHOLAS NABOKOV**

Among the most significant composers of the twentieth century, Shostakovich spent his entire life falling in and out of favour with the ruling Communist Party in Russia. Despite facing enormous pressure from the Russian government over exactly what sort of music he should compose, he still managed to write a stack of hits.

He was born into a fairly well-to-do Russian family, although they suffered at the hands of the Bolsheviks, following the Russian Revolution. He studied at the St Petersburg Conservatoire and was already being hailed as a critical success when his *Symphony No. 1* received its premiere, while he was still a teenager.

Shostakovich was also one of the first great film composers of the 1920s and 1930s – with many of his movie scores still being performed today. These may well have been written by a composer who needed to pay the

> ## DID YOU KNOW?
> **Despite the great distance between Britain and Russia, Shostakovich became good friends with Benjamin Britten – and even dedicated his Symphony No.14 to him.**

bills, rather than out of any great artistic desire, but Shostakovich proved time and time again that he had the knack of knowing how to deliver a catchy melody.

Today, Shostakovich is regarded as being among the finest symphony composers of all time; he wrote fifteen of them in total, which were performed around the world during his lifetime. He manages to span all the emotions in these mighty works, from joyful optimism through to tragedy and anguish. Often his music contained parodies and messages against the oppressive Communist regime.

Despite a prolific output on the symphonic front, he still found time to be something of a ladies' man, marrying three times and enjoying a number of extra-marital affairs. He also played a part in international space history when the first cosmonaut, Yuri Gagarin, sang a song called *'My Homeland Hears'*, written by Shostakovich, over the radio link from his spacecraft back to earth.

unrestrained delight from start to finish. And it's surely the best birthday present for which any budding pianist could wish. For our recommendation below, we've very much kept it in the family.

RECOMMENDED RECORDING
Dmitri Shostakovich jnr (piano); I Musici de Montreal; Maxim Shostakovich (conductor). Chandos: CHAN 10565.

CHART POSITION 40

The Gadfly

Although remembered principally for his large-scale orchestral works and concertos, Dmitri Shostakovich's output for the big screen was also prolific. He was, in essence, the Russian John Williams of his day. Between 1929 and 1970 Shostakovich wrote more than thirty movie soundtracks, but it's his score for the 1955 film *The Gadfly* that remains the big hit in this century.

The film is a proudly boisterous affair: a swashbuckling costume drama depicting the life of a Russian hero in 1830s Italy. The setting of the film gave Shostakovich the excuse to borrow musical ideas from Italian Romantic composers such as Verdi and Bellini, but it's the six-minute *Romance* for violin and orchestra that explains the score's continued popularity today.

Unashamedly inspired by French composer Jules Massenet's soulful *Méditation* from the opera *Thaïs*, it's an elegant, heart-on-your-sleeve melody, which leans and yearns with grace and poise. Twelve sections from the score were subsequently arranged into a suite, and it's in this setting that the film's wider musical content is most likely to be heard

today. The *Romance* also stands alone as a legitimate concert piece in its own right; it is best remembered by millions for its use in the 1980s TV series *Reilly, Ace of Spies*.

RECOMMENDED RECORDING
(*Romance* only) Chloë Hanslip (violin); London Symphony Orchestra; Paul Mann (conductor). Warner: 8573 886552.

CHART POSITION 45

Symphony No. 5 in D minor

To truly understand the music of Shostakovich, we have first to comprehend something of the political climate in which this great composer wrote the majority of his music. For most of his life, Shostakovich studied, worked and composed within the oppressive confines of Josef Stalin's particularly toxic brand of communism. The government was both deeply suspicious of, and threatened by, artistic freedom and creativity. For Shostakovich and his contemporaries, writing music took place in the shadow of judgement that could lead to severe punishment, should they be deemed to have stepped out of line.

That's exactly what happened when, in 1936, Stalin's authorities decreed Shostakovich's music for the opera *Lady Macbeth of Mtsensk* to be inappropriate. Fear gripped the composer: his next work, the *Symphony No. 5*, would simply have to meet with approval. At the same time, though, Shostakovich was no lapdog. He valued his own integrity, and was not about to compose a saccharine work simply to appease the government.

Thankfully, the new piece was a great success, both artistically and politically. Following its premiere in the autumn of 1937, the work's popularity grew rapidly. Today, it remains his best-known symphony. Across four movements, Shostakovich tackles all manner of human emotions. Apparently, at the work's premiere, many members of the audience wept during the sublime third movement.

RECOMMENDED RECORDING
Royal Liverpool Philharmonic Orchestra; Vasily Petrenko (conductor). Naxos: 8572461.
CHART POSITION 151

Jazz Suites

Shostakovich was most definitely a light-and-shade composer. On the one hand, we have the intense, expansive orchestral works, full of grand political gestures and complex musical ideas. On the other, we find the many film scores and the light, jolly *Jazz Suites*, both composed in the 1930s.

Russia was a regressive and disconnected country at this time in its history, deeply unaware of (and unaffected by) most social, cultural and musical developments taking place in the West. Consequently, by the time any appreciation of jazz existed on Russian soil, the bars of New Orleans had been ringing out with the sound of such music for years.

Both of Shostakovich's *Jazz Suites* have a sort of end-of-the-pier quality to them. In truth, they bear the same relationship to authentic jazz as socks and sandals do to high fashion. This is deeply sugary music, created in direct response to the Soviet government's demand that more be done to reflect this emerging genre.

Did Shostakovich compose these suites in a deliberately tongue-in-cheek way, aware of the fact that they contain the kind of jazz that would make Miles Davis turn in his grave? Or

was he musically naive, limited by the Russian communists from the true sound of what he was meant to be emulating? We'll never know for sure – but what we can be certain of is that these tuneful and wholly inoffensive ditties still find an appreciative audience today.

RECOMMENDED RECORDING
Philadelphia Orchestra; Mariss Jansons (conductor). EMI Classics: CDC 5556012.
CHART POSITION 166 (Suite No. 1), 164 (No. 2)

The Unforgettable Year 1919

It's often said that the only truly unforgettable thing about this movie is its soundtrack – in particular, the piano concerto-esque section *The Assault on Beautiful Gorky*. This showy, decadent piece, composed to depict a battle scene, is highly reminiscent of Richard Addinsell's much loved *Warsaw Concerto* – another example of film music that has well and truly outlived the movie for which it was written.

The film itself is a classic piece of Soviet propaganda, portraying Stalin as a hero and a champion of all that is good and right – something that must have been particularly galling for many of the Russians who were subjected to living under his regime. The most popular excerpts from Shostakovich's score were later assembled into a concert suite by his close friend Lev Atovmyan. Aside from *The Assault on Beautiful Gorky*, the most popular section is the lyrical *Romance* for violin and orchestra.

Shostakovich's score certainly has its detractors: critic James Leonard described it as 'simple, shallow and altogether trivial. The themes are standard-issue bombasticities; the piano part is full of nothing but flash superficialities. The trite and tawdry nature of the music makes one regret that Shostakovich was reduced to writing such tripe for the Soviet film industry

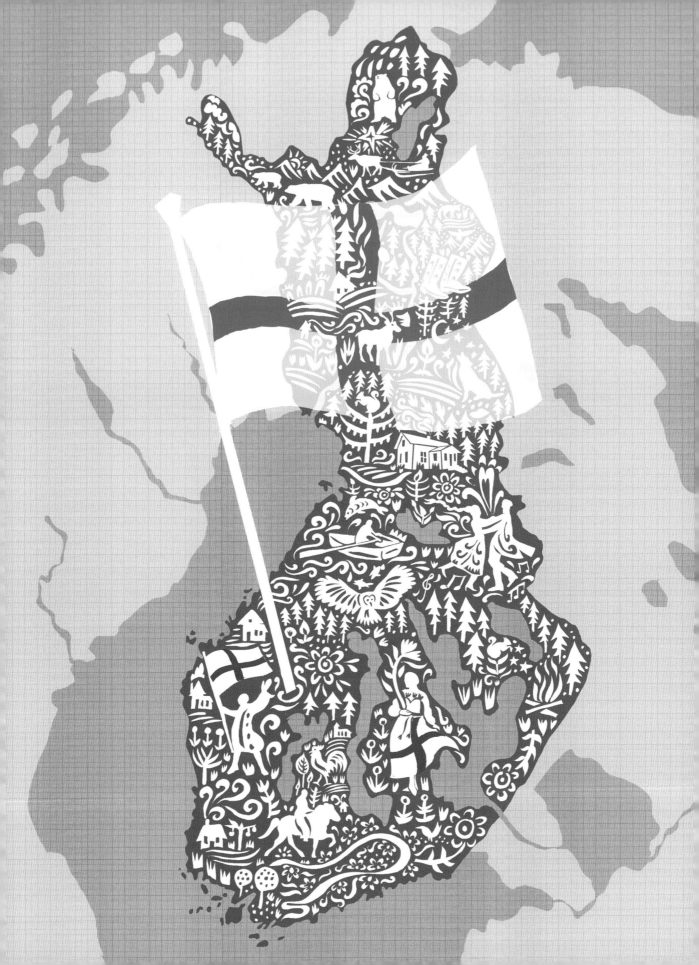

because of the vicious politics of the time.'
RECOMMENDED RECORDING
Moscow Symphony Orchestra; Adriano
(conductor, who goes only by his first name).
Marco Polo: 8223897.
CHART POSITION 207

JEAN SIBELIUS
(1865–1957)

Finlandia

In the summer of 1900, just as the world was beginning to wake up to his music, Sibelius had been on a tour of Europe, ending up at the Exposition Universelle in Paris, where he competed for attention with only the second ever Olympic Games of the modern era. He was certain that he could win a place with his music.

The calling card, which managed to get Sibelius noticed – and to inspire his self-belief – was the nationalistic *Finlandia*, his celebrated tone poem. It was written originally for an event where it was 'understood' as an attack on Russian censorship in Finland. He revised it a year later, its effervescent pride still shouting 'Russia out of Finland' for all those in the know to hear. Sibelius later reworked the central part of the piece into a *Finlandia Hymn*, with words by Finnish poet Koskenniemi (translated here by Keith Bosley in his 1997 anthology, *Skating on the Sea*): 'Finland, behold, thy daylight now is dawning'. That was in 1941 – apt words, indeed, for a work that Sibelius originally called *Suomi herää* ('Finland Awakens').
RECOMMENDED RECORDING
Gothenberg Symphony Orchestra;
Neeme Järvi (conductor). BIS: BISCD221.
CHART POSITION 26

Symphony No. 5 in E flat

Mahler and Sibelius were both masters of the art of composing the symphony, although they sometimes disagreed on the route to take. Sibelius commented that the symphony was closed off, an internal world that made sense only musically, within the work itself. Mahler is said to have famously countered, 'No! The symphony must be like the world. It must embrace everything.'

By the time Sibelius came to premiere his *Symphony No. 5*, on his birthday in 1915, he had in part come round to Mahler's way of thinking – with many of the sections of his new work showing signs of a relaxing of attitude.

Its birth came smack bang in the middle of what must rank as one of the most exciting musical decades of the century: ranging from Stravinsky's *The Firebird* in 1910, through to the modernist composer Edgard Varèse working with the New York Philharmonic in 1919.

Although Sibelius enjoyed near god-like status in his home country, his *Symphony No. 5* was a direct response to not entirely favourable reviews of his *Symphony No. 4*. He even revised the later work, saying, 'I wished to give my symphony another – more human – form. More down-to-earth, more vivid.'
RECOMMENDED RECORDING
City of Birmingham Symphony
Orchestra; Simon Rattle (conductor).
EMI Classics: 50343282.
CHART POSITION 69

Karelia Suite

It's well known that Sibelius held fervent views about his country's position under Russian dominance. He also, in his late twenties and early thirties, became passionate about the micro-nationalist importance of one particular area of Finland, said to be the home of the oldest and most respected aspects of Finnish culture. This area was the Karelia region and the movement campaigning for the area became known as Karelianism.

Much of Karelia lay in Russia, but the fact that part of it was in Finland's eastern tip (focused on Vyborg) was one of the reasons Sibelius accepted a commission to provide music for the students of Helsinki University, in Vyborg. Sibelius mentioned in a letter that 'you couldn't hear a single note of the music – everyone was on their feet cheering and clapping'.

They were staging a historical tableau, and, from the music, Sibelius salvaged three pieces to form an orchestral suite. In the 1990s, a Finnish composer and academic reconstructed more music, which, when recorded, brought the *Karelia Suite* to eleven movements. Most recordings, such as the bright and majestic one below include just the traditional three movements.

RECOMMENDED RECORDING
Helsinki Philharmonic Orchestra; Okko Kamu (conductor). Deutsche Grammophon: 4803297.
CHART POSITION 77

Symphony No. 2 in D

As a symphonic composer, Sibelius must be up there as one of the greenest; he was the biggest recycler in the business. His aforementioned views on the way a symphony should be a sealed unit, generating all its component musical parts from within seem to reach their zenith in this symphony. Its three opening notes more or less appear to form the entire backbone of what was to become one of his most popular works. Of course, you can't question the genius with which it is done. The finale of this symphony particularly has the power to move the listen-

er's emotions. If you listen closely, you will notice that the upward three-note motif from the beginning of the work is still there in the music – and this only adds to the attraction.

It was premiered in 1902, not long after *Finlandia* had its first outing and just before Sibelius's *Violin Concerto* made its debut. Pretty soon, the overtly Nordic sounds led the *Symphony No. 2* to be dubbed the 'Symphony of Independence'. Whether or not Sibelius actually intended this to happen has been open to debate, especially as sketches for it were begun while he was enjoying the beauty of the Italian countryside.
RECOMMENDED RECORDING
Oslo Philharmonic Orchestra; Mariss Jansons (conductor). EMI Classics: 69717802.
CHART POSITION 81

Violin Concerto in D minor

There was a time, in his twenties, when, if he'd been asked the question 'What's your occupation?' Sibelius would have answered 'Violinist'. Having studied the violin from fairly early on, he soon went beyond the merely competent to being really pretty good. The cow standing on his tracks to progress, though, was Martin Wegelius. He was the boss of the Helsinki Institute where Sibelius had gone to learn how to be a better fiddler.

Wegelius began to teach the young Sibelius composition and everything changed in the mind of the pupil. Composition became the only thing. It's true to say that Sibelius never totally left his first love, the violin, behind though – which explains why this concerto is the only one he wrote. How he would have loved to premiere it himself – if only the performance technique had developed at the same pace as his compositional genius.

Jean Sibelius
1865-1957

'Pay no attention to what the critics say. No statue has ever been put up to a critic.'

JEAN SIBELIUS

A violinist and pianist who initially studied composition from books, Sibelius started a law degree before bowing to the inevitable and changing his course to music. He studied in Helsinki, Berlin and Vienna. He was desperate to be a violinist as much as a composer and he auditioned with the Vienna Philharmonic Orchestra in 1891. Sadly, he never made the grade and instead had to settle for writing one of the greatest violin concertos in the world.

Although he was born with the resolutely Finnish-sounding name of Johan Julius Christian Sibelius, he was known early on as Janne to his family and close friends. However, while he was a student, he felt inspired to adopt the same French spelling as had his uncle, calling it his 'music name'. It stuck and he is now known universally as Jean.

By the time Sibelius was thirty-two, he was receiving an annual grant from the Finnish government to remove any money worries that might

DID YOU KNOW?

Sibelius and his wife honeymooned in the Karelia region. Mrs Sibelius was apparently frustrated by her husband's obsession with writing down folk tunes – which he'd later use in his *Karelia Suite!*

otherwise prevent him from composing. He became a much loved national hero over the following decades and was one of Finland's most famous exports – there was even a set of postage stamps issued in his honour.

Sibelius occupies the same sort of position in Finnish musical history as Elgar does in England and Fauré in France. After all, he did compose *Finlandia*, which is regarded as the country's unofficial national anthem.

Sibelius liked to drink and to smoke. He was diagnosed with throat cancer in his forties. The operations to remove the malignant growths were successful and he survived for another half a century. More than twenty years before he died, having made enough money to live comfortably, he simply stopped composing and retired to enjoy the continued adulation of his fellow countrymen and women.

Sibelius was famously dismissive of professional music critics, saying, 'Pay no attention to what the critics say. No statue has ever been put up to a critic.'

In the end, a disastrous premiere led Sibelius into the inevitable revisions that ultimately led to the standard version that is most widely known today (although he would almost certainly have continued to polish the piece anyway). In the 1990s, Leonidas Kavakos was allowed to record the original, which is now on record, and it is said to take even more technical skill than the revised one. Our recommendation below is for the standard rendition, which is in itself truly memorable.

RECOMMENDED RECORDING

Maxim Vengerov (violin); Chicago Symphony Orchestra; Daniel Barenboim (conductor). Warner: 2564693673.

CHART POSITION 83

The Swan of Tuonela

Saint-Saëns famously sets *The Swan*, from his *Carnival of the Animals*, as a solo cello, and ravishingly beautiful it is too. When Sibelius was two-thirds of the way through his musical version of the Finnish tale of *Lemminkäinen*, he was presented with the opportunity to recast the swan as an equally beautiful cor anglais (an instrument similar to the oboe). The difference might be down to the environment: Saint-Saëns's cygnine creation, we would imagine, is very much alive. The Sibelius swan is guarding Tuonela, more or less the Finnish version of Hades, which is surrounded by a dark, wide river.

When it came to composing this piece, the ever diligent Sibelius entered new realms of self-revision, preferring, once he had finished writing the work, not to publish it but to leave it to one side. He then revised it before allowing audiences to hear it. Perhaps this was a self-defence mechanism to save him from public pain? With Sibelius's opulent string writing – there are up to seventeen separate string parts – it has been described as 'Swan

Lake meets *Parsifal*'. It very nearly inspired Walt Disney, too: he produced storyboards for the piece for the original *Fantasia* animated film but the idea never came to fruition.

RECOMMENDED RECORDING

Royal Stockholm Philharmonic Orchestra; Andrew Davis (conductor). Apex: 0927406202.

CHART POSITION 226

BEDŘICH SMETANA
(1824–1884)

Má Vlast

The genre of the symphonic poem was established by the Hungarian composer Franz Liszt: a descriptive, single-movement orchestral piece, telling a story, painting a musical picture, or conveying a certain landscape. And, while Liszt was a master of the form, it was Smetana who undoubtedly composed some of the finest symphonic poems with his set entitled *Má Vlast*.

At over an hour long, *Má Vlast* is a mighty work, comprising six poems in total; but its popularity is due mainly to the second one, *Vltava* – a beautiful, evocative musical painting of the rolling river that passes through the city of Prague. Ebbing and flowing woodwind passages dance alongside the persistent, driving strings, creating a wonderful sense of movement along various parts of the river. During the journey we encounter a hunt, a wedding party and even some dancing water nymphs.

Much is understandably made of Beethoven's deafness – but what many people forget is that the same loss of hearing befell Smetana. Very soon after starting work on *Má Vlast* he was to become completely deaf. Consequently, the vast majority of this music existed only in his head, and he never heard it performed by an orchestra.

RECOMMENDED RECORDING
Prague Philharmonia; Jakub Hrůša (conductor). Supraphon: SU 40322.
CHART POSITION 44

JOHN STANLEY
(1712–1786)

Trumpet Voluntary

Surviving pictures of the English composer and organist John Stanley show clearly the effects of a childhood domestic accident that saw him blinded at the age of two. It is clearly something that never held him back, however, and he became the youngest ever person to get his B.Mus. degree from Oxford University at the age of seventeen. Stanley moved in very auspicious musical circles; he was good friends with Handel, and his teacher, Maurice Greene, was a Master of the King's Musick.

As well as conducting many of Handel's British works, he inherited a few London gigs after Handel's death. These included the oratorio season, which happened around Lent, and the performances of *Messiah* at the Foundling Hospital. Stanley also succeeded William Boyce as Master of the King's Musick when he was sixty-seven (he lived to the very impressive age of seventy-four).

Stanley was most famous in his lifetime, though, as an organist, proving to be a magnet for organ lovers from miles around at his church, St Andrew's in London's Holborn. His

three volumes of organ voluntaries (including the tune featured here) are his most popular legacy. So, although we know this piece as the *Trumpet Voluntary*, it wasn't really initially intended to be played on a trumpet at all.

RECOMMENDED RECORDING
John Filsell (organ). Guild: GMCD7107.
CHART POSITION 262

JOHANN STRAUSS I
(1804–1849)

Radetzky March

Johann Strauss Senior was a major figure in Viennese musical life – but nowadays, he's not the Strauss most people remember. While Strauss the Elder wrote some popular tunes (not least this, his *Radetzky March*), it's his first-born son, Johann Strauss II, who is revered as the 'King of the Waltz'.

Like his son, Strauss Senior made his living not just as a composer, but also as a conductor and violinist. He loved Vienna, having been born a stone's throw from the famous River Danube, and he would regularly walk along the river as a child, enjoying performances from the wandering musicians who worked there.

The *Radetzky March* was composed in 1848 and is so named because of its dedication to Field Marshal Radetzky, a senior member of the Austrian Army who successfully led an assault in Italy that same year. Nowadays, the piece is rarely heard without incessant clapping over the top; it's always played to end the famous New Year's Day Concert in Vienna, with the audience encouraged to applaud the arrival of another year.

There's a bittersweet element to the piece: it was due to be premiered in the autumn of 1849, but Strauss strangely failed to turn up. His publisher later explained, 'During the

instrumentation of the march, Strauss became ill with scarlet fever and died three days later.'

RECOMMENDED RECORDING
Vienna Philharmonic Orchestra; Carlos Kleiber (conductor). Sony: S3K 53385.
CHART POSITION 193

JOHANN STRAUSS II
(1825–1899)

By the Beautiful Blue Danube

If you ever needed proof that Johann Strauss the Younger deserved his nickname 'King of the Waltz', you'll find it in this, his most famous piece of music. Given its popularity today, it's surprising to consider that *By the Beautiful Blue Danube* was by no means an instant hit. This piece of music, so indelibly linked with the city of Vienna, first found favour in Paris after Viennese audiences had slightly turned their noses up at it.

Perhaps the Strauss aficionados of Vienna were used to the shorter, more barnstorming and comical dances that were a staple of this most musical of families; a stately, polite and rather restrained waltz was arguably not what they were expecting when it was composed in 1866. In Paris, though, it was a very different story. *By the Beautiful Blue Danube* was an overnight success: the French embraced Strauss as one of their own, and his dancing melodies became favourites in the city, quickly overshadowing the home-grown talent of French composer Jacques Offenbach – who, up until then, had been the man of the moment.

---

left Johann Strauss II: By the Beautiful Blue Danube

From the shimmering strings at the start, which convey sunlight dazzling on the calm river, Strauss takes us on a gloriously descriptive musical journey through Vienna. Despite its initially frosty reception, the composer's home city eventually came to embrace it, too.

RECOMMENDED RECORDING
Vienna Philharmonic Orchestra; Carlos Kleiber (conductor). Deutsche Grammophon: 4376872.
CHART POSITION 85

Die Fledermaus

'You ought to write operettas, Herr Strauss.' So said French composer Jacques Offenbach to his Austrian counterpart, at a time when Strauss was more known for writing short-form dances. *Die Fledermaus*, his most famous operetta, is primarily loved for what happens before anyone sets foot on the stage: the eight-minute *Overture* is packed full of tunes from start to finish, all of which end up appearing during the course of the action that follows.

Vienna had been captivated by Offenbach's numerous operettas. When Strauss, one of their own, began to embrace this musical form, the public was delighted. Translating literally as 'The Bat', *Die Fledermaus* was written over a two-year period from 1873 and is entirely frivolous in nature. The plot is utterly farcical, focusing on mistaken identity, flirtation and a practical joke that has rather unforeseen consequences. Its utter accessibility – both musically and dramatically – made it a sure-fire hit, and ensured that Strauss was inspired to go on and write operetta after operetta over the next twenty-five years.

Strauss himself was at the podium for the very first performance of *Die Fledermaus*, which took place at the Theater an der Wien on 5 April 1874.

RECOMMENDED RECORDING
Kiri te Kanawa (soprano) as Rosalinde;
Edita Gruberova (soprano) as Adele; Brigitte
Fassbaender (mezzo-soprano) as Orlofsky;
Vienna State Opera Chorus; Vienna
Philharmonic Orchestra; André Previn
(conductor). Philips: 4321572.

CHART POSITION 264

RICHARD STRAUSS
(1864–1949)

Four Last Songs

On his deathbed, Richard Strauss is said to
have uttered the amazing line 'Dying ... is just
as I composed it.' He was referring, directly,
to his tone poem, *Death and Transfiguration*
(*Tod und Verklärung*). Yet, indirectly, he was
also doffing the cap to his *Four Last Song*s,
where, in one, *'Im Abendrot'* ('At Twilight'), he
quotes some of his earlier music, in particular
the *Transfiguration* section.

Strauss had become steadily more unwell
in the run-up to the writing of what we now
call the *Four Last Songs* (there appears to have
been at least a fifth, possibly a sixth planned)
and death was very much on his mind. The
melancholic, autumnal russets and browns
infusing all four works for soprano (or tenor)
and orchestra make for some of the most deli-
cious moments in all music.

It's probably a very subjective call which
version is right for you. Nina Stemme singing with Antonio Pappano's Royal Opera
House Orchestra is wonderful. For a direct
line back to the composer himself, there is
always the remastered Elizabeth Schwarzkopf version with the Berlin Radio Symphony
Orchestra, which comes with its baggage
as well as its beauty. Renée Fleming's perfect rendition is expertly presented with
Christian Thielemann and the Munich Philharmonic Orchestra.

RECOMMENDED RECORDING
Renée Fleming (soprano); Munich
Philharmonic Orchestra; Christian
Thieleman (conductor); Decca: 4780647.

CHART POSITION 60

Der Rosenkavalier

It is beautifully apt that, in 1911, it was a
Strauss who set the Austro-Hungarian Empire alight with a sumptuous, elegant grand
ball of an opera, set in the Vienna of Maria
Theresa. This Strauss, though, was a very different *Kessel der Fische* from the toe-tapping
Johanns I and II. It's as if Richard Strauss has
the entire world of the Johanns captured in a
snow globe which he is shaking in the palm of
his hand (musically speaking, of course).

With its words by Strauss's favourite librettist, Hugo von Hofmannsthal, the premiere
in Dresden of *Der Rosenkavalier* was one of the
composer's biggest successes. It's fair to say
that this particular librettist brought out the
best in Strauss, who not only set his words but
seemed inspired to set the unspoken aspects,
the subtexts, as well. The result is an incredibly
rich score, which feels as if it's pressing on all
four sides of the Viennese ballroom, trying to
get out. For highlights of the opera, including
the amazing duet *'Mir ist die Ehre widerfahren ...'*,
try the 1990s Royal Opera House production
with Ann Murray and Anna Tomowa-Sintow
alongside Kurt Moll. Better still, save yourself
to see it live, where it delights.

Ann Murray (mezzo-soprano) as Octavian; Anna Tomowa-Sintow (soprano) as Marschallin; Kurt Moll (bass) as Ochs; Chorus and Orchestra of the Royal Opera House; Andrew Davis (conductor). Opus Arte: OACD9006D.

CHART POSITION 205

IGOR STRAVINSKY
(1882–1971)

The Rite of Spring

Is this the most influential and important piece of music to have been composed in the twentieth century? Critics and musicologists have argued the point for years, but it's undeniable that the Parisian premiere of Stravinsky's ballet *The Rite of Spring* in 1913 was a momentous occasion – not least because it caused the most famous riot in the history of classical music.

The ballet came as a complete shock for several reasons: firstly, the primeval nature of the subject matter was revolutionary. Music and dancing that depicted pagan fertility rites was hardly run-of-the-mill stuff, even in such a bohemian city as Paris. Stravinsky's earthy, violent music was scandalous for its disregard of accepted ballet forms and its seeming refusal to adhere to any kind of tradition. From the groaning cellos to the aggressive percussion, *The Rite of Spring* did not contain the kind of music or structures that would have been expected. Indeed, by the time the first part of the ballet was over, the police had already arrived and were making efforts to quell the riot among the outraged audience.

The Russian ballet impresario Sergei Diaghilev, with whom Stravinsky had collaborated on *The Rite of Spring*, was far from

upset, though. On the contrary, he exclaimed that the reaction and ensuing pandemonium was 'just what I wanted!'

RECOMMENDED RECORDING
London Philharmonic Orchestra; Kent Nagano (conductor). Virgin: VCK 7915112.

CHART POSITION 149

The Firebird

As you listen to the assured, complex ballet music Igor Stravinsky wrote for *The Firebird*, it's impressive to think that the composer was only twenty-seven when he created it. While Stravinsky was Russian through and through, Paris was a crucially important city for him: it was here that the highly controversial *The Rite of Spring* was premiered in 1913. The city had also hosted the premiere performance of *The Firebird* three years earlier.

The job of writing the music for this Diaghilev ballet was never meant to fall to Stravinsky, though. The first-choice composer was fellow Russian Anatol Liadov, best remembered nowadays for his brooding orchestral piece *The Enchanted Lake*. Liadov suffered a musical version of writer's block and was unable to come up with any music that could suitably convey the centuries-old legend of the firebird. So, straight off the subs bench came Stravinsky, eager to make his mark on the Ballets Russes which Diaghilev ran in Paris.

The premiere of *The Firebird* in 1910 cemented Stravinsky's position as one of the period's most exciting and dynamic composers, and he was revered by the musical elite of Paris. Today, the ballet remains in rep across the world – and the concert suite is regularly performed, too.

RECOMMENDED RECORDING
Philharmonia Orchestra; Esa-Pekka Salonen (conductor). Sony: SBK 89894.

CHART POSITION 212

THOMAS TALLIS
(C. 1505–1585)

Spem in Alium

Does it ever get very 'dog eat dog' in the genteel world of composing? Well, sad to say, it sometimes does. It can be very competitive. Ravel and Debussy were seen to be at odds often; Tchaikovsky writes in his letters about making sure he is the first composer to have a certain instrument; and Tallis? Well, Tallis allowed himself to be almost taunted by visiting Italian composers, who proudly waved their 40-part motets in his face. He simply had to write 'a song of fortie partes, made by Mr Tallys', as it would have been known at the time. Tallis was no spring chicken, either, when he set about finding the choral Holy Grail. Although it's hard to pin down – Thomas Tallis appears to have been an international man of mystery, with no records of him at all before he was an adult – it would appear he was not far off seventy when he set the words of the Matins response 'I have never put my hope in any other but you, O God of Israel'. The music he came up with is simply breathtaking and has captivated new generations down the years.

RECOMMENDED RECORDING
The Sixteen; Harry Christophers (conductor). Coro: COR16073.
CHART POSITION 102

FRANCISCO TÁRREGA
(1852–1909)

Recuerdos de la Alhambra

Spain is to the guitar as Wales is to male-voice choirs. Nearly every well-known piece of music for the instrument seems to have originated in the sun-soaked country, from the much loved concertos of Rodrigo through to this short, unaccompanied miniature by Francisco Tárrega. No one really knows when it was written; all we can say is that its composition is likely to date from the latter half of the nineteenth century.

Despite this beguiling melody sounding beautifully simple, Tárrega really stretches the soloist to the limit with it. For a start, the left-hand positions required of the guitarist are rather awkward, involving all sorts of unusual stretches. On top of that, the use of *tremolo* (very fast, repeated playing of the notes that sit under the main tune) is a technical challenge for any performer. And to top it all, there's a serenity to the melody that has to be retained at all costs if the piece is to sound right – and that's pretty hard to do with everything else that's going on!

The *Recuerdos de la Alhambra* was apparently dedicated to a friend, with Tárrega writing on the original manuscript, 'Since I cannot offer you a present of any worth on your birthday, accept this humble poetic impression, made on my soul by the grandiose marvel of the Alhambra of Granada we both admire.'

RECOMMENDED RECORDING
Julian Bream (guitar). RCA: 09026 618482.
CHART POSITION 183

JOHN TAVENER
(B. 1944)

Song for Athene

Sir John Tavener had this to say about Athene, the inspiration for his most famous work: 'Her beauty, both outward and inner, was reflected in her love of acting, poetry and music.' Rather than being about the Greek goddess of war, as many people presume, *Song for Athene* was written after the funeral of the daughter of a family friend – Athene Hariades – in 1993. She was an actress whom Tavener had heard reading Shakespeare and her death prompted him to amalgamate Shakespeare-derived passages with those of the orthodox funeral service. Although it was not written by the time of

Athene's funeral, its performance at another one, that of Diana, Princess of Wales, brought it to national and international attention. Its sound-world is decidedly individual, refusing to bow down before any one style. It's neither old nor new – it's simply Tavener, haunting his audience and raging at them in turns. One of the features of the music is that it is almost inaudible at times and then suddenly bursts into almost deafening life. Although it's usually a choral piece, special mention should be made of the arrangement made for Nicola Benedetti on the violin, with string accompaniment.

RECOMMENDED RECORDING
Winchester Cathedral Choir; David Hill (conductor). EMI Classics: 5859152.
CHART POSITION 237

PYOTR ILYICH
TCHAIKOVSKY (1840–1893)

1812 Overture

In 1877, within just a few weeks of his wedding to his teenage student Antonia Milyukova, Tchaikovsky had fled the city and found solace in the Russian countryside, where he could reflect on life without the pressures he faced in St Petersburg and Moscow.

It was within this context of personal turmoil that Tchaikovsky composed his most famous and most triumphant of works: the *1812 Overture*. Sadly, though, the process did little to help or heal the composer: he took a great dislike to the piece – which had, after all, been written not through artistic desire but to fulfil a commission.

Given the heartache in Tchaikovsky's life, it's saddening to think that he never realised how his *1812 Overture* would go on to become one of the most adored creations in all classical music. From the introductory

Russian hymn to the bombastic cannonfire that concludes this unashamedly nationalistic concert piece, it's one of the best examples of how Tchaikovsky was a master of orchestration. Next time you hear it performed in a muddy field or at the end of a classical pop concert, take a moment to consider the context in which it was composed. It certainly gives you a different appreciation of this most stunning work.

RECOMMENDED RECORDING

Berlin Philharmonic Orchestra; Claudio Abbado (Conductor). Deutsche Grammophon: 4534962.

CHART POSITION 34

Piano Concerto No. 1 in B flat minor

The thunderously triumphant opening chords of this mighty concerto are among the most famous in all classical music. At the time of composition, though, they were by no means universally loved. When Tchaikovsky played them to the pianist Nicolai Rubinstein, Rubinstein declared it to be 'bad, trivial and vulgar!'

His *Piano Concerto No. 1* was first sketched out during an intensive period of composition at the end of 1874, with the orchestrations then written in the February of the following year. However, after this very productive period, Tchaikovsky evidently wasn't happy: the work was updated some four years later and then revised again as late as 1889.

All three movements of this deeply expressive concerto are sublimely romantic – with both a lower-case and an upper-case R. The expansive, sweeping opening movement is showy; the middle movement, meanwhile, contains soulful melodies with some beautiful interplay between the soloist and orchestra; and the edge-of-your-seat finale is an electrifying thrill from start to finish.

Some eighty-odd years after Tchaikovsky sketched out his initial ideas for his *Piano Concerto No. 1*, it became the first piece of classical music to sell a million records when, in 1958, the pianist Van Cliburn wowed the world with his impassioned recording of the piece.

RECOMMENDED RECORDING

Martha Argerich (piano); Berlin Philharmonic Orchestra; Claudio Abbado (conductor). Deutsche Grammophon: 4498162.

CHART POSITION 38

Symphony No. 6 in B minor
Pathétique

Was it due to cholera-infected water? Could it have been suicide? Or was it, quite simply, the result of a broken heart? All sorts of theories, both credible and anything but, have been espoused when it comes to the reason for Tchaikovsky's death in November 1893.

The premiere of this, his *Symphony No. 6*, took place just over a week before the composer's death. Of all Tchaikovsky's works, this is arguably the one that spans both extremes of the emotional spectrum to the greatest extent. One moment, we're enjoying a graceful

Pyotr Ilyich Tchaikovsky

1840-1893

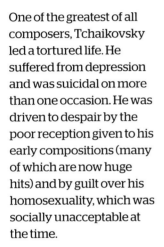

'Truly there would be reason to go mad if it were not for music.'

PYOTR ILYICH TCHAIKOVSKY

One of the greatest of all composers, Tchaikovsky led a tortured life. He suffered from depression and was suicidal on more than one occasion. He was driven to despair by the poor reception given to his early compositions (many of which are now huge hits) and by guilt over his homosexuality, which was socially unacceptable at the time.

As a child, Tchaikovsky's family life was comfortable. He studied law in St Petersburg, next taking a job as a civil servant. He studied music in his free time and eventually enrolled for a course at St Petersburg Conservatoire, where he quickly became a rising star under the tutelage of the great Anton Rubenstein.

He married at the age of thirty-seven, but the relationship was loveless (on his side at least) and the stress began to put pressure on his mental health. Mrs Tchaikovsky, who was a love-struck student, herself ended up in an asylum.

DID YOU KNOW?

Tchaikovsky wasn't afraid of making his views on other composers known. While he once described Mozart as 'the musical Christ', he declared that Wagner simply bored him.

Tchaikovsky's benefactor throughout his life was a rich widow, called Nadezhda von Meck, who insisted they never actually meet, even though she funded him and they corresponded for some fourteen years.

Tchaikovsky had a knack for great tunes and lots of them. His ballets such as *Nutcracker*, *The Sleeping Beauty* and *Swan Lake* are among the most often performed today. He also wrote ten operas, seven symphonies, numerous other symphonic works and noteworthy concertos for both the piano and the violin.

When the composer received his honorary degree from Cambridge University on 13 June 1893, he was in amazing company. Also receiving degrees that day were Saint-Saëns, Bruch and Puccini's librettist, Arrigo Boito.

There is confusion over exactly how Tchaikovsky died – officially, cholera from infected water claimed his life, although there is some evidence that he may have drunk it knowingly.

dance; the next, sombre moods dominate. The symphony's nickname, *Pathétique*, was added by Tchaikovsky's brother, with the blessing of the composer. It suggests pathos in the music – something that is undoubtedly there in spades, but not at the expense of a lightness of touch and, at times, a sense of frivolity. In those moments, at least, the music seems far from autobiographical: if Tchaikovsky was struggling with suicidal thoughts, they're by no means evident throughout.

Tchaikovsky was more than satisfied with this four-movement symphony – but, as was so often and so cruelly the case, the critical reception it received was decidedly muted. Described by some as his farewell to life, in reality we shall never know exactly what inspired the work. What we can be sure of, though, is that it lives on as one of the composer's most adored creations.

RECOMMENDED RECORDING
London Philharmonic Orchestra; Vladimir Jurowski (conductor). LPO 0039.
CHART POSITION 43

Swan Lake

You think ballet, you think Tchaikovsky. The Russian composer was the nineteenth century's true master of dance music. Today, *Nutcracker*, *The Sleeping Beauty* and *Swan Lake* remain sure-fire hits for ballet companies around the world. It's remarkable, then, that when *Swan Lake* was premiered in 1877, the reception it garnered was lukewarm at best. Never mind what the audiences back then thought: it was the dancers who gave the composer a particularly hard time, declaring his music to be simply too difficult to dance to. Music of such richness and depth was not,

---

left Pyotr Ilyich Tchaikovsky: Swan Lake

they thought, the kind that should accompany their balletic moves.

In Russian culture, the swan was the ultimate image of female purity; some have therefore argued that this was the inspiration for Tchaikovsky's music. More likely, though, is that the idea for *Swan Lake* came from a sweet children's dance which the composer first heard at his sister's country house in 1871.

Today, the ballet is adored by young and old: from the graceful *Waltz* in Act I to the playful *Dance of the Cygnets*, this is wonderfully innocent music. Tchaikovsky evidently enjoyed composing the music for *Swan Lake*, writing far more material than would ever be required. Indeed, the version most commonly encountered today is, in fact, an edited one, created after Tchaikovsky's death and considerably shorter than the original, full-length work. It's now the world's most frequently performed ballet.

RECOMMENDED RECORDING
Orchestra of the Mariinsky Theatre; Valery Gergiev (conductor). Decca: 4757669.
CHART POSITION 58

Symphony No. 5 in E minor

For much of his life, Tchaikovsky was inspired on both an emotional and financial level by his patron, Nadezhda von Meck – whom he quite astonishingly never met. Indeed, this was a condition of her patronage.

In the summer of 1888, Tchaikovsky wrote one of his many letters to her, in which he commented, 'I don't know if I have already written that I have decided to write a symphony. At first progress was very arduous, but now illumination seems to have descended upon me. We shall see!' The work in question was this, his *Symphony No. 5*. It had been ten years since the fairly unsuccessful premiere of the *Symphony No. 4* – admittedly punctuated by the composition of the *Manfred Symphony* in 1885 – and Tchaikovsky worked painstakingly hard to ensure that his latest symphonic creation received a favourable response.

Sadly, the reaction to the four-movement *Symphony No. 5* was, at best, muted. Tchaikovsky felt incredibly dejected, even going so far as to distance himself from it for quite some time. After his death, however, the work grew in popularity, with audiences and critics alike acknowledging Tchaikovsky's great skill as an orchestrator and his powerful evocation of the idea of fate throughout the symphony. Today, it stands as one of his most loved large-scale creations.

RECOMMENDED RECORDING
Bavarian Radio Symphony Orchestra; Mariss Jansons (conductor). BR Klassik: 900105.
CHART POSITION 75

Violin Concerto in D

Along with the violin concertos of Bruch and Mendelssohn, this warhorse by Tchaikovsky is one of the most important works for the instrument in the history of Romantic music. It is also a piece that, like the *1812 Overture*, is implicitly linked with Tchaikovsky's emotional turmoil and sham marriage.

Just three months after his union with Antonina Milyukova, Tchaikovsky fled Russia for the countryside. From there, he travelled around Italy and Switzerland, with his trip largely funded by his patron, Nadezhda von Meck. Tchaikovsky's travels ended at Lake Garda, where, among other visitors, he was joined by his former music-theory pupil, the violinist Joseph Kotek.

It's long been argued that Tchaikovsky's feelings for Kotek were much more than platonic. During the stay he confided to a friend,

'I love him very much – but by now quite differently from before.' Whatever the nature of Tchaikovsky's love for him, one thing is very clear: Kotek was the absolute inspiration for the *Violin Concerto*. The young violinist was studying with Joseph Joachim, and eagerly took up the challenge of learning this new work. Interestingly, Tchaikovsky decided to avoid dedicating the concerto to the young soloist. The reason? As he confided to his publisher, '… in order to avoid gossip of various kinds'.

RECOMMENDED RECORDING
Anne-Sophie Mutter (violin); Vienna Philharmonic Orchestra; André Previn (conductor). Deutsche Grammophon: DG 4748742.
CHART POSITION 84

Nutcracker

Audiences in St Petersburg were promised 'a fairy-tale ballet' in the winter of 1892 when, all around the city, posters began to appear advertising the much anticipated new project from Tchaikovsky.

He had been commissioned to set to music a popular family story called *The Nutcracker and the Mouse-King*, a festive favourite which begins on Christmas Eve in the house of two young children, Clara and Fritz. The family is gathered around the Christmas tree. Soon, they welcome the arrival of Uncle Drosselmeyer, who conveniently happens to be a toymaker with some suitable gifts in tow. Over the course of the next ninety minutes, the story encompasses waltzing snowflakes, a handsome prince and some warring mice, as the toys come to life and give Clara and Fritz a Christmas they will never forget.

There is a wonderfully vivid, pictorial quality to Tchaikovsky's colourful music. From the elegant *Waltz of the Flowers* to the thrilling *Russian Dance*, the score is a feast of wonderful melodies. Tchaikovsky had several reservations about it – not surprising, given the less than ecstatic response to some of his earlier works – but the composer evidently had nothing to fear. It has become a perennial Christmas favourite on stage, and the music is adored all year round.

RECOMMENDED RECORDING

Berlin Philharmonic Orchestra; Simon Rattle (conductor). EMI Classics: 50999 64638522.

CHART POSITION 89

Romeo and Juliet

Rachmaninov is often lauded as the Romantic era's finest composer, principally for his ability to express a depth of emotion to which others can only dream of coming close. But no one who listens to Tchaikovsky's *Romeo and Juliet* can be in any doubt that this other Russian composer certainly gives Rachmaninov a run for his money in the heart-on-your-sleeve stakes.

Composed in 1869, and sandwiched between his *Symphonies No. 1* and *No. 2*, this was arguably Tchaikovsky's first true masterpiece. The composer's inspiration was, as the title suggests, the famous Shakespeare play. It was the Russian composer Mily Balakirev who gave Tchaikovsky the idea of taking the English playwright's work and setting it to music. Indeed, he chose to dedicate *Romeo and Juliet* to

Balakirev – a man he looked up to and sought advice from in the early part of his career.

Existing as a single-movement work and lasting around twenty minutes, *Romeo and Juliet* makes full use of the orchestra's sweeping string section. Layer on layer of sumptuous melodies are woven together – with various tunes depicting particular sections of the plot.

As with all too many of Tchaikovsky's works, this one was dismissed at its premiere. But looking back now, with the whole of the composer's career in our line of sight, it's clear that *Romeo and Juliet* was the first true example of Tchaikovsky's emergence as a musical genius.

RECOMMENDED RECORDING

Orchestra of the Academy of St Cecilia; Antonio Pappano (conductor). EMI Classics: 0946 3700652.

CHART POSITION 105

The Sleeping Beauty

Marius Pepita was a phenomenon in the world of Russian ballet. By the time he choreographed *The Sleeping Beauty*, he had overseen more than fifty productions. It's therefore not surprising that the collaboration between Pepita, the country's most exciting choreographer, and Tchaikovsky, the superstar composer, was hotly anticipated.

The two men came together in 1890 to stage this beautifully simple story. The premiere of *Swan Lake* a few years earlier had ruffled a few feathers (if you'll pardon the pun) because it was unusual for a 'serious' composer to embrace ballet. With *The Sleeping Beauty*, Tchaikovsky was proving that the form was indeed one he took seriously, rather than something in which he had only dabbled once out of curiosity.

Writing to the Director of Imperial Theatres about the task of scoring *The Sleeping*

TOP 10 WORKS BY LIVING COMPOSERS

1	Jay Ungar	*The Ashokan Farewell*
2	Karl Jenkins	*The Armed Man (Mass for Peace)*
3	John Williams	*Schindler's List*
4	Howard Shore	*Lord of the Rings*
5	Ludovico Einaudi	*Le Onde*
6	Arvo Pärt	*Spiegel im Spiegel*
7	Karl Jenkins	*Adiemus – Songs of Sanctuary*
8	Philip Glass	*Violin Concerto*
9	John Williams	*Star Wars*
10	Ennio Morricone	*The Mission*

Beauty, Tchaikovsky commented, 'I need sufficient leisure and strength to do it well, because this is not simply a matter of confecting some kind of ordinary ballet music: I have an ambition to write a *chef d'oeuvre* in this genre.' It's worth remembering that, of all his works, the reception *Swan Lake* had received was about the worst imaginable. So, it's not surprising that for his follow-up ballet, Tchaikovsky was determined to prove his worth.

The entire score is a delight – but no section more so than the ravishing *Rose Adagio* from Act I. Proof, if it were needed, that Tchaikovsky's efforts absolutely paid off.

RECOMMENDED RECORDING
Kirov Orchestra; Valery Gergiev (conductor). Philips: 4349222.
CHART POSITION 125

Symphony No. 4 in F minor

Tchaikovsky was on a roll. His *Symphony No. 1* had been a labour of love – but at its premiere in 1868, it was warmly received. *Symphony No. 2* followed five years later, and went down a storm. *No. 3*, revealed to the world just a couple of years after that, received a universal thumbs-up at its first performance. So surely, his *Symphony No. 4* would also be a great success, ensuring the composer's continued upward trajectory?

Sadly for Tchaikovsky, the work received a muted reception when it was first performed. *Symphony No. 4* was a piece that, more than most others, he had given himself to so completely, pouring deep emotions into the composition – emotions that would, in turn, pour back out through the music. How devastating it must have been to feel so unappreciated for his efforts. That's not to say the premiere was a disaster; but to claim it was a triumph would be wholly wrong.

The symphony deals with Tchaikovsky's much loved idea of fate, and was dedicated to his patron Madame von Meck (Tchaikovsky frequently described it to her as 'our symphony'). In 1877, he wrote to von Meck saying, 'This symphony is not a mediocre work, but the best I have done so far.' Despite its initial reception, we can safely say today that Tchaikovsky was right.

RECOMMENDED RECORDING
Vienna Philharmonic Orchestra; Lorin Maazel (conductor). Decca: 4307872.
CHART POSITION 142

Capriccio Italien

Some of the great composers' best creations were inspired by places other than their homelands. Think, for example of Dvořák's *Symphony No. 9* – his musical postcard from America – or of Mendelssohn's brooding *Hebrides Overture*, as fine a musical picture of a stormy Scottish scene as you could wish for. Similarly, Tchaikovsky's orchestral poem *Capriccio Italien* is a richly descriptive portrait of Italy, written when the composer spent three months in Rome in 1880.

His inspiration for the work did not come solely from this relatively brief stay in the capital, though. On the contrary, Italy was Tchaikovsky's favourite holiday destination, and was also a country he turned to for solace and escapism after the break-up of his brief and disastrous marriage.

Despite its single-movement structure, *Capriccio Italien* is a series of musical pictures, drawing on the composer's experiences across the country. It is by no means the most soulful or heart-wrenching of Tchaikovsky's works; instead, this is a more barnstorming, triumphant example of Romantic music. As the composer wrote to his patron, Madame von Meck, 'Thanks to the charming themes, some of which I have taken from collections and some of which I have heard in the streets, this work will be effective.' He wasn't wrong!

RECOMMENDED RECORDING
Montreal Symphony Orchestra; Charles Dutoit (conductor). Decca: 4307872.
CHART POSITION 180

Serenade for Strings

At the very time that Tchaikovsky was composing his nationalistic, powerful and undeniably noisy *1812 Overture*, he was also writing this: the graceful, poised and rather sedate *Serenade for Strings*. It's probably over-interpreting the compositional process to suggest that the *Serenade* acted as a sort of enjoyable musical antidote to the *1812 Overture* – a work Tchaikovsky himself despised – but it's certainly fascinating to hear both works alongside each other and to be able to appreciate two very different sides to this remarkable composer.

Tchaikovsky wrote to Madame von Meck in 1880, making clear his very different feelings for the two works. While the *1812 Overture* was written merely to pay the bills, the *Serenade* for strings was, he said, composed 'from utter conviction. It is a heartfelt piece and so, I dare to think, is not lacking in real qualities'. Those qualities include a hugely impressive command of each string instrument. From the playful lyricism of the violin to the soulful depth of the cello, Tchaikovsky blends each string line into a gloriously rich sound, beginning with the taut opening to the first movement and continuing through the graceful waltz and the dancing finale.

At its premiere, the *Serenade for Strings* was so warmly received that Tchaikovsky had to allow the second movement to be played again as an encore.

RECOMMENDED RECORDING
Royal Philharmonic Orchestra; Daniele Gatti (conductor). Harmonia Mundi: HMU 907394.
CHART POSITION 290

Piano Concerto No. 2 in G

Tchaikovsky certainly set himself an uphill struggle when it came to writing a second piano concerto. His First, premiered in Boston in 1875, is an absolutely electrifying piece – and the audience at its premiere performance thought so too. Tchaikovsky was heralded as a star composer, and one who had an absolute grasp of the piano as an instrument. How on earth could he follow that?

In 1879, *Piano Concerto No. 2* was at an embryonic stage, with several sections having already been sketched out by the composer. Remarkably, he chose to send these sketches to Nicolai Rubinstein – the very man who had rubbished his *Piano Concerto No. 1* as 'utterly worthless' and who, in the process, had caused Tchaikovsky so much personal heartache. Tchaikovsky was evidently not one to bear grudges, though. Despite Rubinstein's initial criticisms of his earlier work, the composer decided to dedicate *Piano Concerto No. 2* to him.

An expansive, three-movement work, the new piece was embraced by the Moscow public when it was premiered in 1882, but it's since gone on to be overshadowed by *Piano Concerto No. 1*. Among the highlights of this follow-up are the beautiful middle movement – effectively a triple concerto for piano, violin and cello – and a dazzling finale, which stretches the soloist to the absolute limit across multiple octaves of the keyboard.

RECOMMENDED RECORDING
Stephen Hough (piano); Minnesota Orchestra; Osmo Vänskä (conductor). Hyperion: CDA 67711/2.
CHART POSITION 298

JAY UNGAR
(B. 1946)

The Ashokan Farewell

When New Yorkers are thirsty, they can simply turn on a faucet and pour themselves a glass of Ashokan water. The Ashokan reservoir is a huge expanse of water some 150 miles north of the city, and not far from the spot where Jay Ungar and Molly Mason have run a 'fiddle and dance' camp annually for more than thirty years. (A recent New Year's dance in the Ashokan Centre boasted 'blues, waltzes, contras and squares').

It all happens amid the beauty of the Catskill Mountains, not too far from Woodstock. On the last night of camp, it is traditional to play Ungar's tune, *The Ashokan Farewell*, a beautiful, slightly mournful waltz, almost in the style of a lament. After it was featured in the landmark American television series *The Civil War*, it suddenly came to international attention.

An arrangement for the Band of HM Royal Marines by Major John Perkins proved a huge hit on Classic FM and has been frequently requested by listeners ever since. The Marines' version is still the benchmark, building up from a haunting solo violin. To hear it in its stunningly raw original version, try Jay and Molly, on violin and guitar. The Catskills virtually appear before your eyes!

RECOMMENDED RECORDING

John Perkins (violin); Band of HM Royal Marines. Classic FM: CFM CD4.

CHART POSITION 87

RALPH VAUGHAN WILLIAMS
(1872–1958)

The Lark Ascending

The George Meredith poem that inspired Vaughan Williams to compose *The Lark Ascending* begins with the words: 'He rises and begins to round/He drops the silver chain of sound/Of many links without a break/In chirrup, whistle, slur and shake.' The composer wrote the piece in 1914, but the outbreak of World War I meant he had to put its premiere on hold. It wasn't until 1921 that *The Lark Ascending* received its first performance, featuring the violinist Marie Hall – the woman for whom Vaughan Williams had written it.

The soaring violin melody ascends so high into the instrument's upper register that, at times, it is barely audible; shimmering strings, meanwhile, provide much of the beautifully sensitive accompaniment, evoking glorious images of the rolling British countryside. Midway through *The Lark Ascending*, Vaughan Williams treats us to an orchestral section that seems to borrow from his love of folk songs; it's not long, though, before the lark returns, with the melody entwining itself around the orchestra and then breaking free, rising to ever loftier heights.

The Lark Ascending is notoriously difficult to play, but the best performances of it are seemingly effortless and free. It remains the composer's most popular work, and seems certain to grace the highest echelons of the Hall of Fame for many years to come.

RECOMMENDED RECORDING
Nigel Kennedy (violin); City of Birmingham Symphony Orchestra; Simon Rattle (conductor). EMI Classics: 5628132.
CHART POSITION 4

Fantasia on a Theme by Thomas Tallis

In 1908, Vaughan Williams travelled to Paris to study orchestration with Maurice Ravel. It proved to be an inspiring experience. When he returned home, he undertook one of his most fruitful periods of composition. The year 1910 saw the premiere of not just his mighty first symphony (*A Sea Symphony*) but of the *Fantasia on a Theme by Thomas Tallis*, too – at the Gloucester Three Choirs Festival.

---

right Ralph Vaughan Williams: The Lark Ascending

This lush, expansive work for string orchestra amply proves that Vaughan Williams's focus on orchestration had paid off. He blends the instruments exquisitely, creating a rich and unmistakably British sound across a fifteen-minute duration. Interestingly, rather than simply being written for a single ensemble, the *Fantasia on a Theme by Thomas Tallis* is, in fact, scored for large string orchestra, slightly smaller string ensemble, and a string quartet, all playing alongside each other. It was the work that was to cement Vaughan Williams's reputation not just at home, but across the rest of Europe, too.

The *Fantasia*'s main theme, heard after the hypnotic opening chords, was discovered by the composer when he was commissioned to put together the 1906 edition of *The English Hymnal*. The process of research served Vaughan Williams incredibly well: many of the tunes he came across were to be put to good use in all sorts of later works.

RECOMMENDED RECORDING
Britten Sinfonia; Nicholas Cleobury (conductor). Classic FM: CFMCD 44.
CHART POSITION 14

Fantasia on Greensleeves

This exquisite four-minute orchestral miniature has far eclipsed the song it was inspired by: namely, *'Greensleeves'*, a traditional melody that was doing the rounds in the days of Henry VIII and which was put to masterful use here by Vaughan Williams. He didn't create it as a stand-alone piece, though; instead, it was initially used in the third act of the composer's Shakespeare-inspired opera *Sir John in Love*.

Vaughan Williams once commented, 'The art of music above all arts is the expression of the soul of the nation.' In this delightful piece,

he manages to capture the very essence of England in music. The serene, pastoral sounds evoke images of bucolic bliss, with lyrical string writing and particularly descriptive flute passages. The title of *Fantasia* is in some ways misleading: the work is neither long enough nor complex enough to deserve the description; instead, it is a rather faithful setting of the original.

The *Fantasia on Greensleeves* uses not only the traditional tune alluded to in the title but also the melody *'Lovely Joan'*, which Vaughan Williams came across in Suffolk. In 1934, under the watchful eye of the composer, Ralph Greaves arranged Vaughan Williams's music into the version we most commonly hear today.

RECOMMENDED RECORDING
English Chamber Orchestra; Daniel Barenboim. Deutsche Grammophon: 4395292.
CHART POSITION 130

Five Variants of Dives and Lazarus

Many of Vaughan Williams's most famous compositions were direct settings of famous or newly discovered folk melodies. In the case of his *Five Variants of Dives and Lazarus*, the inspiration was less literal. As the composer himself explained, 'These variants are not exact replicas of traditional tunes but rather reminiscences of various versions in my own collection and those of others.' The original tune in question, called *'Dives and Lazarus'*, is referenced in sixteenth-century writings but could well have been written earlier than that, and is a musical depiction of the New Testament story of the rich man and the beggar. You may know it by one of its

Ralph Vaughan Williams
1872-1958

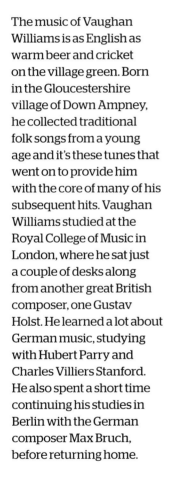

'What we want in England is real music, even if it be only a music-hall song.'

RALPH VAUGHAN WILLIAMS

The music of Vaughan Williams is as English as warm beer and cricket on the village green. Born in the Gloucestershire village of Down Ampney, he collected traditional folk songs from a young age and it's these tunes that went on to provide him with the core of many of his subsequent hits. Vaughan Williams studied at the Royal College of Music in London, where he sat just a couple of desks along from another great British composer, one Gustav Holst. He learned a lot about German music, studying with Hubert Parry and Charles Villiers Stanford. He also spent a short time continuing his studies in Berlin with the German composer Max Bruch, before returning home.

Alongside Elgar, Vaughan Williams ranks as one of the true greats of English classical music; he has become particularly well respected for his symphonies. Politically, he was something of a socialist and he viewed music as being part of everyone's everyday life, rather than being the

DID YOU KNOW?
Vaughan Williams was an outstanding teacher as well as an acclaimed composer. For forty years, he taught composition at London's Royal College of Music.

preserve of an elite. So, he was as comfortable writing short hymn tunes as he was penning long and complicated symphonic works.

Hymns were a speciality for Vaughan Williams and he edited *The English Hymnal* in 1904. Despite being agnostic, he wrote some stunning choral music using Christian themes, as well as composing the opera *The Pilgrim's Progress*, based on John Bunyan's book of the same name.

Vaughan Williams was still composing great music into his eighties. A statue of him remains today at White Gates, his home for many years in Dorking in Surrey.

Since Classic FM began broadcasting in 1992, the popularity of Vaughan Williams has grown steadily each year, with his *The Lark Ascending* regularly topping the annual Classic FM Hall of Fame from 2007 onwards.

Pronunciation tip: 'Ralph', in this instance is pronounced to rhyme with 'safe', as in the actor Ralph Fiennes.

many other names, perhaps *'The Star of the County Down'*.

Much like *The Lark Ascending* and *Fantasia on a Theme by Thomas Tallis*, the *Five Variants of Dives and Lazarus* contains superbly sumptuous string writing, with sweeping melodies stretching across the orchestra, underpinned by deep and resonant harmonies. It was first performed by the New York Philharmonic-Symphony Orchestra in June 1939 under the baton of Sir Adrian Boult. Later that year, Boult conducted the British premiere at Bristol's Colston Hall.

RECOMMENDED RECORDING
Royal Liverpool Philharmonic Orchestra; David Lloyd-Jones (conductor).
Naxos: 8557798.
CHART POSITION 137

English Folk Songs Suite

Vaughan Williams was a proudly British composer. He adored his homeland, having been born in the idyllic Gloucestershire village of Down Ampney. Alongside his fondness for native landscapes, Vaughan Williams was also rather sentimental about Britain's musical history. The existence of military bands was something he recognised as being crucially important to the UK's cultural and community life. So, in 1923, he composed his *English Folk Songs Suite* for them.

Today, it's the orchestrated version of the work, assembled by Gordon Jacob, that we most commonly hear. Beginning with the sprightly march *Seventeen Come Sunday*, Vaughan Williams then treats us to the beautifully melancholic *My Bonny Boy*, before concluding in rousing fashion with another march, *Folk Songs from Somerset*. The suite isn't restricted to those three melodies alone, though. Instead, all sorts of British folk songs appear along the way, some of them overt

and others hidden within this boisterous and catchy set of tunes.
RECOMMENDED RECORDING
Academy of St Martin in the Fields; Neville Marriner (conductor).
Classic FM: CFM FW 043.
CHART POSITION 187

The Wasps

It was thanks to Cambridge University that Ralph Vaughan Williams wrote the music for a satirical production of the Aristophanes comedy *The Wasps*. He was invited to compose it by the fabulously named Cambridge Greek Play Committee, which, incidentally, is still going strong, albeit it under a slightly different name. For proof, just take a look at www.cambridgegreekplay.com – a website of which Vaughan Williams would surely have approved!

Vaughan Williams had studied at Trinity College, Cambridge, in the 1890s, and had gone on to become one of the most exciting composers of his generation. Several of Vaughan Williams's composition tutors – among them, Charles Villiers Stanford and Hubert Parry – had been similarly commissioned by the Greek Play Committee in years gone by, so Vaughan Williams was following in illustrious footsteps.

For decades after writing the music for *The Wasps*, the *Overture* was the only section to be regularly performed. In 2005, the Hallé Orchestra and their conductor Sir Mark Elder recorded the complete incidental music, making it widely available for the first time since its composition.

Symphony No. 5 in D

On the warm evening of 24 June 1943, Vaughan Williams stood on the podium at the Royal Albert Hall in front of the London Philharmonic Orchestra to conduct the premiere performance of his *Symphony No. 5*. The work had been a relatively long time coming. It was eight years since his *Symphony No. 4* and, given the many periods of intense orchestral composition in Vaughan Williams's career, many were surprised that his follow-up hadn't come sooner.

Britain was in the middle of fighting the Second World War. The balmy, sun-hued sounds of this piece offered a short musical escape from the struggles and tragedy of war. The warm orchestral colours and stirring clarion calls from the wind section display a composer who was very much in tune with those around him.

Dedicated to Sibelius, *Symphony No. 5* is powerful and joyful in equal measure: the mark of a mature and much-loved composer, and the summation of everything he had learned during his long and happy musical career to date.

RECOMMENDED RECORDING
Philharmonia Orchestra; John Barbirolli
(conductor). EMI Classics: CDM 5651102.

CHART POSITION 273

A Sea Symphony

Much is made, entirely understandably, of Vaughan Williams's musical studies during his time as an undergraduate in Cambridge, but little is mentioned of his focus on literature and poetry. And yet, when considering his deeply evocative work *A Sea Symphony*, these studies were of the utmost importance.

In 1892, Vaughan Williams had been introduced to the poetry of Walt Whitman by the soon-to-be-famous atheist philosopher and fellow Cambridge graduate Bertrand Russell. Whitman's work was to have a beguiling effect on the young composer. In 1903, he started work on a set of pieces originally titled *Songs of the Sea*, all of which set Whitman's poetry to music. These songs morphed into an *Ocean Symphony* – which, in turn, eventually became *A Sea Symphony*, the creation we know and love today.

The different sections of the symphony are evocatively titled (for example, the slow movement 'On the beach at night, alone') and it took Vaughan Williams more than six years to complete. It was derivative, too, as the composer himself was all too happy to point out: 'The Elgar phrase which influenced me most was "Thou art calling me" in *Gerontius*,' he later wrote. 'I am astonished to find on looking back on my earlier works how much I cribbed from him.'

RECOMMENDED RECORDING
Joan Rodgers (soprano); William Shimmell
(baritone); Royal Liverpool Philharmonic
Orchestra and Chorus; Vernon Handley
(conductor). EMI Eminence: EMX 2142.

CHART POSITION 275

A London Symphony

Vaughan Williams is often depicted as an inherently pastoral composer. After all, he started life in a vicarage in the quaint-sounding village of Down Ampney in Gloucestershire. Listening to works such as *The Lark Ascending* and *Fantasia on Greensleeves*, the temptation to caricature Vaughan Williams as a country boy is all the more appealing.

And yet, while being an unashamed lover of all things rural, Vaughan Williams was also an enthusiastic embracer of city life. At the start of his first marriage, he and his wife settled in Chelsea; when he later remarried, London was once again home; and Vaughan Williams also spent a happy and fruitful time studying at the Royal College of Music, just opposite the Royal Albert Hall.

Of the nine symphonies he wrote, *A London Symphony* was the composer's favourite. Beginning with a musical portrayal of the River Thames in the lower strings, we then take in Piccadilly, Bloomsbury Square and various other portraits of city life, including the repeated chiming of Big Ben. Listening to this work, you cannot help but feel that Vaughan Williams was, for part of his life at least, very happy to count himself as a Londoner.

RECOMMENDED RECORDING

Hallé Orchestra; John Barbirolli (conductor). EMI Classics: CDM 7641972.

CHART POSITION 279

GIUSEPPE VERDI
(1813–1901)

Nabucco

Nabucco is the opera that brought Verdi back from the brink. He had been ready to give up composing for good. It was by no means solely the critical failure of his previous opera, *Un giorno di regno*, that was responsible, either. After all, Verdi had endured the worst of times not long before. As well as the death of both his children, he had lost his wife.

The public hammering over *Un giorno di regno* saw Verdi inside his agent's office,

telling him his musical career was over. Suddenly envisaging the death of Italian opera or his 10 per cent, or both, the agent proffered a copy of a libretto by a writer named Solera. 'Read it,' he begged him. The story goes that Verdi read it on his journey home and by the time he had arrived at his house, the words *'Va, pensiero'* ('Chorus of the Hebrew Slaves') had captured his imagination. He was back. And when the opera was a smash in Milan in 1842, its name clipped from *Nabucodonosor* (Nebuchadnezzar) to simply *Nabucco*, then he was back with a vengeance!

RECOMMENDED RECORDING

Matteo Manuguerra (baritone) as Nabucco; Renata Scotto (soprano) as Abigaille; Veriano Luchetti (tenor) as Ismaele; Elena Obraztsova (mezzo-soprano) as Fenena; Nicolai Ghiaurov (bass) as Zaccaria; Robert Lloyd (bass) as the Gran Sacerdote; Ambrosian Opera Chorus; Philharmonia Orchestra; Ricardo Muti (conductor). EMI Classics: 4564472.

CHART POSITION 48

Requiem

Requiems come in all shapes and sizes. Some, like Fauré's, are serene, hardly so much as raising their grief-stricken voices. Others, like Mozart's, are melancholic and rousing by turn, snapshots of the composer's music at the time, more than any great comment on the theme of mortality and death. Verdi's, however, fits into a category that's almost a one-off, with Berlioz's *Requiem* possibly the only other major companion work. It's the 'blockbuster' category.

Verdi's *Requiem* is a huge, great wind-machine of a thing, often labelled an opera in all but name. Verdi had written a *Libera me* as a part of what was meant to be a joint Requiem by him and several other composers, in honour of Rossini. When all that fell through, his

Libera me was sent back to him. In his sixties and prompted by the death of his friend, the writer Manzoni, he set to work on surrounding it with its other constituent parts. It was a huge hit. In performance, it can be impressive simply to see the eight trumpets, often lined up round the stage, but when they play alongside a chorus marked *fff* (that's four times as loud as 'loud') well, it's simply staggering.

RECOMMENDED RECORDING
Christine Brewer (soprano), Karen Cargill (mezzo-soprano), Stuart Neill (tenor); John Relyea (bass-baritone); London Symphony Orchestra and Chorus; Colin Davis (conductor). LSO Live: LSO0683.
CHART POSITION 55

La traviata

The mid- to late-1840s was a period when Verdi's career was going through the roof. Behind him, by this point, were the sad times when he had lost his wife and children and he was busy rebuilding his personal life with the help of a soprano called Giuseppina Strepponi. Strepponi herself was not having the best time of it, with her voice past its peak: one particularly tough season saw her booed off the stage in Palermo. So it was that, after a couple of years as companions in Paris, the two set up home back in Verdi's native Bussetto, unmarried and causing a bit of a rumpus in the process. It's against this backdrop that the wily Verdi found himself curiously re-attracted to the Dumas story of 'the fallen woman' in *La Dame aux camélias*.

The opera premiered in 1853, with a disastrous first night. The composer wrote to a friend '*La traviata* last night a failure. My fault or the singers'? Time will tell!' Indeed it did. It's been a roaring success ever since.

RECOMMENDED RECORDING
Anna Netrebko (soprano) as Violetta; Rolando Villazón (tenor) as Alfredo; Vienna Philharmonic Orchestra; Carlo Rizzi (conductor). Deutsche Grammophon: 4775933.
CHART POSITION 86

Aida

It's fair to say that Verdi was playing hard to get when it came to *Aida*. He was being pursued seemingly constantly by Ismail Pasha, the Khedive of Egypt and Sudan, to write for various state events, the opening of the Suez Canal being one of them. When the Cairo Opera House was being unveiled in 1869, Verdi finally agreed to compose something. Even then, he asked for a phenomenal fee, almost as if trying to price himself out of the market. Fee agreed, though, he set about working on an opera with a specially commissioned Egyptian archaeology theme. Sadly, the Franco-Prussian war displaced the best-laid plans; costumes and sets got stuck in Paris. In the end, Cairo opened with Verdi's *Rigoletto*, which was by then eighteen years old.

Aida made it to Cairo only in 1871, nearly two years late. Sadly, a century later almost to the day, the Khedival Opera House, as it was known, was completely destroyed by fire. A new opera house opened in 1988, the funds a gift from the people of Japan.

RECOMMENDED RECORDING
Leontyne Price (soprano) as Aida; Robert Merrill (baritone) as Amonasro; Jon Vickers (tenor) as Radames; Rome Opera Orchestra and Chorus; Georg Solti (conductor). Decca: 4607652.
CHART POSITION 95

Giuseppe Verdi
1813–1901

'It may be a good thing to copy reality; but to invent reality is much, much better.'

GIUSEPPE VERDI

The fact that when we think of Italy we think of opera is in no small part due to this mischievous-looking man, considered by many to be the greatest of all Italian opera composers.

Big tuneful hits fill his twenty-six operas and the majority of them remain on the bill of fare at opera houses around the world today. When *Aida* received its premiere in Italy, the audience loved it so much that the standing ovation lasted for no fewer than thirty-two curtain calls. Another of Verdi's major works, the *Requiem*, is regarded as one of the greatest pieces of choral work ever written.

When this most Italian of Italian composers was born, he was recorded in the baptismal register not as Giuseppe Fortunino Francesco Verdi but as Joseph Fortunin Francois. The town clerk in his native

Le Roncole was French, as, indeed, was the town: Le Roncole was then part of the Departement Taro, part of the First French Empire.

DID YOU KNOW?

Verdi accomplished many things at a young age: he was playing the keyboard aged three, learning the organ at the age of 10, and was married by the time he was 22.

Verdi was a talented child and was playing the organ in his local church while his age was still in single figures. After studying in Milan, his first opera was well received. But, away from work, his life took a tragic turn for the worse, with his two young children and his wife dying in quick

succession. At the time, he was trying to compose his first comic opera. Perhaps quite understandably, it wasn't a great success, being booed by the audience at its premiere.

Shortly afterwards, Verdi was asked to write the music for the libretto of *Nabucco* by the famous La Scala opera house in Milan. It was a roaring success and Verdi's career was back on track. In fact, he could do no wrong and his hit operas were staged around the world just as fast as he could get the music down on the manuscript paper. *Rigoletto*, *Il trovatore*, *Don Carlos*, *La forza del destino* – all were smash hits.

Verdi lived a long life and his final opera came in the decade before his death. *Falstaff* was based on Shakespeare's *The Merry Wives of Windsor*. It was a masterpiece of comic opera.

Rigoletto

'Use four legs, run through the town and find me an influential person who can obtain the permission for making *Le Roi s'amuse*'. It's a great line, and one that shows how determined Verdi was to get his hands on Victor Hugo's *Le'Roi s'amuse*. Hugo's work was already pretty controversial, having been dogged by interference from the censor in his native Paris. The man with the blue pencil didn't feel that the portrayal of the eponymous monarch as a womanising cynic, lacking moral fibre, was the way to present kings.

In the end, Verdi switched his characters around, with the king becoming the Duke of Mantua. Womanising, immoral dukes didn't appear to cause the same level of offence. It was first performed, pretty much at the height of Verdi's popularity, at Venice's La Fenice Opera House in the March of 1851. Contemporary accounts say that it was a massive success, and some report that the bigoted Duke of Mantua's aria *'La donna è mobile'*, was being sung in the streets the next day.

RECOMMENDED RECORDING
Joan Sutherland (soprano) as Gilda; Luciano Pavarotti (tenor) as the Duke of Mantua; London Symphony Orchestra; Richard Bonynge (conductor). Decca: 4142692.
CHART POSITION 232

La forza del destino

Whether the makers of a certain famous brand of beer intended it or not, there is a rather nice musical pun involved in choosing the central theme of the *Overture* from *La forza del destino* for their 'stellar' advertising. After his *Un ballo in maschera* (*A Masked Ball*) in the 1850s, Verdi had pretty much retired to his farm in Sant'Agata, and was overcome with acute writer's block. Telling friends that his composing days were over, he simply tended the farm and smiled that cheeky smile of his. It took the temptation of a large commission from Russia to get the blood pumping to his writing hand again. Soon, he was thinking of quite a few ideas for a new work, partly based on a Spanish play called *Don Alvaro*, by Angel de Saavedra, Duke of Rivas. Verdi insisted that his librettist, Francesco Piave, somehow combine a work by Schiller called *Wallenstein's Lager*. There are some great 'highlights' versions of the opera, but if it's the *Overture* in particular you are after, Claudio Abbado conducts the Berlin Philharmonic in this and some other choice Verdi opera overtures and preludes.

RECOMMENDED RECORDING
Berlin Philharmonic Orchestra; Claudio Abbado (conductor). Deutsche Grammophon: E4576272.
CHART POSITION 295

ANTONIO VIVALDI
(1678–1741)

The Four Seasons

Vivaldi's output of concertos is, by anyone's standards, staggering, with a total of 350 of them under his belt. Around 230 of these are for the violin. Although we're not talking concertos in the sense of the huge, full-bosomed Romantic beasts of, say, Tchaikovsky, Grieg or Rachmaninov, we are still in the realms of phenomena here. Vivaldi wrote so many concertos that, much like Haydn and his symphonies, he tended to resort to nicknames rather than numbers, for ease. His names came from various sources, too, sometimes programmatic and descriptive, occasionally crediting a soloist (the

---

right Antonio Vivaldi: The Four Seasons

Antonio Vivaldi

1678–1741

'He is an old man, who has a prodigious fury for composition. I heard him undertake to compose a concerto, with all the parts, with greater despatch than a copyist can copy it.' CHARLES DE BROSSES

Despite the fact that Vivaldi wrote somewhere around eight hundred different works, his music was rarely played from his death in 1741 right through to the middle of the twentieth century, due largely to an astonishing piece of classical vandalism, which saw masses of his manuscripts deliberately locked away for a century or so. He then had something of a comeback and now sits near the top of the list of most performed Baroque composers.

To say that Vivaldi was prolific would be an understatement, with more than five hundred concertos, a clutch of operas and a large pile of sacred and secular vocal works to his name. And that's before we get onto the hundred or so other instrumental pieces that he penned.

Vivaldi's father was a violinist and Antonio followed in his footsteps. Vivaldi's skill on the instrument meant that

DID YOU KNOW?

Vivaldi was a talented composer – as he made clear to anyone who would listen. He once claimed he could compose an entire concerto faster than it could be written down!

he knew exactly how to compose music that got the most out of virtuoso performers. He became a teacher at the Ospedale della Pietà, an orphanage for young girls. Much of the music he composed was for performance by the

highly talented group of youngsters in his care.

Were there to be a 'Musical Redheads Hall of Fame', he'd be up there with Cilla Black and Mick Hucknall. He appears to have enjoyed a lifestyle that was every bit as flamboyant as the rock and pop stars of the twenty-first century. Vivaldi is still referred to in musical circles as the 'Red Priest' and even though he was a man of the cloth, he used to tour with both a top soprano and her sister. Despite his denials, everyone thought that there was more to this threesome than just trio sonatas. And they say blondes have all the fun.

Although he was born some 300 miles away on the other side of the Alps, Vivaldi ended up in the next graveyard along from Mozart in Vienna. Both of them were in paupers' graves.

Concerto 'Il Carbonelli' was a dedication to the fiddler Giovanni Carbonelli, who ended his days here in the UK).

With *The Four Seasons* – rediscovered only in the twentieth century – we have not one, not two, but three sets of titles. There are the original twelve concertos called 'the contest between harmony and invention'. There's the first four of those, our heroes the *Four Seasons*; and then there are the occasional half-titles, spotted around the works. For even more colour, the second movement of *Spring* is part-labelled 'the barking dog'; while one section of autumn says 'the drunks have fallen asleep'.

It is still Nigel Kennedy's 2 million-selling version that sounds the best to our ears.

RECOMMENDED RECORDING
Nigel Kennedy (violin); English Chamber Orchestra. EMI Classics: 5562532.

CHART POSITION 21

Gloria in D (RV 589)

Let's face it: Vivaldi is never going to be signing copies of his latest CD in a branch of HMV or anywhere else. There are those that use this fact as an example of classical music's limits. Nonsense. It is a beauty beyond belief, prompting a frisson of sheer delight, when these limits are cracked open and a new work by a long-gone composer is discovered.

So, take heed if ever you're flicking through old music manuscripts. Be alert for anything saying 'Vivaldi's Gloria'. For while it is well known that the beloved *Gloria in D* is one of a pair – the other not nearly so often performed – what is sometimes overlooked is

that it was one of a threesome. Would that it might turn up.

What makes the *Gloria in D* shine out is its sheer exuberance and sense of the unique. It really is a work full of character, which, from its opening rush, never stops.

RECOMMENDED RECORDING
Concerto Italiano; Roberto Alessandrini (conductor). Naïve: OP30485.

CHART POSITION 117

Mandolin Concerto in C (RV 425)

Vivaldi was known to have benefited from several great violinists where he worked, at the Ospedale della Pietà in Venice. One in particular, by the name of Anna Maria, was the dedicatee of more than 30 of his 230 violin concertos. One suspects that his choices when it came to mandolin players were much more limited. He wrote only two works with mandolin in them and only one for the solo instrument. Having said that, the one he did write is one of the best concertos from his entire output.

It comes from a vintage Vivaldi year, 1725, when he would have been forty-seven. In the same twelve-month period, he also produced *The Four Seasons*. Although they were written for the Ospedale della Pietà, they were done so in a slightly unusual way. With his stock high, Vivaldi had embarked on a series of travels, overseeing old works and pitching for new ones. It was during this time that the Pietà commissioned him to supply a massive number of new pieces by post. Nice work, if you can get it.

RECOMMENDED RECORDING
Ugo Orlandi (mandolin); I Solisti Veneti (orchestra); Claudio Scimone (conductor). Apex: 2564612642.

CHART POSITION 145

Motet in E (RV630)

In the years leading up to the turn of the millennium, *'Nulla in mundo pax sincera'*, the opening section of Vivaldi's *Motet in E*, was very much associated with an Australian jumping up and down on a trampoline in a dodgy raincoat. Thankfully, this period has lapsed. But the memory lingers, as they say. It came about when the piece received a fresh lease of life as part of the soundtrack to the 1996 Scott Hicks film, *Shine*, about the life of pianist David Helfgott. Although Rachmaninov and his *Piano Concerto No. 3* were the main recipients of the film's inherited limelight, *'Nulla in mundo pax sincera'* was certainly back on the map. The title translates as 'There is no true peace left in the world' and it goes on 'free from bitterness: pure and true peace, sweet Jesus, lies in you'.

The setting, for soprano with just two violins, a viola and basso continuo (an interchangeable low line, usually taken up by the cello), adds a beautiful sparseness to a tune that is already exquisitely icy. If you try Emma Kirkby's version on the album below, you also get the other two sections of the motet, a recitative and a concluding *Alleluia*.

RECOMMENDED RECORDING

Emma Kirkby (soprano); Academy of Ancient Music; Christopher Hogwood (conductor). Decca: 4557272.

CHART POSITION 169

Lute Concerto in D

(RV 93)

Although we associate Vivaldi mainly with Venice because he spent pretty much the first forty years of his life there, he did, inevitably, get itchy feet as he became older. As well as wanting to travel, he was also keen to oversee productions of his operas, not just in order that they came out well, but also so that he might pitch for new work in different geographical markets. In his fifties, his reputation as a composer preceded him and Vivaldi was able to travel quite a lot. The job at the Pietà was still assured via that unique contract to supply new tunes in the post, so he was able to zip around with relative freedom, often with an eyebrow-raising entourage of two soprano sisters in tow, to spread the Vivaldi word.

This Concerto comes from this globe-trotting period (or, at least, Europe-trotting period). It was written in Bohemia, although its three short movements never saw publication in his lifetime. If it's an authentic sound and perfectly judged playing that you want, try a version by Ugo Orlandi (mandolin) and I Solisti Veneti. For a modern take, transposed to guitar, try Los Romeros – the talented Romero family recommended below – and their arrangement, with more Vivaldi works alongside.

RECOMMENDED RECORDING

Los Romeros (guitars); Academy of St Martin in the Fields; Iona Brown (conductor). Philips: 4681462.

CHART POSITION 235

Concerto in G, for two mandolins (RV 532)

It must have been an amazing day for the music registrar at the library in Turin. In 1926, a party from the local Salesian community – a mission of priests founded by St John Bosco in nearby Monferrato – knocked on the door to check on the value of their collection of manuscripts. As a charitable brotherhood, they had inherited the collection from the family of one Count Giacomo Durazzo, a famous arts patron. They now needed money to fund some much needed renovations to their buildings. As a result of their questions, the library in Turin contacted Durazzo's descendants in Genoa, too. Soon, hundreds of previously unknown Vivaldi manuscripts were uncovered, now known as the Mauro Foa and Renzo Giordano Collections.

Among the dazzling jewels in this collection is this double concerto for two mandolins, which quickly became a twentieth-century favourite, a pleasure that had been denied to music-lovers of the preceding two hundred years. An astounding story, but at least one with a happy ending. Now, numerous Vivaldi works take their rightful place in the classical world.

RECOMMENDED RECORDING
James Tyler (mandolin); Robin Jeffrey (mandolin); English Concert; Trevor Pinnock (conductor). Archiv: 4473012.

CHART POSITION 289

RICHARD WAGNER
(1813–1883)

Tristan and Isolde

'Since I have never in my life known the true happiness of love, I wish to erect a monument to this, the most beautiful dream of all, in which love will be fully satisfied from beginning to end. I have made a sketch of a *Tristan and Isolde* in my head; the simplest yet most full-blooded conception. With the black flag that waves at the end I shall then enshroud myself and die.' How on earth was the Hungarian composer Franz Liszt meant to respond to that particular letter from his friend and fellow composer Richard Wagner in 1855?

The extreme nature of Wagner's pronouncement is ultimately matched in the ground-breaking, powerful music he composed for this, his opera *Tristan and Isolde*. The composer went on to state that this was a tale of 'the bliss and wretchedness of love', and one that could end only with 'one sole redemption – death'. So at the outset, we know this is no light-hearted affair.

Most famous for its *Prelude*, in which we find the much-analysed 'Tristan Chord' –

which was to confound and fascinate critics and musicologists in equal measure – *Tristan and Isolde* is opera on an absolutely epic scale – and none the worse for that.

RECOMMENDED RECORDING

Plácido Domingo (tenor) as Tristan; Nina Stemme (soprano) as Isolde; Ian Bostridge (tenor) as Hirt; Orchestra and Chorus of the Royal Opera House, Covent Garden; Antonio Pappano (conductor). EMI Classics: 5580062.

CHART POSITION 92

Tannhäuser

Wagner didn't really do understate. His works were epic in scale, fantastically mythological in plot, and revolutionary in both length and orchestration. In the case of *Tannhäuser*, even the word 'opera' wasn't deemed to be sufficient: Wagner initially referred to it as a 'romantic grand opera' but then elevated the work to a 'consummate drama', as he described it to his wife Cosima in 1882.

Tannhäuser and the Song Contest at the Wartburg, to use its full name, is a three-act opera set in the thirteenth century. It encompasses goddesses, nymphs, sirens, knights and a whole host of other fantastical characters. The opera's *Overture* is its most famous section: the

Richard Wagner

1813–1883

'Wagner has lovely moments but awful quarters of an hour.'

GIOACHINO ROSSINI

Think Wagner; think 'extreme'. His music is extreme, and it tends to elicit extreme reactions from listeners. It's love or hate with him. Fellow composer Rossini believed that 'Wagner has lovely moments, but awful quarters of an hour.' People rarely use the word 'quite' in connection with Wagner.

Despite his genius, he was a deeply flawed and unpleasant character – racist, anti-Semitic, Machiavellian and a serial philanderer with a monstrous ego. Without doubt an awful man. Nevertheless, the music he wrote was his one redeeming feature and you should try it before you completely make up your mind about him. His greatest achievement is the four operas that make up *The Ring Cycle*, which together last for more

than fifteen hours. No, that's not a misprint.

> ## DID YOU KNOW?
>
> **Despite his great successes in the concert hall and in the opera house, Wagner was never able to stay out of debt during his lifetime.**

In a book filled with people who were certainly not backward about coming forward when it came to pushing their own talents to the hilt, Wagner takes the biscuit. In terms of control-freakery, he is without parallel. Not only did he compose the music and write the librettos for his operas, he also

controlled the staging and performances, taking on the role of director and conductor. He even ended up building his own concert hall, nearly bankrupting some of his backers in the process.

One of the stranger uses of Wagner's music came in the cartoon *What's Opera, Doc?* Bugs Bunny and his lifelong adversary Elmer Fudd can be heard singing along to parts of *Die Walküre* and *Tannhäuser*, giving many youngsters their first taste of opera.

The *Siegfried Idyll* is possibly the most special birthday present ever. Wagner wrote it for his new wife, Cosima. He smuggled a chamber orchestra of musicians onto the landing outside her bedroom in 1870 and had them play this new work for her. Definitely one better than breakfast in bed.

shimmering, dramatic chords give way to a series of thrilling and expansive themes, which very much set the scene for the action that follows. The woodwind convey chanting pilgrims (listen out for the sombre sound of the clarinets and bassoons), while the aching and arching string lines allude to sexual temptation and lust. In just under fifteen minutes, Wagner certainly manages to cover a lot of ground!

The composer himself conducted the premiere of *Tannhäuser* at Dresden's Royal Saxon Court Theatre, on 19 October 1845. In between finishing the score and conducting the first performance, he had been on a long holiday to the spa city of Marienbad, along with his wife, his dog and his parrot.

RECOMMENDED RECORDING
(highlights only) Bayreuth Festival Orchestra and Chorus; Wolfgang Sawallisch.
Philips: 4346072.
CHART POSITION 94

Die Walküre

At around five hours in duration, Wagner's opera *Die Walküre* is an epic work in its own right – but it's only one of four instalments of the composer's mighty *Ring Cycle*. And while the entire opera is packed full of thrilling music, one particular five-minute orchestral firework is the reason for its truly widespread popularity. The *Ride of the Valkyries*, which acts as the curtain-raiser to Act III, has been included in countless television programmes, commercials and movies – most notably, *Apocalypse Now*, in which the music is put to gripping effect during the opening of helicopter fire on a village in Vietnam.

Die Walküre has far more to offer than just The *Ride of the Valkyries*, though. Telling the

story of the curse-inflicting Wotan, king of the gods, the opera is a stunningly powerful setting of the Norse mythology with which Wagner was fascinated. If you can't spare the full five hours to listen to the opera in its entirety, you might want to try a few of the most famous musical sections: in particular, the thrilling *Wotan's Farewell* and the aptly named *Magic Fire Music*, which displays the composer's absolutely assured grasp of orchestration and musical colour better than many of his non-operatic works.

Die Walküre was premiered in Munich in March 1870, and remains one of the most popular operas in the world today.
RECOMMENDED RECORDING
Poul Elming (baritone) as Siegmund; John Tomlinson (bass) as Wotan; Nadine Secunde (soprano) as Sieglinde; Bayreuth Festival Orchestra; Daniel Barenboim (conductor).
Teldec: 4509911862.
CHART POSITION 97

Siegfried

Like *Die Walküre*, *Siegfried* is a mammoth opera in its own right, but can really be understood only in the context of the entire *Ring Cycle*, where it falls as the penultimate work in the set. Think of it as a sort of nineteenth-century version of *The Lord of the Rings* trilogy, albeit with a fourth instalment.

The fantastical, mythological nature of the plot makes it almost impossible to sum up succinctly, which is surely one of the reasons why the opera lasts for well over four hours. Briefly, we once again meet Wotan, now called the Wanderer – whom we left at the end of *Die Walküre*, despairing about the fate of his beloved Brünnhilde. As Wagner himself wrote to the German musician August Roeckel, 'After his parting from Brünnhilde, Wotan truly is nothing but a departed spirit.'

Siegfried's principal focus is not Wotan, though, but the legendary Norse character Sigurd, a national hero depicted in all sorts of art forms.

The orchestral *Preludes* to Acts I and III are much loved in their own right, and Wagner's use of musical themes to depict plot lines is once again enthralling. Only one opera in the *Ring Cycle* was to remain: *Götterdämmerung*, which was to premiere in 1874 and which brought this extraordinary twenty-six-year project to a close.

RECOMMENDED RECORDING
Siegfried Jerusalem (tenor) as Siegried; Graham Clark (tenor) as Mime; John Tomlinson (bass) as The Wanderer; Bayreuth Festival Orchestra; Daniel Barenboim (conductor). Teldec: 4509941932.
CHART POSITION 188

Lohengrin

Nowadays, Wagner is principally remembered for his *Ring Cycle*. And yet, during the composer's lifetime, *Lohengrin* was the most frequently performed of all his operas. By the late nineteenth century, the opera had gained almost cult status among the musical elite, after its first performance in Weimar in 1850 with Franz Liszt on the podium. In 1893 the prominent New York music critic Henry T. Finck described it as 'the most popular work in the world's operatic repertory'. Amazingly, though, Wagner himself was prevented from attending because of his status as a political refugee in exile, banned from his home country of Germany.

Lohengrin's popularity was not particularly embraced by the composer, though. On the contrary, he vented his frustration the year after its premiere, writing, 'If I could have everything my way, *Lohengrin* – the libretto of which I wrote in 1845 – would be long forgotten

in favour of new works that prove, even to me, that I have made progress.'

The barnstorming orchestral *Prelude* to Act III is a vividly colourful section of the opera, which stands on its own as a classic example of Wagner's ability to stir and inspire with his thrilling use of every part of the orchestra.
RECOMMENDED RECORDING
Kurt Moll (bass) as King Heinrich; Cheryl Studer (soprano) as Elsa; Siegfried Jerusalem (tenor) as Lohengrin; Vienna Philharmonic Orchestra; Claudio Abbado (conductor). Deutsche Grammophon: 4378082.
CHART POSITION 194

The Mastersingers of Nuremburg

Between 1856 and 1868, Wagner took a substantial break from his *Ring Cycle*, in part to focus on this opera *The Mastersingers of Nuremburg*, and also to devote time to his masterpiece *Tristan and Isolde*.

Wagner was a canny composer: he realised that the Act I *Prelude* to *The Mastersingers of Nuremburg* was a fine concert work in its own right, so much so that he tweaked it for performance separate from the opera itself. The themes for the *Prelude* had come to the composer relatively easily but it took him many months to compose the music for the remainder of the opera. That gives a plausible reason as to why, in the *Prelude*, there are no obvious references to the musical motifs depicting the main character, the cobbler-poet Hans Sachs. Quite simply, Wagner hadn't come up with them when the *Prelude* was composed.

Much of the *Prelude* was written on the road, as Wagner travelled from Venice to Vienna on 12 November 1861. Perhaps surprisingly, *The Mastersingers of Nuremburg* is a comedy (a term used loosely), and where the *Ring Cycle* seems initially impenetrable, this opera is both warm and accessible – not just in the *Prelude*, but in the music that follows, too.

RECOMMENDED RECORDING
Elisabeth Schwarzkopf (soprano) as Eva; Otto Edelmann (bass) as Hans Sachs, Erich Kunz (baritone) as Beckmesser; Bayreuth Festival Orchestra and Chorus; Herbert von Karajan (conductor). EMI Classics: CHS 7635002.
CHART POSITION 217

Götterdämmerung

On 17 August 1876, Wagner's extraordinary twenty-six-year project, the *Ring Cycle*, came to its mighty conclusion when the fourth and final instalment, *Götterdämmerung*, was premiered in Bayreuth. It was an extraordinary occasion in musical history: the first complete performance of the *Ring Cycle*, a creation that still captivates with its potency today.

Such is the mythological nature of the story, it is almost impossible to sum up the epic plot in a succinct way. What we can say, though, is that this immense tale of Norse mythology set to music was universally acclaimed when Hans Richter conducted its premiere performance. Before Wagner, opera had been a relatively predictable art form: male lead and female lead fall in love, everything looks rosy, and barely ten minutes later everyone's in tatters as at least one of the main characters has died (usually because of suicide or murder).

Through the *Ring Cycle*, Wagner took the notion of opera and extended its possibilities ten-fold. He also demonstrated his complete grasp of writing for the human voice: it is almost impossible to listen to *Brünnhilde's*

Immolation Scene from Act III and not feel the hairs on the back of your neck stand up as this dramatic soprano solo thrills and chills in equal measure.

RECOMMENDED RECORDING
Éva Marton (soprano) as Brünnhilde; Siegfried Jerusalem (tenor) as Siegfried; Thomas Hampson (baritone) as Gunther; Bavarian Radio Symphony Orchestra and Chorus; Bernard Haitink (conductor). EMI Classics: CDS 7544852.
CHART POSITION 230

WILLIAM WALTON
(1902–1983)

Crown Imperial

William Dunbar gets the credit for the title to this work. This man of arts and letters, who was known as the 'rhymer of Scotland', was a friend of Robert Blackadder, the beautifully named Archbishop of Glasgow. It was Dunbar who wrote 'In Honour of the City', about London, which contained the lines 'Empress of townes, exalt in honour, In beawtie beryng the crone imperiall, Swete paradise precelling in pleasure, London, thou art the flour of Cities all.' From here, Walton took his idea for the title of this 1937 work. He wrote it for the coronation of Edward VIII, but in the end used it for the coronation of George VI. Said to have been modelled on the *Pomp and Circumstance Marches* of Elgar, it was performed again at the coronation of Queen Elizabeth II in 1953. At the time, much was made of the absence of Elgar's music at the

1953 coronation, with *Crown Imperial* being called the old wine to go alongside his new, *Orb and Sceptre*.

RECOMMENDED RECORDING
Royal Philharmonic Orchestra; André Previn (conductor). Telarc: CD80125.
CHART POSITION 198

Spitfire Prelude and Fugue

Leslie Howard as R. J. Mitchell. David Niven as his test pilot. *The First of the Few*. It sounds, and is, a product of its time, a flag-waving morale-booster movie on the subject of the Supermarine Spitfire. For Walton, movies were his bread and butter. Yes, he was lucky enough to enjoy the support of various patrons along the way – particularly Lady Alice Wimbourne. Indeed, by way of answering the question 'What did you do in the war, Uncle William?', when the Queen's Hall was destroyed in 1941, it was the very same air raid that took out Walton's house, too. Consequently, the composer moved in with his patron and continued composing. It's said that when a friend passed on the artistic desires of the director (also Leslie Howard) for the music, Walton turned to him and replied, 'Ah, Leslie wants lots of notes. I see!' The film came out in 1942, and the *Spitfire Prelude and Fugue* was premiered by the Liverpool Philharmonic Orchestra, at the city's Philharmonic Hall, in January 1943.

RECOMMENDED RECORDING
Academy of St Martin in the Fields; Neville

Marriner (conductor). Chandos: CHAN8870.
CHART POSITION 281

CHARLES-MARIE WIDOR
(1844–1937)

Organ Symphony No. 5 in F minor

The French composer Charles-Marie Widor wrote a total of ten organ symphonies – but sadly, it is only the *Toccata* from *No. 5* that retains any kind of popular appeal today. It's quite some popular appeal, though, being one of the most regularly requested wedding-day pieces in the world. Many a bride and groom have left the church to the sound of 'the Widor', as it's often called. It certainly provides something of a challenge for your average parish organist to pull off successfully!

The *Toccata* first became popular around 1880: the combination of rather frantic right-hand decorative lines with sturdy, anthemic melody notes from the pedals of the organ became a pretty instant hit. Although referred to as a 'symphony', this work does not fit that title in the traditional sense – and nor do Widor's other organ symphonies, for that matter. Rather, we can only assume that the term is intended to convey the composer's full use of the organ's range and musical colour, in much the same way that other composers employ all elements of the orchestra's possibilities when writing a standard symphony.

Widor himself was a master of the instrument: he succeeded his fellow French composer César Franck as Professor of Organ at the Paris Conservatoire.

RECOMMENDED RECORDING (TOCCATA ONLY)
Stephen Cleobury (organ). Decca: 4600212.
CHART POSITION 57

JOHN WILLIAMS
(B. 1923)

Schindler's List

The line from Steven Spielberg to the people saved from death by Oskar Schindler (*Schindlerjuden*, as they were known) is indirect but tangible. One of those whom he saved, Poldek Pfefferberg, told the story to Thomas Keneally, who published his *Schindler's Ark* book in 1982. Pfefferberg met with Spielberg and implored him to turn it into a film. Spielberg knew inside that he would, but told Pfefferberg it would happen in ten years' time. In the end, the film, with the title *Schindler's List*, saw the light of day in 1993, winning seven Oscars, seven Baftas and three Golden Globes.

To provide the music for so moving a film, Spielberg turned to his favourite composer, and John Williams came up with one of his most fitting and heart-wrenching scores. The violinist Itzhak Perlman was hired to perform the plaintive melody that runs through the film. The score was one of the Oscar-winning aspects of the movie, helping it to become one of the most successful in cinema history (with a budget of $22 million, its total revenues topped $321 million).

RECOMMENDED RECORDING
Itzhak Perlman (violin); Pittsburgh Symphony Orchestra; John Williams (conductor). Sony: S2K 51333.
CHART POSITION 120

Star Wars

It's easy to forget, in these days of seemingly ubiquitous *Star Wars* clones and all of the merchandise associated with a big movie release that, back in the Silver Jubilee year of 1977, *Star Wars* was simply a brilliant movie and

not a franchise. By that time, John Williams had already composed several successful film scores, including *The Poseidon Adventure*, *The Towering Inferno* and *Jaws*. But, he had yet to sample the superstardom that the six-part *Star Wars* series would afford him.

Harking back in scale and grandeur to the swash-buckling scores of Korngold and Steiner, Williams's music touched a nerve with modern cinema audiences. When matched with George Lucas's sci-fi modernism, his sweeping neo-Romantic manuscripts resulted in movie superstardom. They came complete with leitmotifs (musical identifiers) for many of the principal characters, just as Wagner had used before him. When the franchise extended to cover two sequels and three prequels, Williams was always there, providing the perfect accompaniment.

From Britain's point of view, it was the start of an association with the London Symphony Orchestra that would last through all six films. There are numerous sets of the *Star Wars* soundtracks. We've opted for the version of *Star Wars* that was remastered in 2004. The original and best.

RECOMMENDED RECORDING
New London Children's Choir; London Voices; London Symphony Orchestra; John Williams (conductor). Sony: SK89932.
CHART POSITION 158

Harry Potter

What is there to say about the *Harry Potter* phenomenon that has already not been said? Any book that can spawn its own age (the 'Harry Potter generation', so they say) must have accumulated all there is to be said on the subject. It was in 2001 that the first film, *Harry Potter and the Philosopher's Stone* was released, four years after Bloomsbury published

John Williams
b. 1923

'So much of what we do is ephemeral and quickly forgotten, so it's gratifying to have something you have done linger in people's memories.'

JOHN WILLIAMS

One of the most successful composers of the twentieth and twenty-first centuries, John Williams has been nominated for the Oscars forty-three times, winning the top prize five times. He also has nineteen Golden Globe nominations and three victories to his name. He's also been nominated for thirteen Emmy Awards, winning twice.

Williams was born in New York in 1923. He moved with his family to Los Angeles in 1948. He joined the American Air Force, before moving back to New York to study at the Juilliard School. While there, he made money working as a jazz pianist in many of the clubs in Manhattan. Finally, he made the move back to Los Angeles, where he started to work in the film and television industry. Throughout the 1960s, he wrote the theme tunes of many successful American television programmes.

DID YOU KNOW?

John Williams has an extraordinary work ethic: he still composes two film scores every year, even though he's now well into his seventies.

It was in 1973 that John Williams met Steven Spielberg – the man with whom he would have the greatest creative partnership of his long career. Their first collaboration was on the film *Sugarland Express*. After that, they worked together time and time again, building into one of the most enduring and successful director–composer partnerships anywhere in the world of film. As well as the soundtracks that have been voted into the Classic FM Hall of Fame, he's also written the music for blockbusters such as *Jaws*, *Superman* and *E.T.*

Many composers today use computers to help them compose their music, but John Williams prefers to sit at a piano to work out the tune and use a pencil and paper to write down what he's composed. It's hard work too – he might have only eight weeks to write around two hours of music for a full orchestra for a film. He works long hours in his small office in the Dreamworks studios in Los Angeles.

J. K. Rowling's novel. John Williams was drafted in to write the first score, which he did in Los Angeles and Tanglewood (where he has homes) before recording the soundtrack in London in August 2001. Instantly, his themes became radio hits, and the basis for the next six films in the series, despite the fact that Williams himself dropped out of overall responsibility for the scores after number three (*Harry Potter and the Prisoner of Azkaban*). All the *Harry Potter* film soundtracks are still available with new music for each one by Patrick Doyle, Nicholas Hooper and Alexandre Desplat respectively. The final film, *Harry Potter and the Deathly Hallows Part 2*, sees Frenchman Desplat writing the soundtrack once again.

RECOMMENDED RECORDING

London Symphony Orchestra; John Williams (conductor). Atlantic: 7567930865.

CHART POSITION 186

Saving Private Ryan

The story is probably very familiar, by now. Amid the carnage of the Omaha beachhead assault of 1944, the camera follows Tom Hanks and his men as they wander the beach at the start of the film, before the search begins for the sole surviving brother of three fallen soldiers – the 'Ryan' of the title. *Saving Private Ryan* won five Oscars in 1998. Although Best Sound was one of the Oscar spoils – an odd one to major on you might think – Best Soundtrack was not. John Williams came away empty-handed this time. The job for Williams here was a tricky one. Spielberg wanted to keep much of the film silent, to concentrate on the true horrors of war and to make sure that the harsh and real sounds of death were heard (and it clearly worked, hence the Best Sound Oscar). The limits this put on Williams were considerable, but he still managed to come away with a moving theme, played over the end credits and soon becoming a stand-alone hit. The wordless chorus with a trumpet and snare-drum combination certainly tugs at the heart strings.

RECOMMENDED RECORDING

Tanglewood Festival Chorus; Boston Symphony Orchestra; John Williams (conductor). Dreamworks: DRMD 50046.

CHART POSITION 213

HANS ZIMMER
(B. 1957)

Gladiator

The German composer Hans Zimmer is a particularly versatile musician: one minute he's the keyboard player for the band The Buggles (they of 'Video Killed the Radio Star' fame); the next, he's writing film music for *The Da Vinci Code*, *Pearl Harbor* and *Gladiator*, his most successful movie soundtrack by a country mile.

Released in 2000, the film confirmed Zimmer's status as one of the most important movie composers of his generation. This epic Roman adventure, directed by Ridley Scott, demanded equally majestic and regal music. As the soundtrack proves, Zimmer amply rose to the challenge. Of the entire score, the section entitled *Earth* is the most popular and well known.

Zimmer was nominated for an Oscar for the *Gladiator* score, for which he was assisted by Lisa Gerrard and Klaus Badelt, most famous now for his music for *Pirates of the Caribbean*. *Gladiator* was a phenomenally successful film overall, garnering twelve Academy Award nominations, winning five of them, and taking millions of dol-

lars at cinemas worldwide. The soundtrack, meanwhile, continued to appear in the classical charts a decade after the film's release – proof, if it were needed, of the music's rare ability to live on beyond the initial hype surrounding the movie in question.

RECOMMENDED RECORDING
Lyndhurst Orchestra; Gavin Greenaway (conductor). Decca: 4765223.
CHART POSITION 196

DOMENICO ZIPOLI
(1688–1726)

Elevazione

Very little is known about the Italian Baroque composer Domenico Zipoli, whose stately *Elevazione* became something of a classical music hit in the 1990s thanks to its exposure on Classic FM. Zipoli received lessons from some of the best composers of his day – not least Alessandro Scarlatti – but he wasn't to remain in Italy for long. Music was, in one sense, only a hobby for Zipoli, for it was his

right Hans Zimmer: Gladiator

calling as a Jesuit missionary that defined much of the composer's life.

Since 1715, Zipoli had been the sole organist at the Jesuit Church in Rome; he studied to become a Catholic priest but, tragically, died from tuberculosis before he could become ordained. By that time, the composer had gained a considerable following in South American countries, where his choral music – all but forgotten now – was regularly performed.

Elevazione is scored for oboe, cello, organ and strings; its sedate pace and stately sound have guaranteed its use in both weddings and funerals in recent years. Since being championed by Classic FM, the piece has appeared on countless classical compilations over the last fifteen years – although, still, *Elevazione* remains something of an enigma. Beyond its instrumentation, very little is known about the piece.

RECOMMENDED RECORDING

Robert Truman (cello); Consort of London; Robert Haydon-Clark (conductor).
Sony BMG: 4800249.

CHART POSITION 171

25 Recordings
You Should Own

1	Sergei Rachmaninov	*Piano Concerto No. 2 in C minor* Soloist: Stephen Hough. Hyperion: CDA 675012.
2	Ralph Vaughan Williams	*The Lark Ascending* Soloist: Nigel Kennedy. EMI Classics: 5628132.
3	Wolfgang Amadeus Mozart	*Requiem* London Philharmonic Orchestra and Choir. EMI Classics: 5209492.
4	Edward Elgar	*Cello Concerto in E minor* Soloist: Natalie Clein. EMI Classics: 5014092.
5	Henryk Górecki	*Symphony No. 3 (Symphony of Sorrowful Songs)* Soloist: Dawn Upshaw. Nonesuch: 7559 792822.

See individual entries for full recording details.

6	Ludwig van Beethoven	*Symphony No.6 (Pastoral)* Budapest Festival Orchestra. Channel Classics: CCS SA 30710.
7	Pyotr Ilyich Tchaikovsky	*1812 Overture* Berlin Philharmonic Orchestra. Deutsche Grammophon: 4534962.
8	Richard Strauss	*Four Last Songs* Soloist: Renée Fleming. Decca: 4780647.
9	Richard Wagner	*Tristan and Isolde* Orchestra and Chorus of the Royal Opera House, Covent Garden. EMI Classics: 5580062.
10	Max Bruch	*Violin Concerto No. 1 in G minor* Soloist: Nigel Kennedy. EMI Classics: 5574112.
11	Dmitri Shostakovich	*Symphony No. 5 in D minor* Royal Liverpool Philharmonic Orchestra. Naxos: 8572461.
12	Marie Joseph Canteloube de Malaret	*Songs of the Auvergne* Soloist: Veronique Gens. Naxos: 8557491.
13	Johannes Brahms	*Symphony No. 4 in E minor* Berlin Philharmonic Orchestra. EMI Classics: 50999 26725420.
14	Erik Satie	*Gymnopédies* Soloist: Pascal Rogé. Decca: 4102202.
15	Johann Sebastian Bach	*St Matthew Passion* English Baroque Soloists; Monteverdi Choir. Deutsche Grammophon Archiv: 4297732.

16	Felix Mendelssohn	*Elijah* Orchestra of the Age of Enlightenment; Edinburgh Festival Chorus. Decca: 4556882.
17	Joaquín Rodrigo	*Concierto de Aranjuez* Soloist: Julian Bream. EMI Classics: CDC 7546612.
18	Camille Saint-Saëns	*Symphony No. 3 in C minor (Organ Symphony)* Soloist: Michael Matthes. Deutsche Grammophon: 4358542.
19	Gustav Holst	*The Planets* London Philharmonic Orchestra. EMI Classics: 6278982.
20	Antonín Dvořák	*Symphony No. 9 in E minor (From the New World)* Oslo Philharmonic Orchestra. EMI Classics: 5008782.
21	Nikolay Rimsky-Korsakov	*Scheherazade* Kirov Orchestra. Philips: 4708402.
22	George Frideric Handel	*Zadok the Priest* Choir of King's College, Cambridge. EMI Classics: 2289440.
23	Frédéric Chopin	*Piano Concerto No. 2 in F minor* Soloist: Eldar Nebolsin. Naxos: 8572336.
24	Jean Sibelius	*Symphony No. 5 in E flat* City of Birmingham Symphony Orchestra. EMI Classics: 50343282.
25	Thomas Tallis	*Spem in Alium* The Sixteen. Coro: COR16073.

Acknowledgements

Our biggest thanks of all must go to the Classic FM listeners, without whom there would be no Classic FM Hall of Fame. It is a real thrill for us to be able to broadcast a new chart over the Easter weekend each year and we remain just as excited as anyone else, as we wait to discover the nation's favourite classical works each year.

Writing a book is a long process, which involves many more people than just those with their names on the cover. We are indebted to Lorne Forsyth at E&T Books for his unstinting support of this project from our first discussions about writing it. We are also grateful to Mark Searle for setting us on our writing pathway and to our editor Olivia Bays, who has so expertly guided us through the process of turning our manuscript into the finished item, and also to Nick Sidwell for his work behind the scenes.

Enormous thanks are due to Global Radio's Founder and Executive President Ashley Tabor, to Group Chief Executive Stephen Miron, and to Director of Broadcasting Richard Park, for their encouragement. Thanks also to Giles Pearman, Buffie du Pon, Racheal Edwards, Andrea Flamini, Felix Meston and John Chittenden. Among the Classic FM programming team, we must thank Nick Bailey, Jamie Beesley, Fiona Bowden, Laurence Llewelyn-Bowen, John Brunning, Stuart Campbell, Chris Chilvers, Jamie Crick, Nick Ferrari, Mark Forrest, Nigel Gayler, Howard Goodall, Matt Gubbins, Owen Hopkin, Alex James, Jane Jones, Myleene Klass, David Mellor, Anne-Marie Minhall, Phil Noyce, Nicholas Owen, Emma Oxborrow, Alexandra Philpotts, Rupert Reid, Oliver Melville-Smith, John Suchet, Margherita Taylor, Natalie Wheen and Andrew Wright – all of whom work incredibly hard to make the Classic FM Hall of Fame the success it is each year.

About The Authors

Darren Henley is the Managing Director of Classic FM. Responsible for producing the first Classic FM Hall of Fame in 1996, he looked after the chart for the next eleven years of its life. He was named Commercial Radio Programmer of the Year in 2009. Darren advises ministers in the Department for Education and the Department for Culture, Media and Sport on music and cultural education. He studied politics at the University of Hull and is currently undertaking postgraduate research in music at the University of York. He is an Honorary Fellow of Canterbury Christ Church University. This is his twentieth book about classical music and musicians.

Sam Jackson is the Executive Producer at Classic FM in charge of all aspects of the station's music output. He has been the producer of the Classic FM Hall of Fame since 2008 and is closely involved with the station's large-scale music events and with the network of Classic FM orchestras around the country. After graduating from the University of York with a first-class degree in music, Sam worked as the producer of many of Classic FM's biggest programmes. He is a proficient piano and clarinet player and writes regularly for *Classic FM Magazine*.

Tim Lihoreau is Classic FM's Creative Director, but will be better known to many listeners as the presenter of the station's *Brighter Breakfast* programme each weekend morning. Tim has won a multitude of awards for his radio writing and production on both sides of the Atlantic, as well as being the author of eleven books. His *Modern Phobias* has been translated into eleven languages. With a degree in music from the University of Leeds, he was a professional pianist before moving into radio. Along with his wife, he runs three amateur choirs in his home village in Cambridgeshire and regularly plays the organ at his local church.

Index